POMPEII HERCULANEUM MT. VESUVIUS

205 Color illustrations

BONECHI

Text by Stefano Giuntoli.
Editorial assistance: Monica Bonechi.

Translated by Studio Comunicare, Florence

*Photographs from the Archives of
Casa Editrice Bonechi taken by*
Archivio Fotografico
dell'Osservatorio Vesuviano,
Foto Antonio Biasucci, Gianni Dagli Orti,
Paolo Giambone, Cesare Tonini,
Foto Tripodi, Foto Amendola,
Foto De Gregorio Andrea.

ISBN 88-7009-738-2

*   *   *

Diffusion:
VI.MAR. di SCALOGNA Vincenzo & F.S.A.
Via Nolana Trav. Tirone 215
80045 Pompei (NA)
Tel. 081-8635315

INTRODUCTION

"Who lives down there in the abyss? Live there a new people hidden under the lava? Does the past retrace its steps? Oh, come thou Greeks and Romans! Behold: ancient Pompeii is resurrected, the city of Hercules rises once more!»: thus sang Schiller in his poem "Pompeii and Herculaneum".

The story of humanity is full of moving and touching episodes: the rediscovery, or more precisely the resurrection, of Pompeii and Herculaneum are among the most important.

Today Mt. Vesuvius, in all its calm majesty, looms over the countryside speckled with spots of greenery and houses: grapevines cling to its ample sides and the broom once more flowers. It is hard to imagine today that this serenely beautiful landscape was once the setting for tragedy and death, violence and destruction.

But the ruins of Pompeii and Herculaneum stand as witnesses. For what happened in Pompeii and Herculaneum may be unique in history: not only did a civilization die here, as was the case elsewhere in analogous situations, but daily life came to a sudden standstill. People died on the thresholds of their houses, the loaves of bread stayed in the oven, and the dogs remained chained outside the door and the slaves in their bonds. The coins still lay on the table in the taverns, and the papyrus scrolls on the shelves of the libraries. These walls still bear the election slogans and phrases of love and of derision.

The catastrophe took place so unexpectedly that the daily course of life, the activities of hundreds and hundreds of

people, was suddenly interrupted. Nor does it mean much that death came differently to Herculaneum and to Pompeii. Little does it matter if here there was a hope, the barest hope, of flight, while rivers of mud flowed down and covered the city, while there the chances of escaping from the sulphurous vapors and the impalpable layer of ashes which slowly suffocated and covered everying were null. Their fate was the same, they were condemned, the two of them. And for both, the resurrection after almost 1700 years was to be the same.

The only thing that had survived the appalling tragedy was the precise, on the spot, account of Pliny the Younger, who even though he lost his uncle in the catastrophe, diligently, reported the details of that dramatic summer day in A.D. 79.

The accuracy, the wealth of details, the precision of his account have without doubt been of great aid to archaeologists and scholars.

Pliny observed and described a terrible natural phenomenon, while thousands of persons died buried under a blanket of lava, ashes and lapilli and "many raised their hands to the gods, but almost all were convinced that the gods were there no longer."

The man who rediscovered Pompeii and Herculaneum in the 18th century did more than just bring to light two buried cities: he tied together, as if by magic, a broken thread, once more took up a discourse that had been cut short, in other words he gave life back to all those whom the gods had deprived of life.

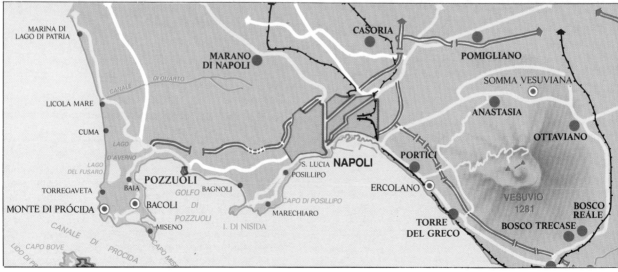

MARINA DI
LAGO DI PATRIA

CASORIA

MARANO
DI NAPOLI

POMIGLIANO

SOMMA VESUVIANA

CANALE   DI QUARTO

LICOLA MARE

ANASTASIA

CUMA

OTTAVIANO

LAGO
D'AVERNO

LAGO
DEL FUSARO

PORTICI

S. LUCIA NAPOLI
POSILLIPO

POZZUOLI

ERCOLANO

TORREGAVETA

BAIA

GOLFO

BAGNOLI

VESUVIO
1281

MONTE DI PRÓCIDA

BACOLI

DI

BOSCO
REÁLE

MISENO

POZZUOLI

CAPO DI POSILLIPO

MARECHIARO

BOSCO TRECASE

I. DI NISIDA

CANALE   DI   PROCIDA

CAPO BOVE

CAPO MIST

TORRE
DEL GRECO

LIDO DI PR

VESUVIUS

Mount Vesuvius rises 1200 m above the Gulf of Naples. The whole area was inhabited in very ancient times because of the beauty of its landscapes, the fertility of the ground and the mildness of its climate. The history of the eruptions of mt. Vesuvius is probably one of the most famous and fascinating.

There are several volcanos in Italy, in particular in Tu-scany, Latium and Campania. They are often situated near areas which were inhabited from the beginning of civilization but which were no longer active when the areas were civilized. In some cases their activity was infre-quent and caused only slight damage. That is the reason why Amiata, Cimino, the Alban hills, Roccamorfina and Ischia – these are just few examples – are not famous for their volcanos.

The Phlegraean Fields, that is the north-western area near Naples, in which the craters were originated by eruptions over a period of 20,000 years, are famous for the so-called

5

bradyseism. This phenomenon, which consists in a slow vertical rising of the ground, has caused risings and a whole series of consequences in the area around Pozzuoli. The last manifestation of the phenomenon took place in the years 1982-84 and caused a rising of about 1,5 metres with evident negative consequences on the social and economic tissue. The activity of Vesuvius seems to follow a determined cycle. At the beginning there is a violent explosion, which is sometimes followed by streams of lava. The first cycle which has so far been identified dates back to about 25,000 years ago. This was followed by other eruptive cycles and long periods (in some cases centuries) of quiescence. The most important eruptions, that is on the basis of the amount of the erupted material, took place in Mercato, approximately 8,000 years ago, and in Avellino, approximately 3,800 years ago. Each volcanic episode has been given the name of the place in which the complete sequence was observed.

After the eruption in Avellino the activity of the volcano seemed to die down and in fact the first historical records classify Vesuvius as no longer active. In the 1st century B.C. the volcano looked like a mountain and was covered with wild vines. In fact the rebel gladiator Spartacus and his comrades, who took refuge on mt. Vesuvius, used their branches to build ladders and surround the Roman troops so they could flee. According to Plutarchus this episode took place in 72 B.C.

The igneus nature of these rocks was discovered in 50 B.C. by the famous Greek geographer Strabo but no one suspected the volcano was going to be active again. In 63 A.D. very violent earthquakes shook all the Vesuvian area but Vesuvius still appeared a flat and common mountain.

The eruption which took place on 24th August 79 A.D. is the most famous eruption in ancient history. Today this episode is still full of fascination despite the fact it completely destroyed Pompeii and Herculaneum. The letters of Pliny the Younger and Tacitus give a detailed description of the events. The letters describe the circumstances which led to the death of Pliny the Elder, who devoted his life to studying natural phenomena. Pliny the Younger's description is a record of exceptional importance because

A striking panorama of Naples during the eruption of mt. Vesuvius in 1944.

it contains significant details on the phenomenon. He describes the appearance of the pine-like eruptive cloud which usually originates from high energy explosions, now known as Plinian explosions. It is reasonable to believe that Pliny the Elder died of suffocation like most of the people whose bodies have been reconstituted in plaster during the excavations.

It has been calculated the volcano erupted about 3 cubic km of lava in a period of 30 hours. Therefore the eruption of Pompeii was the most violent and destructive among those studied so far, and among those which have taken place in densely-populated areas.

Pompeii was buried by pyroclastic rocks, resulting from the explosion, whereas Herculaneum was covered by a mud avalanche. Both towns were cancelled from the face of earth and remained so until in the 18th century they were first excavated.

Other volcanic events occurred at intervals of centuries followed by a new period of quiescence, which, according to Sir William Hamilton, plenipotentiary minister in Naples and husband of the famous Lady Hamilton, lasted from 1139 to 1631. In 1631 in fact there was a violent explosion which has been identified with the last cycle of the activity of Vesuvius.

The volcanic phenomena have been described by several authors so that it is now possible to put the various phases into a chronological sequence: lava eruptions of great extent are generally followed by more or less violent explosions; the last one was witnessed in 1944.

If we observe the Vesuvius crater now from the top it seems incredible that the volcano could have caused so much destruction. The vapours issuing from the main crater are the only sign of its activity.

The volcano is now in a quiescence phase which is the closing phase of an eruptive cycle. Basing our considerations on the history of this volcano we can predict that there will be no eruptions in the near future. New eruptions should take place in the third millennium of our era. Nature, however, does not follow strict rules. Therefore the volcano could at any time restart its eruptive cycle although it seems quite improbable.

Marino Martini
Professor of Volcanology University of Florence

The mouth of the volcano in an eruptive phase.

On the following pages an aerial view showing the enormous crater of the volcano.

Opposite: above, a view of Vesuvius;
below, the striking volcanic rock of the mountain.

The interior of the crater seen from on high.

GUIDE FOR THE VISIT

Generally those who plan to visit the crater of Mt. Vesuvius take the road, open both to cars and busses, which leaves Herculaneum or Torre del Greco and climbs up to the parking lot at the base of the «Great Cone», but there is also a private road which goes up from Boscotrecase.

The Volcanological Observatory of Mt. Vesuvius lies at an altitude of 609 m. and can be reached by turning off the main road. Another turn, further on, leads to the chair lift, no longer in use, which had replaced the old funicular immortalized in the song Funiculì-Funicolà. Inaugurated in 1880, it was closed in 1944 after a series of eruptions.

As one climbs, the vegetation progressively changes and becomes more sparse. The flourishing orchards, favored by the fertile lava soil, on the lower part of the volcano, give way to barren stretches of broom and grass and lichens.

A farflung stupendous panorama accompanies the visitor: the eye ranges from the Gulf of Naples with the Phlegraean Fields and the islands of Ischia and Procida up to the Sorrentine peninsula and Capri.

From the parking place at an altitude of 1000 m. the excursion continues on foot up a steep path which, after about an hour's walk, reaches the edge of the crater.

Here, after the ticket office, there is a large open area (with a coffee bar and souvenir shop) which provides an exceptional view of the interior of the crater.

The inner walls, of stratified rock, descend to a depth of 200 meters, surrounding the gigantic terminal opening of the volcano which is almost circular in form and has a diameter of about 600 meters.

A complete turn around the crater takes about an hour on foot along a path, at times rather dangerous, which runs along the edge, and which can only be undertaken accompanied by one of the guides available in the large square near the guardhouse.

STRATIGRAPHY OF VOLCANIC LAYERS

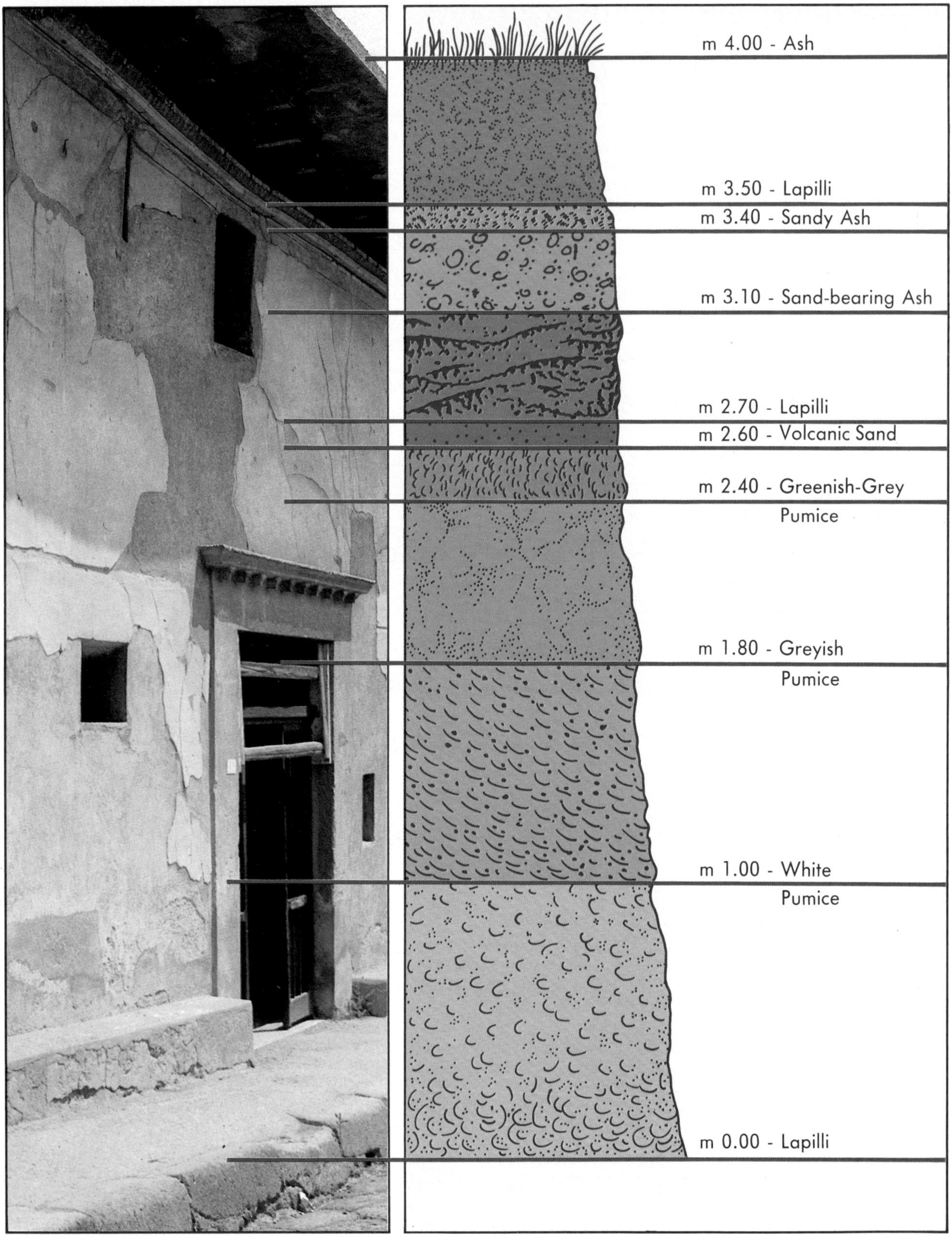

m 4.00 - Ash

m 3.50 - Lapilli

m 3.40 - Sandy Ash

m 3.10 - Sand-bearing Ash

m 2.70 - Lapilli

m 2.60 - Volcanic Sand

m 2.40 - Greenish-Grey Pumice

m 1.80 - Greyish Pumice

m 1.00 - White Pumice

m 0.00 - Lapilli

POMPEII

In the picture, a 19th-century reconstruction of the
Temple of Venus in Pompeii.

INTRODUCTION

HISTORICAL SURVEY

*It is difficult to say just how large any protohistoric set-
tlement on the ridge of lava where Pompeii was to rise
may have been. Not enough has been found in the way
of pottery that can be referred to the inhumation culture
of the Iron age pit tombs (a fossa, 9th-7th cent. B.C.),
but in any case the lack of water here makes it unlikely
that an inhabited center of any size existed before the
middle of the 7th cent. B.C.*

*In the course of the 8th cent. B.C. Greek (Ischia and Cu-
mae) and Etruscan colonization (Capua) in the territory
of Campania stimulated the development of Pompeii as
a city around the area of the Forum. A point of encounter for important trade routes, it became a clearing station for traffic towards the hinterland. Up until about the
middle of the 5th cent. B.C. the city was dominated polit-
ically by the Etruscans, whose presence is verified by the
finds of bucchero with Etruscan inscriptions. In the
course of the 6th cent. B.C. the influence of the Greek*

*culture is also documented by the terracottas which deco-
rated the Temple of Apollo, by important ceramics and
architectural elements that were part of the so-called
Doric Temple. During the 5th cent. B.C., after the defeat
of the Etruscans by the Greeks of Cumae and the Syracu-
sans in the battle of Cumae in 474, the entire fertile Campanian countryside was occupied by Samnite peoples
from the mountain hinterlands, both as a result of military operations and through a slow gradual penetration
and assimilation with the local population. This was
probably when Pompeii spread out over the entire lava
ridge and was surrounded by walls.*

*It was in the 4th cent. B.C. that Pompeii began its great
urban expansion along a grid layout, and the buildings
began to be constructed in limestone. A new series of
conflicts broke out in that same century between the
Samnites who had become city dwellers and new waves of
Samnite peoples from the mountains. The intervention of
Rome played a determining role and at the end of these
struggles, known as Samnite wars (343-290 B.C.), Rome*

The Style IV fresco inside the House of the Vettii, depicting Apollo overcoming the Python. Right: detail of a room decorated with Style II simulated architecture.

dominated all of Campania. The part played by Pompeii was minor, both here and in the war with Hannibal (218-201 B.C.). In fact, while victorious Rome subjected most of the Campanian cities which had sided with Hannibal to heavy sanctions and deprived them of their liberty, the position of Pompeii was not particularly unfavorable. To the contrary, with the dominion of Rome over the Mediterranean, merchandise moved more freely and in the course of the 2nd cent. B.C. the city's economic growth accellerated, particularly with the production and exportation of wine and oil. This state of well-being was reflected in the spurt in public and private building: in this period the Temple of Jupiter and the Basilica were built in the area of the Forum, which, together with the Triangular Forum, was restructured, while in the field of private undertakings a patrician dwelling such as the House of the Faun competes both in size and magnificence with the dynastic palaces of the Hellenistic East. Pompeii sided with the Italic allies in the battle for the right to Roman citizenship which led to the Social Wars (90-89 B.C.).

In 89 B.C. the city was besieged by Sulla and conquered without particular consequences. It was transformed into a municipium *and governed by the magistrature of the* quattuorviri *between 89 and 80 B.C., when it was turned into a military colony named Cornelia Veneria Pompeianorum by Publius Cornelius Sulla, nephew of the dictator. This was when the* ordo decurionum, *or local senate was formed, through the admission of pro-Sullan elements to whom the principal magistratures were also entrusted. Economically the city continued to flourish and new important public buildings, such as the Amphitheater and the Odeion, were created.*

The Imperial period opened with the entrance into Pompeii of new families favorable to Augustus and a wholehearted adhesion to the new political ideology manifested in a propagandistic public building program, such as the Building of Eumachia and the Temple of the Fortuna Augusta. After an obscure period of political crises under Claudius, the situation was fully normalized under Nero. It was under his reign, in A.D. 59, that the bloody riots in the Amphitheater between Pompeians and Nucerians took place. In A.D. 62 a disastrous earthquake heavily damaged the buildings in the city. The following years were dedicated to the challenging job of rebuilding, which was still in progress when Pompeii was completely buried under a dense hail of volcanic cinders and ash in the fatal eruption of Vesuvius on August 24, 79 A.D. A moving eyewitness account of the tragedy has been left us in two letters sent to Tacitus by Pliny the Younger.

14

THE STYLES OF PAINTING

Style I (or "incrustation") spread through the Roman world in the 2nd cent. B.C. when it became fashionable to paint the inner walls of private dwellings as well as of public and religious buildings. This decorative mode was of Greek derivation, directly inspired by the isodomic masonry technique of 6th and 5th cent. B.C. architecture, and used polychrome stucco to reproduce the projecting elements such as the dado, the middle zone in large panels, the upper zone in smaller panels, the cornices, and sometimes the pilasters which articulate the walls vertically. The lively color contrasts are no more than a translation into the pictorial idiom of the Hellenistic innovation of employing various types and colors of marble, in the realization of the single elements.

Style II (or "architectural") became popular in the years when Sulla's military colony was established (80 B.C.). The decoration on the walls proposed perspective views with architectural elements illusionistically articulated on different planes with foreshortenings and complex perspective effects which culminated in breaking through the wall towards an imaginary open space. The immediate models were the illusionistic stage sets of the Hellenistic-Roman theater and the new "baroque" fashions of 2nd-1st cent. B.C. architecture.

Style III (or "ornamental") was a reaction to the baroque solutions of the illusionism of Style II, together with the preference for academic classicism typical of the art of the Augustan period. The walls are once more simple flat surfaces which mark the boundaries of an enclosed space and are subdivided horizontally and vertically into monochrome areas articulated by slender architectural and decorative elements. The focal point is a painting in the center, generally of mythological, religious or idyllic subject, set inside an aedicule flanked by panels with small scenes suspended in the center which depict miniature figures and landscapes; in the upper zone slight perspective architectural elements in the manner of Style II occasionally survive. Worthy of note are the frequent use of Egyptian-style decorative elements and the appearance of an impressionistic technique typical of Alexandrine "impressionistic" painting, which in a certain sense contrasts and enlivens the sober balanced classicism of Style III.

Style IV, which became popular in the period of Claudius and Nero, exhibits the typical eclecticism of Roman art in its broad variety of decorative schemes inspired by both Style II and Style III. The colors are more decided and tend to contrasting lively color effects, the decorative elements multiply and crowd together, alternating with illusionistic architectural views and pictures of mythological subjects often painted in the impressionistic technique. A particular type is that of suspended carpets with small pictures and figures in the center, inspired by the Hellenistic fashion of hanging decorative tapestries on the walls.

DOMESTIC ARCHITECTURE

Pompeii, thanks to the exceptional completeness of archaeological documentation, provides a fairly exhaustive picture of the evolution of domestic architecture of the "Italic" type, both as regards upper class houses as well as the more modest dwellings. The basic nucleus for all further development was the atrium house, of which one of the oldest and most important examples in Pompeii is the House of the Surgeon dating to the 4th cent. B.C. Domestic life revolved around the atrium which had two basic functions: it provided light for the house, which was conceived of as a closed organism with high enclosing walls, through an opening in the roof, and it collected rain water in an impluvial basin at the center of the floor under this opening, from whence the water was carried off into a cistern. The lararium for the tutelary gods of the household was in the atrium and in the earlier examples the kitchen with the hearth, around which the family consumed its meals, was also there. A short corridor (fauces) led to the atrium around which there was a series of small rooms which served as bedrooms (cubicula), as well as two open areas at the ends of the side walls, used for the ancestor cult (alae). The back wall was occupied by the tablinum, a room originally used as bedroom for the husband and wife and later transformed into a dining room or reception hall. Next to it was a corridor which led to the hortus, a small garden enclosed by a high wall.

15

The small entrance portico to the presumed shrine of Isis inside the House of Octavius Quartio.

In the 2nd cent. B.C., after Rome's conquests in the East, the influence of Hellenistic architecture led to the fusion, in the ambience of the patrician dwelling, of the atrium house with the Greek type centered around the peristyle, a courtyard garden, often with basins, surrounded by a columned portico off which the various rooms opened. Another element adopted at this time by the Italic house was the triclinium, *a dining room generally situated next to the* tablinum *and with three convivial couches from which meals were taken in a reclining position in Greek style. The introduction of the peristyle in place of the original* hortus *led to the development of other rooms for daily use (*diaetae*) and reception (*oeci*) next to it, as well as occasionally the creation of baths. As time passed the layout of the various elements became more complex. A particularly significant example is the imposing House of the Faun.*

*The houses of the lower classes of small shopkeepers, ar-*tisans, freedmen, were much smaller and simpler in plan. Often they were lined up in a single large building with the various entrances on the facade. Inside, the various rooms were articulated around a covered atrium without an *impluvium (*atrium testudinatum*), with a first floor facing onto it, used for the bedrooms. The increase in population in Pompeii in Imperial times meant that housing was in great demand and as a result apartment houses of as many as three floors were built.*

The shops, workshops, laboratories, of which Pompeii furnishes us with an exceedingly vivid and significant picture, were often part and parcel of the owner's living quarters, which were behind the shop or on the floors above.

It was also fairly frequent to find shops set up in rooms that opened off on either side of the entrance to an upper class dwelling and which were rented out by the owners of the house.

MOSAICS

The oldest type of decorated pavement is the *opus signinum, well represented in pre-Sullan Pompeii. This type of pavement consists of fragments of bricks and potsherds set into a layer of lime, in which white tesserae of "palombino" were sometimes inserted to create a regular dot effect or a carpet of geometric pattern. At the same time the* emblemata *made their appearance - small pictures set at the center of the pavement and depicting scenes that were inspired by the models of great Greek painting. In Sulla's time the mosaics reflected the taste for the schemes of Style II wall painting, with illusionistic perspectives in boxes made of tesserae that became gradually lighter in color and with patterns of rhombs with borders of cubes and perspective meanders. Toward the end of the republican period simpler black and white mosaics became popular. They had geometric decorations and figures, surrounded by borders of wave meanders, dentate bands, checkerwork. Sober geometric mosaics also characterize the period of the early empire; with the Claudio-Neronian period there is an increase in traditional ornamental elements which crowd the composition, while the figured mosaics reflect the luminarist acquisitions that had been experimented in contemporary Style IV painting.*

SCULPTURE

The sculpture found in Pompeii generally falls into a category of artisan production that satisfied requests of a decorative, celebrative-political, religious, and sepulchral nature.
Pompeii was after all a provincial city, where the clients were prevalently middle class and there was no particular demand for real works of art.
This explains the essentially "practical" nature of Pompeian sculpture which consisted primarily of small-size statues although there were also figures that were larger than life such as some of the examples from the Temple of Jupiter. Copies of famous works, such as that of the Doryphorous, are extremely rare. A variety of materials was used for the sculpture: marble, tufa, limestone, terra cotta, bronze.
The discovery of fragments from various statues as well as famous pieces such as Apollo playing the lyre, the so-called Caligula on horseback, Apollo and Artemis archers, show that bronze was more common than previously thought.
Portraiture appeared after the establishment of Sulla's colony, initially in the field of funerary and honorary sculpture, and then, after the empire, with the representations of the various members of the imperial family.

The elegant mosaic in chiaroscuro, depicting tragic masks and garlands, found in the House of the Faun and now in the Museo Nazionale in Naples.

Public buildings

Temples

Stores

Private buildings

Houses of dignitaries

Areas to be excavated

1 - Porta Marina
2 - Suburban Villa
3 - Antiquarium
4 - Temple of Apollo
5 - Basilica
6 - Public Buildings on the South Side of the Forum
7 - Building of Eumachia
8 - Temple of Vespasian
9 - Sanctuary of the Lares Publici
10 - Macellum
11 - Temple of Jupiter
12 - Arches on the North Side

of the Forum
13 - Horrea
14 - Via dell'Abbondanza
14 - Intersection of Holconius
15 - Triangular Forum
15 - Doric Temple
16 - Large Theater
17 - Odeion
18 - Gladiators Barracks
19 - Temple of Isis
20 - House of Menander
21 - House of the Ceii
22 - House of the Diadoumeni

23 - Fullonica Stephani
24 - Shops of Via dell'Abbondanza
25 - Thermopolium with Lararium
26 - Thermopolium of Asellina
27 - Election slogans
28 - House of Trebius Valens
29 - House of Paquius Proculus
30 - House of Octavius Quartio
31 - House of Venus in the Shell
32 - House of Iulia Felix
33 - Amphitheater
34 - Large Palaestra
35 - Necropolis of Porta Nocera
36 - Stabian Baths

37 - Via Stabiana
38 - Lupanar
39 - Via degli Augustali
40 - Pistrinum of the Vicolo Torto
41 - House of M. Lucretius
42 - House of the Silver Wedding
43 - House of the Centennial
44 - House of M. Obellius Firmus
45 - House of the Golden Cupids
46 - House of the Great Fountain
47 - House of the Dioscuri
48 - House of the Vettii
49 - House of the Faun
50 - Temple of Fortuna Augusta

51 - Arch of Caligula
52 - Forum Baths
53 - House of the Tragic Poet
54 - Bakery of Modestus
55 - Via Consolare
56 - House of Sallust
57 - Porta Ercolano
57 - Via dei Sepolcri
58 - Villa of Diomedes
59 - Villa of Mysteries

19

PORTA MARINA

As the name indicates, this was the gate facing the sea, set in the western side of the hill on which the town rose. It is the most recent of Pompeii's city gates, built in *opus incertum* in lava stone. It consists of two passageways with barrel vaults, one meant for pedestrians and one for vehicles and animals.

Later these two passageways were joined at the back in a single vaulted gallery, which is what we see today.

In the 1st cent. B.C. various villas were built near the city walls on this side with its magnificent panorama of the coast.

SUBURBAN VILLA

This villa near the Porta Marina was discovered after the bombardment of 1943. It dates to the Imperial period and is set against the outer side of the city walls, whose function had changed with the *pax augustea* and from here it enjoyed a marvelous view of the sea. The building seems to have been abandoned after the earthquake of A.D. 62.

Stretches of walls can still be seen behind a long colonnaded portico, in front of which is a garden that covers an older road that led to the Porta Marina. A series of rooms opens off the portico: the main room is a large triclinium with an antechamber, originally paved with hexagonal tiles and a complex painted decoration which represented one of the first examples of Style II (late 1st cent. B.C.), restored in Style IV in the middle of the 1st cent. A.D. The main band on the walls, surrounded by elegant accessory decoration, is occupied by three large pictures of Cretan subjects: Theseus killing the Minotaur with Athens in the background; Theseus abandoning Ariadne on the island of Naxos; and Icarus and Daedalus. The upper band contains cupboard doors with portraits of poets.

Next to the triclinium is a cubicle with an alcove with white-ground walls and another alcove with two small pictures of mythological subject. Behind the cubicle a second triclinium looks out through a three-light opening onto another garden. The fresco on the walls depicts a satyr and a maenad.

The two vaulted passageways of the Porta Marina, for pedestrians and for vehicles.

A room in the Antiquarium.

ANTIQUARIUM

The Antiquarium in Pompeii, at present being reorganized, was founded in 1861 and rebuilt with new museum installations after being destroyed by bombs in World War II. The Antiquarium contains material from the different phases of life in the city and the surroundings, thus supplying an explanatory chronological survey of the cultural vicissitudes of this exceptionally well-documented archaeological site.

The protohistoric phase is represented by tomb furnishings from the inhumation cemetery in the Valle del Sarno, dating to the Iron Age between the 9th and the 8th cent. B.C. The archaic period is represented by terracottas from the Doric Temple and the Temple of Apollo, as well as Corinthian pottery, Attic black-figure and red-figure pottery, and Etruscan bucchero, dating to between the 6th and 5th cent. B.C. From the Samnite period there are the tufa pediment and the altar from the Temple of S. Abbondio dedicated to Dionysius (3rd-2nd cent. B.C.) and figured capitals with Dionysiac subjects dating to the same period and from the entrances of some of the houses on the Via Nolana.

From the Roman period are a cloaked statue of Livia, Augustus' wife (from the Villa of the Mysteries), and the portraits of Marcellus, Augustus' nephew, of C. Cornelius Rufus (from the house of the same same), of

Vesonius Primus (from the House of Orpheus). Domestic ware, tools and instruments for work, the remains of food such as carbonized loaves of bread, eggs and other things also date to Roman times. Casts of some of the bodies of the victims of the eruption are also to be found here.

TEMPLE OF APOLLO

This imposing religious complex stands along the western side of the forum but does not communicate with it. The fact that Corinthian, Attic black-figure and red-figure pottery and Etruscan bucchero with dedicatory inscriptions have come to light in the area of the temple testifies to the existence of a cult of Apollo in Pompeii, undoubtedly imported from Greece via the Greek colonies in Campania as early as the first half of the 5th cent. B.C. The ground plan as we know it dates back to no earlier than the Samnite period (2nd cent. B.C.) and was inspired by Hellenistic models. It was frequently modified until the restoration after the earthquake of A.D. 62, and this had not yet been terminated when the eruption of A.D. 79 took place.

The actual temple stands at the center of a peristyle of 48 columns with the entrance on the south side, from the Via Marina. Originally the colonnade of the portico was

Above, the portico of the Temple of Apollo with the statue of the god and, below, the remains of the sanctuary and the altar.

Opposite: the bronze statue of Apollo near the portico of the sacred area.

The interior of the Basilica.

Doric with a Doric entablature with metopes and tri-glyphs, on top of which stood another tier of smaller columns. After the earthquake, a heavy layer of stucco transformed the columns into the Corinthian style, the entablature was redecorated with a frieze of griffins supporting garlands and the upper tier of columns was not replaced.

The original aspect of the complex was considerably modified when openings the sanctuary had on the east side, overlooking the forum, were walled up and transformed into niches decorated in Style IV painting with subjects from the Iliad. Around 2 B.C. the *duoviri* M. Holconius Rufus and C. Egnatius Postumus had a high wall raised on the west side. As explained in an inscription, it was built so that the sanctuary could not be seen from the windows of the houses that faced in this direction. The temple was thus isolated at the center of an enclosing wall, completely altering the idea behind the original Greek architectural model upon which it was based. Various statues were found in front of the columns of the portico: the bronze statue of Apollo with a bow was near the east side, while on the west the statue of his divine sister Diana was situated, with an adjacent cult altar. Both statues have now been replaced by copies. The marble statues of Venus and Hermaphrodite may have been set along the south side temporarily while the nearby Temple of Venus to which they probably belonged was being remodelled. Lastly, on the east side there was also a herm with a youthful version of Hermes, of the type associated with the god as protector of the palaestra.

The Temple of Apollo is a peripteral structure with six Corinthian columns on the front and nine on the sides, set on a podium with an entrance staircase on the front. The cella is paved with a central carpet of rhombs in polychrome stone mosaic bordered by three bands. The outer one was decorated with a meander design in perspective. Near the entrance, in the pavement, a dedicatory inscription in Oscan referring to the *quaestor* Oppius Campanus was found. The oval tufa *omphalos* inside the cella is the symbol of the Delphic Apollo. The cult statue has not been found and all that remains is the base at the back wall. The temple is architecturally heterogeneous, for it includes elements appertaining to the Etruscan-Italic tradition such as the podium and the flight of stairs on the front, and Greek, such as the peripteral module and the Corinthian order.

In front of the building is the marble cult altar with the dedicatory inscription of the *quattuorviri* M. Porcius, L. Sextilius, Cn. Cornelius, and A. Cornelius, figures who belonged to the early phases of Pompeii's political history when it was a Sullan colony (80 B.C.). The sundial, dedicated by the Augustan *duoviri* L. Sepunius Sandilianus and M. Herennius Epidianus was set on an Ionic column near the temple stairs.

The interior of the Basilica with the Tribune at the back.

BASILICA

The Basilica, identifed as such by graffiti on the intonaco of the walls (*bassilica*), stands near the west corner of the Civil Forum. It is one of the oldest known examples of this type of building, the beginning of a long tradition which would evolve in its final form into the model for the Christian basilicas.

In Pompeii the Basilica can be dated to the last quarter of the 2nd cent. B.C. on the basis of roofing tiles with the factory mark in Oscan *Ni-Pupie*, the name of a magistrate in the Samnite period, and of inscriptions scratched into the oldest intonaco of the walls, also written in Os-

can. The building already reflects some of the structural conventions later codified by Vitruvius in his *De Architectura* for the basilicas, but differs in the proportions of the volumes and because the entrance is on the short side, overlooking the Forum, instead of on the long side; as a result the tribunal is also on the short back wall, on an axis with the entrance.

The main entrance consists of five openings scanned by piers, which lead to an uncovered vestibule, to the south of which is a room with a deep well for water inside. The vestibule leads to the real entrance to the Basilica which has a facade raised up on four steps, with four Ionic columns flanked by two side doors. The interior has a nave and two aisles: the nave is bordered on its four sides

The recostruction of the interior of the Basilica.

Opposite: a stretch of the portico in the Forum with the Temple of Jupiter in the background.

by twenty-eight large columns, each built of tiles which were cut along the flutes and then covered with stucco. A row of Doric half columns is set along the aisles. Originally they were topped by a second tier of Corinthian half columns. The roof must have been with a single truss and the intercolumniations between the half columns of the upper tier must have been left open to allow light to enter the Basilica.

There were two secondary entrances at the center of the long sides. The back wall was occupied by a tribunal, a podium with an elevation of two superposed tiers of six Corinthian columns; two rooms at the sides have entrances framed by an Ionic column and two Doric half columns in the corners. In the space between these two rooms and the tribunal, two flights of stairs lead to an underground vaulted room. The tribunal, access to which was via two wooden staircases, was reserved for the judges who directed the trials from here and pronounced their verdicts. The Basilica played a leading role in the civil and commercial life of the city. Justice was administered here, but important business meetings were also held, the most pertinent economic and legal affairs were handled and authoritative scholars have found a comparison to modern Wall Street quite apt. The numerous graffiti found on the walls inside, which were originally decorated in Style I, are now in the Museo Nazionale in Naples. The subjects were varied ranging from witty to erotic to political.

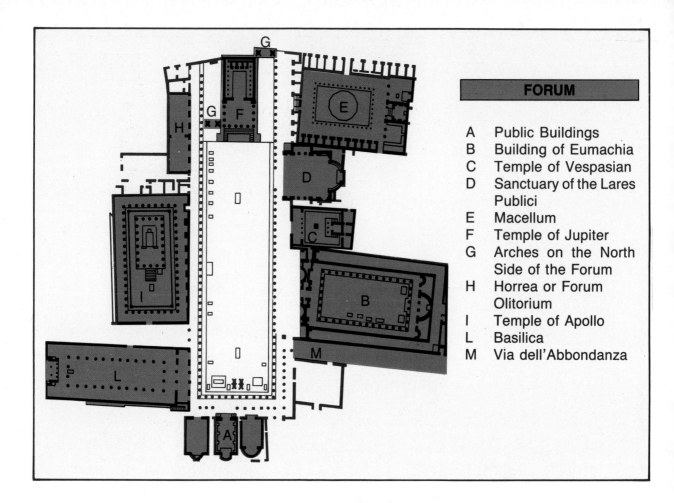

FORUM

A Public Buildings
B Building of Eumachia
C Temple of Vespasian
D Sanctuary of the Lares
   Publici
E Macellum
F Temple of Jupiter
G Arches on the North
   Side of the Forum
H Horrea or Forum
   Olitorium
I Temple of Apollo
L Basilica
M Via dell'Abbondanza

THE FORUM: GENERAL BACKGROUND

The Forum of Pompeii occupies an area which lies at the confluence of important old communication routes between that city and Naples, Nola and Stabia. It was the center of the city when it was first founded, and even after the great expansion of Pompeii it continued to play a fundamental role in the politcal, religious, and economic life of the city even though it now lay on the outskirts. Unfortunately most of what we know is limited to the more recent phases of the layout of the Roman Forum, both as far as the shape and size of the piazza are concerned as well as for the types of buildings which surrounded it. Up until the 2nd cent. B.C., a relatively late period, the area of the Forum, which was certainly smaller than it is now, was used only for markets. It was not enclosed by porticoes and seems to have been surrounded by a series of shops and modest buildings, the foundations of which indicate that the square was irregular in shape. But the religious complex of the Temple of Apollo already existed in the 6th cent. B.C. It was originally in communication with the piazza and still consti-

tutes part of the western side, although the orientation diverges slightly.

The great transformation of this market place into a monumental area to be used as the site for public buildings and official religious structures took place in the 2nd cent. B.C. The piazza was enclosed on three sides by two tiers of porticoes in tufa, Doric below and Ionic above, separated by an entablature of metopes and triglyphs. A Latin inscription found in front of the Basilica informs us that this portico was built by the quaestor *Vibius Popidius. Now the office of* quaestor *is not among those documented in Roman Pompeii, but since the inscription is in Latin and not in the Oscan tongue, the portico was probably built some time around the conquest by Sulla, and certainly before its institution as the colony of Cornelia Veneria Pompeianorum in 80 B.C. The paving of the piazza in slabs of tufa, about 40 cm. lower than the present level, also belongs to this phase. The base of the portico is raised above the level of the piazza by three steps, thus closing the area of the forum to wheeled traffic.*

It was also in the course of the 2nd cent. B.C. that the Fo-

Above, a stretch of the Forum and, below, the south side with the public buildings.

rum acquired its definitive size: the north side was shut off by the creation of the large Temple of Jupiter (later transformed into Capitolium), while the south side was enlarged by building the Basilica, seat of the administration of justice and commerce, the Comitium for the elections and the three municipal buildings. A mensa ponderaria (weights and measures standard) already existed in the Samnite period, set in a niche in the external wall of the enclosure of the Temple of Apollo. The Samnite weights and measures were then modified according to those of the Augustan period.

In the years after the establishment of Sulla's colony, building activity was concerned primarily with the theaters and the realization of the Amphitheater. In the early Imperial period new buildings also appeared in the Forum. The east side of the square was occupied by the Building of Eumachia, the wool market, probably meant for more important commercial transactions, by the Temple of Venus and the Sanctuary of the Lares Publici (protecting divinities of the city). In the Augustan period the repaving of the piazza in travertine was begun as well as the replacement of the tufa portico with one in travertine, never completed because of the earthquake of A.D. 62 and the eruption of A.D. 79. The orators' tribune (suggestum), situated on the west side of the piazza, is also incomplete. None of the many statues whose bases are still visible in the area of the Forum was ever found. They may have been damaged and were never set up again after A.D. 62.

Above, the south side of the Forum and, below, the model of the area.

PUBLIC BUILDINGS

Three buildings of almost identical size, meant to house the principal magistratures of the city, are lined up along the south side of the Forum. All three reveal remodelling in brick that dates to after the earthquake of A.D. 62. The eastern building, towards the Via dell'Abbondanza, is the one that suffered least damage. It is a rectangular building with an apse at the back. It was here that the *duoviri*, the principal magistrates of the city, exercised their functions. The building in the center has a podium and a series of piers along the interior side walls. The supposition is that the civic administrative documents were kept in wooden cupboards which would have been set into the niches that were thus formed. The western building was the headquarters of the *decurioni* who comprised the *Curia*, the city's senate. There are niches for statues in the side walls and in the apse at the back.

A stretch of the portico in front of the building of Eumachia.

BUILDING OF EUMACHIA

The large building situated on the eastern side of the Forum, between the Temple of Vespasian and the Comitium, was built, according to the two inscriptions on the architrave of the portico in front of it and near the entrance on Via dell'Abbondanza, by the priestess of Venus Eumachia, patron of the *fullones*, who dedicated it to the *Concordia Augusta* and the *Pietas*. These were programmatic concepts bound to Tiberius and his mother Livia and the building must be dated to this period.

The facade, rebuilt in brick after the earthquake of A.D. 62, is preceded by a portico with two tiers of columns and has two large raised niches at the sides which were meant for the auctioneer at public auctions. Another two semicircular niches are framed by a pair of smaller niches which contained the statues of Aeneas, Romulus and, probably, of Caesar and Augustus. Extant inscriptions on the bases of the first two list the deeds of the personages represented (*elogia*) and thus clearly indicate that

it was modelled on the Forum of Augustus in Rome. The entrance is framed by a particularly fine marble cornice, decorated with scrolls and birds, which must have belonged to the first phase of the building for it is too short. A corridor flanked by two rooms, in one of which is to be found the large container for urine which the *fullones* used to cleanse the cloth, leads to a large interior courtyard with a two-tiered colonnaded portico on four sides. On the back part a porch-like structure marks the presence of the large apse behind, preceded by two columns topped by a pediment, containing the cult statue of the Concordia Augusta. A cryptoporticus lit by large windows runs along three sides behind the walls of the porch. In the back wing, behind the apse, is a niche with a statue of Eumachia dedicated by the *fullones*.

Just what the building was used for is problematical. Its obvious propagandistic intent in favor of the imperial family leads one to believe that it must have been something more important on an economic and commercial level than a simple wool market, a hypothesis some of the evidence has engendered.

The area of the Temple of Vespasian.

TEMPLE OF VESPASIAN

It is situated on the eastern side of the civil Forum between the Sanctuary of the Lares Publici and the Building of Eumachia. The limited space available determined the irregularity of the plan, set at an angle with respect to the axis of the square of the Forum.

The facade is in brick, parallel to the axis of the portico, projecting forwards more than the adjacent Building of Eumachia. An entrance door here leads into a vestibule and then to the court preceded by four columns, with perimetral walls in blocks of tufa reinforced at the corners and with piers in brick. The walls were simply intonacoed and decorated with a pattern of large blind windows framed by pilaster strips and with triangular and curved pediments set over them. A provvisory system for channeling rain water had been installed in the courtyard in preparation for the paving that was to come.

The temple stands at the center of the back wall of the courtyard, with a cella in brick with two antae, set on a tall podium and accessible from the back via two side-stairs. The cella, which still has the base on which the cult statue was set inside, was originally preceded by a tetrastyle porch.

A marble altar, its four sides decorated with reliefs, stands at the center of the courtyard in front of the aedicule. The principal side depicts a scene of sacrifice of a bull: a priest, *capite velato* (with his head covered), performs libations on a tripod, assisted by *camilli* with objects for the rite; behind him are two lictors and a flute player. In front of the priest is the *victimarius* with a two-edged axe and an assistant leading the bull to sacrifice. In the background of the scene is depicted a tetrastyle temple to be identified with the aedicule of the back side. The reliefs on the north and south sides show the objects used in cult ceremonies: the augur's curved staff, the box which contains the incense, the small tablecloth, the patera for the libations, the pitcher, the ladle. Lastly, on the relief facing the temple aedicule there are two laurel trees, attribution of the emperor Vespasian (formerly of Augustus), between which is hung a garland of oak leaves, the civic garland which since Augustus has been the symbol of imperial authority. The temple then was dedicated to the Genius of Vespasian and had not yet been finished when the eruption of A.D. 79 took place. A door in the back wall of the courtyard leads to three rooms used by the personnel in charge of the temple and as storerooms.

HORREA OR FORUM OLITORIUM

This building is situated along the west side of the Civic Forum to the north of the Temple of Apollo. An open portico, it faces on the Forum square and on the facade has eight large piers in brick which frame eight entrances. It was to house the warehouses and the grain market, but it had not yet been finished when the eruption of A.D. 79 struck. The internal walls are of rough masonry with no trace of intonaco and the roof had not yet been built. At present, covered by a modern shed roof and closed by a gate, the portico is used as the storeroom for the archaeological finds. It contains a large quantity of amphoras and pottery of daily use, oil presses, capitals and architectural elements as well as casts of the victims of the eruption from the Antiquarium. Of particular interest is the 'muleteer' who, crouched up, tries to protect his face with his hands from the terrible exhalations. He was found next to the skeleton of his mule, under the portico of the Large Palaestra. Inside a case is the cast of a dog who was chained near the entrance of the House of Vesonius Primus, struck as he tried in vain to free himself.

Above: a millstone, architectural fragments, stone weights and amphorae inside the Forum Olitorium. Below: the piers on the facade of the Horrea.

MACELLUM

The Macellum, or the food market of Pompeii, stands in the northeast corner of the Forum. It was set here for two reasons - firstly because a supply center was needed in a central zone of the city, and secondly because its position at the edge of the Forum square would not obstacle its functions.

Its orientation does not lie on an axis with that of the Forum and in an attempt to compensate for this the shops decrease in depth from north to south. The building has three entrances, the main one on the west side divided into two passageways by an aedicule set in the center. From here there is access to the rectangular courtyard which originally had colonnaded porticoes on four sides, as indicated by the remains of travertine steps which must have served as stylobate for the columns, of which however no traces have been found since the building was being reconstructed after the damages suffered in the earthquake of A.D. 62.

At the center of the courtyard twelve bases housed the supporting posts of the conical roof of a twelve-sided building used as a fish market, which was cleaned by the flow of a fountain as shown by the great quantity of fishbones and scales found in a drainage channel which began at the center of this area.

The portico in front of the shops of the Macellum.

The remains of the temple of Jupiter.

TEMPLE OF JUPITER

On the short south side of the Forum square, the temple is dedicated to the Capitoline triad of Jupiter, Juno and Minerva. It was first built around the middle of the 2nd cent. B.C. as part of the enlargement and new orientation of the forum.

The podium, built in *opus incertum*, dates to the founding of the temple and inside houses rooms (*favissae*) comprised of three aisles and covered with vaulting which were to be used as storage chambers for the ex-votos and as storerooms. The temple was prostyle with six Corinthian columns on the front and three on the sides, and with piers at the outer corners of the cella, with composite capitals. In its earlier 2nd-cent. B.C. version the pronaos and the cella were shorter than what we see now and the entrance staircase on the front reached up to what is now the second intercolumniation. The cella had no aisles and was without an internal colonnade.

With the second phase, dated to the 2nd cent. B.C., the temple assumed its present size, with a very deep pronaos and the staircase which is divided into two flights below so as to include at the center a platform on which the altar was set. There must have been equestrian statues on either side of the staircase, for which only the bases remain. The cella was divided into three aisles by two rows of columns set in two tiers, Ionic below and Corinthian above, set along the side walls. The side aisles were thus extremely narrow.

The first wall decoration was painted in Style I in faux marble incrustation, probably replaced in the Sullan period by paintings in Style II. At the back of the cella a tripartite podium, with an elevation of half columns and three-quarter columns at the corners, held the statues of the Capitoline triad, of which a large head of Jupiter still remains.

A third phase in the restoration of the temple took place in the time of Tiberius. The tripartite podium of the cella was enlarged and faced in marble, the pronaos was repaved in travertine, the external walls and the podium were freshly stuccoed and the interior walls of the cella were redecorated with Style III painting.

An idea of what the Temple of Jupiter looked like can be had from a representation in the household shrine of the House of Caecilius Iucundus, in which the equestrian statues on either side the staircase are also visible.

This page: the honorary Arch of Drusus. Opposite: the two sides of the honorary Arch of Tiberius or Germanicus.

ARCHES ON THE NORTH SIDE OF THE FORUM

The northern side of the Civil Forum is shut off by the mass of the Temple of Jupiter, flanked by two honorary arches in brick. Nothing is left of their original marble revetment. The western arch, situated at the height of the temple colonnade, was dedicated to Drusus; it originally had a pendant arch on the other side of the temple, which was torn down so as to leave open the view of the arch behind attributed to Tiberius or to Germanicus.

It was built further back from the temple and constituted a monumental entrance to the Forum. The uncertainty of the attribution is due to an inscription by Germanicus in which his son Nero is named, that was found nearby and which probsbly belonged to the arch. On either side of the passageway, facing the Forum, are two niches in which the statues of Nero and Drusus werw set. They were Germanicus' sons but also heirs to the throne after the death of the son of Tiberius. The bases of the marble columns which decorated the front and back of the arch are still extant. The attic must have been crowned by an equestrian statue of Tiberius or Germanicus.

VIA DELL'ABBONDANZA AND INTERSECTION OF HOLCONIUS

The Via dell'Abbondanza was one of the two principal *decumani* of the city (the other consisted of Via di Nola and its extensions into Via della Fortuna and Via delle Terme), in other words the east-west street axis which traversed the entire urban area, even if in Pompeii the orientation is more southwest-northeast. The western stretch of Via dell'Abbondanza connects Via Stabiana, that is the *cardo maximus*, with the Forum square, after which the street continues as Via Marina, leading out of the Porta Marina. This first stretch of Via dell'Abbondanza, which belongs to the earliest phases of Pompeii's city plan as it grew up around the area of the Forum, later, when the city's town plan was considerably enlarged, was continued beyond the Via Stabiana, following a course that was exactly parallel to the *decumanus* of Via di Nola, until it reached the Porta di Sarno. This large thoroughfare connected the most important centers of city life with each other, from the Forum, to the Stabian Baths, up to the zone of the Amphitheater and the Large Palaestra. The maximum width was about 8.50 m. and it seems that in the stretch towards the Forum it had been newly paved by the *aedili*. The intersection formed by the crossing between Via dell'Abbondanza and Via Stabiana, that is between the *cardo maximus* and the *decumanus maximus* is known by the name of Holconius for on a base near one of the four piers which supported a four-sided arch there was originally the wreathed statue of M. Holconius Rufus, one of the outstanding political figures in Pompeii of the Augustan period. The house attributed to him stands nearby. On one side of the intersection is the fountain with a basin in which is represented the *Concordia Augusta* with a cornucopia, erroneously identified with the personification of Abundance, from which the street takes its conventional name.

Via dell'Abbondanza and the fountain from which it takes its name.

Above, the Intersection of Holconius and, below, a shop nearby.

TRIANGULAR FORUM
AND DORIC TEMPLE

The so-called Triangular Forum is situated on the far end of a lava outcrop to the southwest of the Large Theater and the Quadriporticus of the Gladiators, in a striking position overlooking the plain below. This area came to look as it does now in the Samnite period, in the 2nd cent. B.C., as part of the town-planning project for the restructuration of the theater area.

The complex can be reached through a propylaeum with six Ionic columns and a fountain in front, which opens in the northern tip of the triangular piazza. It has a portico with ninety-five Doric columns on three sides, while the southwest side has been left open with its fine panorama towards the sea. Right inside the entrance, near the north portico, were a fountain and the base of a statue

The interior of the cavea of the Large Theater.

dedicated to Marcellus, Augustus' grandson. The archaic Doric Temple stands in the center of the piazza, with nothing left now but the foundations. To judge from the few surviving architectural elements, it was founded in the second half of the 6th cent. B.C. It is difficult to establish what the original plan was, for it is poorly preserved and was frequently remodelled in the course of the centuries. Renovation dating to four different phases has been identified, to between the end of the 6th and the 2nd cent. B.C. Two divinities, Hercules and Minerva, represented in some of the antefixes, were probably worshipped here.

The double rectangular enclosure in front of the facade of the temple probably represents the *heroon* for the cult of the mythical founder of the city. Three tufa altars are found next to it. Not far from the *heroon*, a *tholos* with seven Doric columns encloses a well cut into the lava rock. As shown by an inscription in Oscan, this building was built by the *meddix* (an important public office in the Samnite period) Numerius Trebius. Near the northwest corner of the temple a semicircular bench with lion feet (*schola*) and a sundial behind it were set up in the Augustan period by the *duoviri* L. Sepunius Sandilianus and M. Herennius Epidianus, both of whom also dedicated the sundial in front of the Temple of Apollo.

LARGE THEATER

Built in the Hellenistic period, between the 3rd and the 2nd cent. B.C., the theater of Pompeii obviously assimilated all the architectural canons of the Greek theater, which remained basically the same despite the various modifications the building was subject to. The *cavea* was in fact set into the natural slopes of the lava ridge and not raised on masonry substructures; the orchestra is in horseshoe shape and not semi-circular, a mode which was also of Greek origin and which was to encounter greater favor in the Roman-Italic ambience. Moreover the specific position of the building can be traced back to the sacral character of the theater performances which was strongly felt in the Greek world, and which is here manifested in the fact that it communicates directly with the so-called Doric Temple and the ancient sacred area of the Triangular Forum which it included.

The theater as we see it now has many elements due to restoration carried out in the Augustan period, as stated in various inscriptions, under the patronage of Marcus Holconius Rufus and his brother Marcus Holconius Celer, members of a wealthy family who held the most important civic offices in the city.

Above, the interior of the Odeion and, below, one of the kneeling atlantes figures decorating the head of the cavea.

ODEION OR SMALL THEATER

Situated near the Large Theater, the construction of the *odeion* had evidently already been foreseen in the town plan of the entire area in the Samnite period, even though it was not to be built until Pompeii was transformed into a colony by Sulla (80 B.C.).

Two inscriptions inform us that the two Sullan *duoviri* Q. Valquo and M. Porcius were responsible for having the structure built. It consists of a theater *cavea* inserted into a square perimetral wall on which the roof rested. The Odeion was in fact meant for a more intimate type of spectacle, such as musical auditions, poetry recitals, mime. The seating capacity is about 1500.

GLADIATORS BARRACKS

A large quadriporticus stands behind the stage of the Large Theater and is connected to it, in line with the Vitruvian canon which, according to the Greek model, provided for a porticoed area in which the spectators could walk and converse during the intervals between spectacles. This example in Pompeii is one of the oldest

*Above: the large quadriporticus of the Gladiators Barracks.
Below: the helmet of a gladiator found here (Museo
Nazionale, Naples).*

known in Italy for this type of building and it dates to the
early 1st cent. B.C. The quadriporticus, composed of 74
Doric columns, can be reached from an entrance with
three Ionic columns set near the north corner. After the
earthquake of A.D. 62 the complex lost its original function and was turned into barracks for gladiators. The
monumental entrance was walled up and a guard post
was set near an entrance doorway. In this phase a series
of rooms on two floors was realized. The northeast side
houses the sector for the mess with a spacious exedra
preceded by four piers which comprised the dining room,
and a large kitchen with annexed storerooms. The apartment of the *lanista* or instructor was on the top floor
while the gladiators were lodged in the cells arranged
along the sides of the quadriportico. In some of them hel-
mets and richly decorated parade armor was found, as
well as eighteen cadavers and the skeleton of an infant in
a basket.
An exedra at the center of the southwest side has frescoes
in Style IV depicting Mars and Venus and trophies of
gladiators' arms. A room in the southwest side served as
a prison as shown by the iron shackles fastened to a
beam, although the four bodies found here were not
chained.

The Temple of Isis.

TEMPLE OF ISIS

It is situated to the north of the Large Theater, between the Samnite Palaestra and the Temple of Jupiter Meilichio. As we are told in an inscription on the architrave, this religious complex was restored after the earthquake of A.D. 62 by a private individual, the wealthy freedman Numerius Popidius Ampliatus in the name of his son Numerius Popidius Celsinus. The temple was first built around the end of the 2nd cent. B.C. The sacred area is bounded by a high wall with a colonnaded quadriporticus inside, at the center of which the temple stands. The ground plan is unique - the cella, which is wider than it is deep, is set on a tall podium and is preceded by a pronaos with four columns on the front and two on the sides. The main entrance consists of a flight of stairs on the front of the building, while a subsidiary staircase is on the south side. Two niches with triangular pediments, on either side of the cella outside the columns of the pronaos, housed the statues of Harpocrates and Anubis, divinities connected with the cult of Isis. On the exterior wall of the back of the temple there is a third niche for the simulacrum of Dionysius between two ears in stucco, symbols of the god's benevolence in giving petitions a hearing.

A podium whose hollow interior was meant for the cult statues is in the cella. When excavations were in course, a large marble hand, two human skulls, and other ritual objects were found here. The decoration on the outside of the temple consisted of white stucco panels and a polychrome frieze of volutes. The walls of the portico were painted with a pattern of red panels, at the center of which were priests of Isis, framed by architectural elements and small landscape scenes. A statue of Venus and the bronze herm of C. Norbanus Sorex, an actor, were found in the south corner, while a statuette of Isis dedicated by the freedman L. Caecilius Phoebus was found near the west corner. The entrance to the courtyard, flanked by two piers with engaged half-columns, is at the center of the east side.

A shrine with a fresco, now transferred, depicting a priest before Harpokrates, is in the wall across the way.

A square unroofed building in the southeast corner of the courtyard is the so-called *Purgatorium*, in which purifica-

*The large peristyle around the garden of the
House of Menander.*

tion rites were held. A staircase leads to a vaulted subter-
ranean chamber, which contains a basin for lustral water.
The facade has a broken triangular pediment and a frieze
with two processions of priests converging towards the
center. Mars with Venus and Perseus with Andromeda
are shown on the side walls.

The most important of the various altars set up in the
courtyard and between the columns of the portico is the
one between the *Purgatorium* and the temple. The remains of the sacrifices were collected in a well that was
fenced off in the northeast corner of the courtyard.

A series of living quarters for the priests opens off the
south wall of the portico, whiile the west wing is almost
completely occupied by the elevation of the *Ecclesiasterion* with five arched entrances. This large hall was where
those initiated in the cult of Isis met. When it was discovered, the names of Numerius Popidius Celsinus, his
father, and his mother Corelia Celsus, could be read on
the pavement. The walls are frescoed with five panels of
sacred subjects in Egyptian style and representations of
Io in Egypt and Io in Argos. The remains of an acrolythic
statue were found in front of this room. Two other rooms
which communicated with the *Ecclesiasterion* were clearly used for cult purposes.

HOUSE OF MENANDER

As indicated by a bronze seal found in the servants'
quarters, this imposing mansion belonged to Quintus
Poppaeus, a member of the important *gens* of the Pop-
paei related to Nero's second wife, Poppaea. The first
version of the house, limited to the rooms articulated
around the atrium, dates to the middle of the 3rd cent.
B.C. It was renovated a century later, but the ground
plan and the decoration as we know it date to the early
Augustan period when a revolutionary enlargement of
the dwelling was terminated with the addition of the
peristyle, the baths and the servant's quarters. At the
time of the eruption the decoration and some of the structures were being restored.

Benches for the *clientes* were built along the facade. The
entrance is framed by two Corinthian piers. The vestibule
leads to the large Tuscan atrium, with a marble basin for
rain water (*impluvium*) in the center and the walls frescoed in Style IV with medallions containing the head of
Zeus-Ammon and tragic masks. Set into the west corner
is a lararium in the form of a small temple with a double
pediment.

The remains of the facade of the House of the Diadoumeni with the columns of the corinthian atrium.

HOUSE OF THE DIADOUMENI

This large house, built in the Samnite period in the second half of the 2nd cent. B.C., must have belonged to Marcus Epidius Rufus or Marcus Epidius Sabinus, to judge from the number of times these two names appear in the election propaganda on the facade and on the walls of the neighboring buildings.

Outside, a two-step podium runs along the facade, an unusual architectural feature. Beyond the entrance vestibule is an atrium of Corinthian type of an imposing size, with sixteen columns with Doric capitals set around the impluvium basin in the center. This is the most striking of the rare Corinthian atriums in Pompeii (in other words with a row of columns set along the sides of the impluvium). All around were various rooms, but unlike the canonic scheme, here the *alae* were at the center of the side walls instead of at the back. They were preceded by a pair of Ionic columns and the corner piers had capitals with the heads of maenads or divinities.

In the *ala* of the northwest side there is a shrine which the dedicatory inscription on the podium tells us was erected by two freedmen named Diadumeni (hence the name of the house) in honor of the Lares and the Genius of their master Marcus, certainly one of the two public personages cited above.

FULLONICA STEPHANI

This is the only one of the laundries in Pompeii that had not simply been adapted from a building that was already there, but was an actual restructuring of a patrician house, rationally conceived to best fulfill this new function. It was excavated in 1911 and was found in good shape so that the specific uses of the various rooms could be identified.

Both the final phase in the preparation of fabrics, the end process for removing the last traces of dirt, as well as the public service of washing and pressing garments, took place in the *fullonicae*. The name of the probable owner of this laundry, a man named Stephanus, has been deduced from the programs of election propaganda that are painted near the entrance, which also inform us that women as well as men worked in the *fullonica*.

The entrance door was normally closed from the outside by a latchbolt. During the excavation a skeleton was found inside, with a considerable sum of money nearby (1089.5 sesterces), which may have been the laundry's last intake, unless it was the patrimony of a simple fugitive who had sought refuge here. The entrance is very wide facilitating the movement of the clients. The remains of a press (*torcular* or *pressarium*) for "ironing" clothes was found in the first room. From here to the atrium

The atrium of the Fullonica Stephani with the tub for washing the cloth.

where the impluvium basin at the center has been transformed into a tub for washing, with the addition of a parapet. The roof of the atrium does not slope down but is flat with a skylight in place of the *compluvium* (the only known example in Pompeii) to provide a surface where the cloths could be spread out to dry in the sun.

Beyond the small garden with the peristyle are the other installations: three tubs for washing, intercommunicating but without a drainage system, and five oval basins for trampling (*lacunae fullonicae* or *saltus fullonici*) where the workers washed the fabric by trampling on it after having soaked it in a mixture of water and degreasing alkaline substances such as soda and human or animal urine. Containers for the urine used in washing were found near these basins. It is a curious fact that while af-

ter Vespasian the urine was available from the public latrines which he had created involving the payment of a tax, before that the *fullones* invited their clients or simple passersby to urinate in amphoras from which the neck had been removed and which were set in the lanes and near the entrances of the *fullonicae*.

The next step in the procedure was to soften the fabrics which had been hardened by the urine by treating them with a special type of clay (*cretae fullonicae*) and then to the scutching and a thorough rinsing that would eliminate the substances used in the previous steps. These procedures were then followed by carding to raise the nap, clipping, brushing and finally pressing. This *fullonica* also had service rooms for the personnel such as a latrine and a kitchen.

A stretch of Via dell'Abbondanza.

SHOPS OF
VIA DELL'ABBONDANZA

In 1911-1912 excavation campaigns were begun in Pompeii aimed at uncovering a long stretch of Via dell'Abbondanza and the buildings which lined it, in the direction of the Porta di Sarno. The excavation and careful restoration have provided us with a vivid image of what daily life was like in one of the main thoroughfares in the city, with its shops and their signs to attract clients, its two-story buildings with balconies overlooking the street, the election and propagandistic inscriptions on the walls, the graffiti left by passersby.

In the years after the earthquake of A.D. 62 the Via dell'Abbondanza was apparently becoming the real heart of commercial activity in Pompeii, especially in the area around the intersection with the Via Stabiana. Shops above all were being rebuilt or newly constructed, while the actual dwelling houses had not yet been restored when the eruption took place in A.D. 79. This, for example, was the case with the bakery of Sotericus, the only one facing onto this street, realized after A.D. 62 by adapting two ruined houses. Next to it is the *caupona* (tavern) which also belonged to Sotericus, with a sign that was originally painted with the personification of Roma-Virtus wearing a helmet and where the obscene graffiti left by the clients refer to the amatory services provided by the waitresses and the hostess. In addition to various taverns, a wide variety of shops lined the Via dell'Abbondanza: laundries, dyers, workshops where felt was made, smithies - in one, which belonged to a man named Verus, was found a *groma*, an instrument used by surveyors in measuring lots of land. In the stretch of street near the Porta di Sarno, already in the suburbs, the shops become less frequent and the houses, like the one of Octavius Quartio and Iulia Felix, resemble suburban villas in their size and layout more than city dwellings.

THERMOPOLIUM WITH LARARIUM

This thermopolium is situated in Via dell'Abbondanza and has the usual L-shaped counter, with the long side facing the entrance and the other side at right angles towards the interior, with built-in holes for the containers for drinks and hot food served there. A similar simple counter runs along one of the side walls.

When it was excavated, the last day's earnings, 683 sesterces in small coins, were found in one of the jars in the counter. A lararium with a temple-like facade in stucco, with small Corinthian columns and a triangular pediment, is on the back wall. Inside is a white-ground band in which the Genius of the owner of the shop, flanked by the Lara, is depicted offering libations in favor of the gods. Below are painted two serpents moving towards an altar, a subject commonly found in domestic shrines, symbol of fertility and procreative power.

A door near the lararium leads to a back room which communicates with the atrium of the house of the owner of the thermopolium, the entrance to which is in a secondary side street off Via dell'Abbondanza. A cubicle is decorated with pictures of birds on white walls, while the tablinum has as yet no painting. A triclinium with fine late Style III wall painting opens onto a small garden. The dado is painted with plant motifs while, above, a shrine is flanked by architectural views, panels with a picture in the center, candelabra. A painting depicting the Rape of Europa, who is shown on the back of a bull, is still intact at the center of one wall. The small garden, in which numerous amphoras were found, also houses a summer triclinium.

HOUSE OF TREBIUS VALENS

A multitude of inscriptions covered the facade of this house, but they were unfortunately lost in the bombardment of 1943.

In the front, the house is laid out around an atrium with a basin in the center, surrounded by the various rooms. The first cubicle on the left in decorated with full Style II paintings with the name of the owner of the house, Valens, scratched into one of the walls. In another cubicle, on the right, the discovery of a casket with precious objects and ointment jars would seem to indicate that it was the mistress's bedroom. On this side there is also a rectangular hall with birds and other animals painted on the black-ground walls.

Above, the triclinium of the house of Trebius Valens.

A section of the frescoes in the presumed shrine of Isis in the House of Octavius Quartio, situated at the western extremity of the viridarium.

*The colonnade and the pergola with the biclinium on the
east side in the House of Octavius Quartio.*

HOUSE OF OCTAVIUS QUARTIO OR OF LOREIUS TIBURTINUS

This large patrician mansion takes its name from a fictive Loreius Tiburtinus, the result of the fusion of the names of two people which appeared in the election slogans on the facade. It actually belonged to Octavius Quartio whose bronze seal was found in a cubicle where a kiln had been temporarily set up for the redecoration of the walls which was being carried out at the time of the eruption of A.D. 79. The dwelling consisted of two nuclei: the first dating to the Samnite period was traditionally centered around the atrium, the second was inspired by the more varied and animated architectural idiom of the 1st cent. A.D.

The entrance, near which are seats for the *clientes*, is flanked by two *cauponae* (taverns) which communicated with the inside of the house. The impression of the tall door reinforced with bronze bosses still exists. The vesti-bule leads to the Tuscan atrium with a central impluvium, transformed into a flower bed. The arrangement of the cubicles and the *alae* is standard, even if the left *ala* had become a simple passageway to the adjacent quarter with kitchen and latrine.

The new quarter, articulated around a small *viridarium* with porticoes on three sides, is situated on the other side of the atrium. The room at the center of the west side may have been a shrine to Isis, to judge from the decoration of tendrils, trophies and figurines, a priest of Isis with cult instruments whom an inscription below identifies as Amulius Faventinus Tiburs. Two paintings on the front show Diana at the bath and Actaeon torn to pieces by his dogs. On the east side an *oecus* has the upper walls decorated with scenes from the mythical saga of Heracles against Laomedon, while the lower walls show a series of episodes involving Achilles (funeral games in honor of Patrocles, Priam asking for the body of Hector, etc.). Outside are paintings of Orpheus soothing the animals with his lyre and Venus gliding over the surface of the ocean in a shell.

AMPHITHEATER

Pompeii's amphitheater was built immediately following its foundation as a military colony by Sulla in 80 B.C. by the *duoviri* Quintus Valgus and Marcus Porcius, who also had the Odeion built. It is the earliest of the amphitheaters we know of (the Amphitheater of Taurus, the first one to be built in stone in Rome, dates back to no earlier than 29 B.C.) and is therefore particularly important in providing a picture of this type of typically Roman architecture. Campania moreover has been indicated as the place of origin for gladiatorial games, of which evidence exists as far back as the 4th cent. B.C.

The Amphitheater is situated in the southeastern zone of Pompeii, chosen because the area was still free of buildings at the time and because the earthfill inside the city walls could be used as a substructure for the eastern part of the *cavea*. The arena was excavated about six meters deep below the existing level of the land and the earth was then used as a landfill to support the western half of the building. A containing wall with buttresses and blind arches was erected here, constituting the principal facade of the complex. Two double stairways on the west and two simple stairways on the north and south led to an uncovered corridor which served the *summa cavea*. Access to the *media* and *ima cavea* was through four corridors which led to the *crypta*, a covered gallery, also vaulted, which runs along the lower steps of the *media cavea* and opens through arches on two orders of seats. The two main corridors also open into the entrances to the arena set at the ends of the principal axis and were paved for the use of wagons. While the north corridor regularly follows the axis of the arena, the other corridor crosses the west side of the building and then turns at a right angle, leading out at the far south of the arena, since there could obviously be no opening on the side that was backed up against the city walls.

Inscriptions inform us that the two niches set on either side of the north corridor, which was the main entrance to the arena, housed the statues of Caius Cuspius Pansa and his son of the same name. They both held important civic offices, including those of *duoviri* and were honored by the city for having restored the Amphitheater after the earthquake of A.D. 62.

The arena is elliptical and surrounded by a parapet more than two m. high, originally painted with scenes of the hunt and of matches. The *ima cavea* was for persons of rank and was divided into sectors: the central part of the first four rows consisted of four wide platforms for the *bisellia*, those on the east reserved for the decurions and those on the west for the *duoviri* and the contracters of the spectacles. The *media* and *summa cavea* were divided into *cunei* by flights of stairs. As can still be seen, not all the sectors here had stone seats, but there were prevalently wooden tiers.

A view of the Amphitheater (80 B.C.).

Two views of the so-called "garden of fugitives".

NECROPOLIS OF PORTA NOCERA AND GARDEN OF THE FUGITIVES

A necropolis consisting of a series of tombs bordering the Via Nocera lies right outside the Porta Nocera. There are various types of sepulchres: chamber tombs, cube tombs (a dado), altar-shaped, aedicule tombs, hemicycle, etc. ranging chronologically from the Republican period to the last years of Pompeii.

At the point where this street intersects with the street that runs down from the Porta Nocera stands a travertine cippus which informs us that the military tribune Titus Suedius Clemens was charged, by decree of the Emperor Vespasian, with reestablishing the boundaries of the public soil.

Near the cippus is a low building, called « garden of the fugitives », in which casts of some of the victims of the eruption are kept. The thirteen bodies discovered here were those of inhabitants who died from the poisonous sulphur fumes borne by the wind. Their bodies, which were imprisoned in the ashes and pumice that solidified as time passed, left cavities in the earth which in the course of the excavations were filled with plaster, thus providing us, after centuries, with the shapes of the ancient inhabitants of Pompeii.

STABIAN BATHS

These baths take their name from the fact that they are situated on a city block bordered by Via Stabiana and Via dell'Abbondanza. They are the oldest baths in Pompeii and four different building phases can be identified. The oldest part seems to date to the late 4th cent. B.C. and consisted of the palaestra, a series of cells with tubs along the north side and a well to furnish water. It was at this time that the palaestra was built in a trapezoidal form due to the presence of two old streets and the garden of a house that was later torn down.

The general layout of the bath however dates to the 2nd cent. B.C. as confirmed indirectly by an inscription of the *duoviri* of Sulla's colony C. Uulius and P. Aninius who state that they have reconstructed the palaestra and the porticoes and have created a *laconicum* for sweat baths and a *destrictarium* for cleansing the body. The entrance is on Via dell'Abbondanza and from here access is to the courtyard of the palaestra with colonnaded porticoes on three sides and the entrance framed by two piers, a motif also found on the portico of the opposite side. At the center of the west side is a swimming pool (*natatio*)

A view of the area occupied by the palaestra and the relative colonnade inside the Stabian Baths.

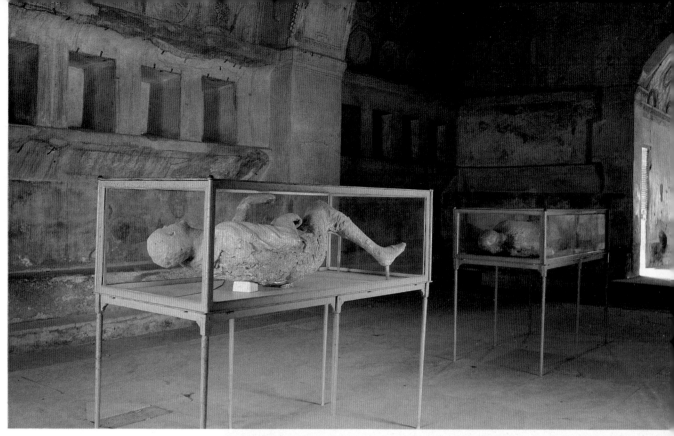

Two sections of the apodyterium.

flanked by two rooms where the clients washed before entering the pool, and by a dressing room. These rooms are decorated with polychrome stuccoes that can be dated to the years after the earthquake of A.D. 62. The actual baths were on the east side and were divided into two opposing non-communicating sectors, one for men and one for women, with the *praefurnium* for heating set at the center and used by both. Entrance to the men's baths was from the southeast corner of the

Above: a secondary entrance on the western side of the Stabian Baths. Below: the fountain on Via Stabiana.

portico where a sundial with a dedication in Oscan was found. A passageway with a barrel vault decorated in polychrome stucco with figured medallions leads both to the *apodyterium* (dressing room), with niches in which to put the clothing and also with a stuccoed vault, and to the circular *frigidarium*. The latter, with a domed ceiling painted blue to represent the starry skies, was orginally the *laconicum* built in Sulla's time, and only later turned into the cold baths. Next comes the *tepidarium* for luke-warm baths, with a pool on the short side, and then the *calidarium*, which, like the preceding room, has the pavement raised up on *suspensurae*, and walls with airspaces for the passage of hot air; a pool for hot baths is on the short side, while across from it is the *labrum*, a circular pool for cold baths.

VIA STABIANA

This street is one of the three *cardines* of Pompeii (the others are Via di Mercurio - Via del Foro - Via delle Scuole and Via di Nocera), the streets that cross the city on a north - south axis. The route followed by Via Stabiana, which lies in the valley between the two lava ridges on

Above: the intersection between Via Stabiana and Via del Tempio d'Iside. Below: a stretch of the Via Stabiana.

which Pompeii is situated, has been used since oldest times, since it joined the city to Stabia and Sorrento and the coastal route that joined Naples to Stabia also passed along it for a stretch. It then joined Pompeii to its river port on the Sarno, an important trade route; traces of a suburb with mercantile installations and warehouses were found on this line about one kilometer from Pompeii in the hamlet of Bottaro.

As part of the town plan of Pompeii, it was used as the north - south artery and lengthened so that it joined the Porta di Stabia with the Porta Vesuvio and the two eastern *decumani* running east - west, the Via Nolana and the Via dell'Abbondanza, crossed it so as to create a regular grid plan which was to condition all future development of the city. The Via Stabiana was the means of communication between the areas where large numbers of persons congregated, such as the Stabian Baths and the Central Baths, situated along the street, and the zone of theaters and the Temple of Isis. It was also extremely important as a thoroughfare for trade, confirmed by the wear the basalt pavement shows near the gates. After A.D. 62 the area around the intersection with Via dell'Abbondanza became the principal center of trade and economic life in the city.

LUPANAR

The *lupanar* on Insula VII is the only one of the twenty-five houses of prostitution known in Pompeii which was built specifically as such. The others are to be found on the first floors of the inns or taverns or even in private homes, or consisted simply of a room with a bed, accessible directly from the street. As customary this brothel was situated at the intersection of secondary streets.

This brothel has ten rooms, five on the lower floor and five larger ones on the upper floor, with a balcony in front that acted as a passageway and which could be reached by an independent flight of wooden stairs. A Priapus with two phalluses was painted next to the entrance on the ground floor, shown beside a fig tree, holding his two male members. The rooms have masonry beds on which mattresses were spread. Erotic scenes which probably indicated the "specializations" offered to their clients were painted above each door. The interior of the brothel must have been redecorated shortly before the eruption, for there is the impression of a coin dating to later than A.D. 72 in the intonaco of one of the rooms. On the other side of a wall on the ground floor there is a latrine. A large number of inscriptions, over 120 of which are still legible, were scratched into the walls both by the client and by the girls who worked there as prostitutes. We can

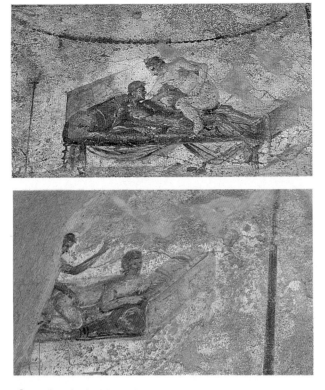

Opposite: the building of the lupanar and the vestibule with various rooms on either side.
This page, below: the fresco with the biphallic Priapus in the lupanar and, above, erotic scenes painted above the doorways of the rooms.

still read the boasts of faithful clients, exclamations of satisfaction, complaints because of having contracted venereal diseases, expressions of specific desires, coarse word-plays, etc. We find that many of the girls had foreign Greek or Oriental names, a sign of the fame enjoyed by "exotic" prostitutes. The client could also have boys. The prices were very low, one of the reasons being that these brothels were frequented by the lowest levels of society and by slaves. On the average the cost of a sexual service was two *asses*, the equivalent of the cost of two cups of wine.

Caligula had ordained a tax on prostitution, which corresponded to the price charged one client per day. Prostitutes could not testify in court, nor, after legislature passed by Domition be the recipient of an inheritance, even if they had stopped practicing this profession. Only marriage might make it possible for them to acquire the rank of *matrona*.

The Pistrinum of the Vicolo Torto.

PISTRINUM OF
THE VICOLO TORTO

This bakery belonged to N. Popidius Priscus for it is connected to his house by a door set at the back of the complex. The machinery for the production of bread consists of four millstones in porous lava, very compact resistent stone so there were no risks of its losing tiny fragments in the grinding process which might be mixed with the flour. The form of these mills resembles an hourglass with a biconical or hollow *catullus* which rotates above on a cone-shaped pivot (*meta*), set on a base in masonry and surrounded by a paved floor on which the animals yoked to the beams inserted in the *catullus* walked.

The wood-burning oven is next to the grindstones. It is in concrete and set into a square chamber with a vent at the top so the air needed for combustion could circulate inside and it had a chimney. On the front the loaves were put in through an arched opening in brick. A masonry tub was used for washing the grain. Two rooms next to the oven were destined for the storage of the bread after it was baked and as granary.

This bakery served only for the production and wholesale distribution of bread which may also have been sold by itinerant venders since it had no actual shop open to the public.

Above: the fresco of the wedding of Mars and Venus in the House of M. Lucretius and, below, a medallion of Mercury in the same house.

HOUSE OF M. LUCRETIUS

This house is attributed to M. Lucretius because his name appears as addressee on a letter depicted, with a kit for writing letters, in a wall painting in a room near the garden. He was an important figure who held the office of *decurion* in the city and was a priest of Mars.

This patrician house had fine wall paintings, now mostly in the Museo Nazionale in Naples. In the atrium there are still some frescoes in Style IV with imaginary architecture, and in the tablinum the Triumphs of Bacchus with a satyr and a Victory. There must also have been various panel paintings in the tablinum which unfortunately have been lost.

The atrium lacks a central impluvium and it is therefore to be supposed that it was not covered with the customary shed roofs that sloped down towards the interior, but was covered by a roof that completely covered the house with a watershed towards the exterior (*atrio testudinato*). The lararium is in the atrium and the large tablinum opens in

Above: a fresco landscape inside the House of M. Lucretius and, below, the fresco with Narcissus at the spring.

the back wall, beyond which a lovely garden stretches out in scenic perspective on a higher level. With herms and statues of satyrs, cupids, and various animals set among the beds, at the back was a fountain with mosaic decoration, where the water poured out of a goatskin held by a marble silenus.

HOUSE OF THE SILVER WEDDING

The name derives from the fact that the house was excavated in 1893, the year in which the monarchs of Italy celebrated their silver wedding anniversary. The house was built in the Samnite period in the second cent. B.C., and its last owner was L. Albucius Celsus.

The vestibule leads into an imposing austere tetrastyle atrium, with an impluvium in the center and a marble

Two rooms with frescoes in the House of the Silver Wedding.

pedestal which served as a fountain. The compluvium roof has palmette antefixes and lion-head gutter spouts. At the back are the tablinum and two other rooms, beyond which is the peristyle of Rhodian type, with a higher ceiling on one side, making it sunnier, supported by large Doric columns unlike those on the other sides. The garden is in the center and glazed Egyptian-type statuettes of animals were found here.

A kitchen and a bath consisting of an *apodyterium*, *tepidarium* and *calidarium* open off the west arm of the peristyle, while a pool in a garden behind served as a *frigidarium*. A summer triclinium is next to the baths. At the back an exedra with yellow walls decorated with garlands and wreaths is flanked by two cubicles, also decorated in Style III painting. The west side houses an *oecus* with a vaulted ceiling supported by four columns, with wall paintings in Style II and a mosaic pavement. On this side there is an entrance to another larger garden with a pool in the center and the remains of an open-air triclinium.

Above: the niche nympheum with the waterfall in the House of the Centennial and, below, a medallion in the same house with a fresco landscape.

HOUSE OF THE CENTENNIAL

This vast house owes its name to the fact that it was excavated in 1879, the 18th centennial of the eruption which buried Pompeii. It was built in the 2nd cent. B.C. and its history includes phases of restructuring and renovating in the Imperial period. It is comprised of two dwellings articulated around two Tuscan atriums with impluvium at the center.

The large main atrium with its mosaic pavement has walls decorated with pictures in Style IV painting of theater subjects. At the back wall is the tablinum flanked by two rooms, one with white-ground walls and one with black-ground walls. The garden surrounded by a peristyle is situated behind the tablinum. The famous bronze of the Satyr, with a goatskin, which decorated the edge of the swimming pool was found here. At the back of the peristyle is a nymphaeum with a niche decorated with mosaics, from which a waterfall cascaded into a basin set at a lower level. The small cryptoporticus which supports the niche has paintings of naturalistic subjects while the upper parts of the walls in the courtyard are frescoed with hunts of wild beasts.

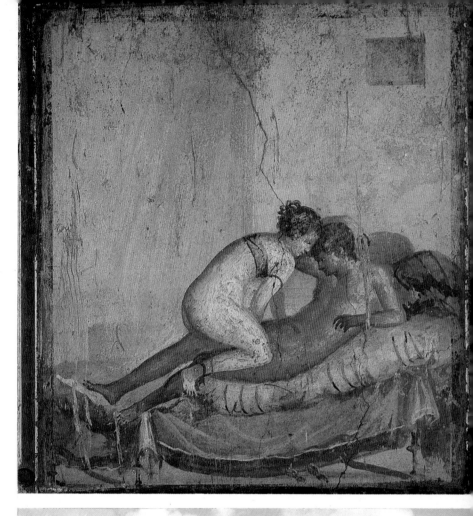

Various rooms decorated with paintings of a mythological nature, an isolated cubicle with erotic pictures, a bath, belong to the southwest quarter, access to which is through a secondary entrance. The painting with Bacchus and Vesuvius covered with forests, now in the Museo Nazionale in Naples, comes from the lararium in the atrium.

HOUSE OF M. OBELLIUS FIRMUS

The house belonged to M. Obellius Firmus, whose name appears several times in the election inscriptions found on the walls of the neighboring buildings and even inside the house itself. The building technique and the ground plan date the building to the Samnite period.

At the front it consists of two entrances and two atriums. The main one is tetrastyle with columns in tufa and a centralized plan and with a traditional layout of rooms - a series of cubicles at the sides, the *alae* and the tablinum at the back. The temple-like lararium is in the southwest corner, while there is a safe near the south wing. The secondary atrium is of the Tuscan type and also follows the canonic plan as much as the restricted space permits.

The back half of the house consists of a peristyle with columns on three sides and a large garden. A series of rooms is set along the southwest side. These include a kitchen, a small bath, a cubicle with an alcove decorated with pastoral scenes, an *oecus*. Adjacent to the garden are a cubicle and a communicating *oecus* with wall decoration of particularly fine quality: a swamp landscape and two *pinakes* (pictures) with an offerer and Cybele in the cubicle and imaginary Style II architecture in the *oecus*.

HOUSE OF THE GILDED CUPIDS

The house belonged to Gneo Poppaeo Abito, perhaps related to Poppaea, Nero's wife, and it is without doubt one of the most interesting in Pompeii as regards the elegance and refinement of the architectural and decorative aspects typical of the spirit and artistic taste of Nero's time. It is not large and has a rather irregular ground plan, dictated by the space available and the lay of the land.

In the front the house has a vestibule and an atrium with a central rather small impluvium. Only three rooms face onto the atrium, two cubicles on either side of the vesti-bule and a tablinum at the back with paintings that represent the meeting between Paris and Helen in the presence of Eros.

But the real heart of the dwelling is the peristyle: the garden has a pool at the center surrounded by flower beds and, originally, statuettes of animals, herms, reliefs. The back wall is raised to increase the scenographic effect and at the center has a pediment on fluted piers with an *oscillum* (marble disk against the evil eye) hanging from the architrave. Theater masks are also hung in the intercolumniations of the portico as a finishing touch to the refined decoration of the ensemble.

A triclinium on the east side of the peristyle enjoys a view of the garden and is decorated with Style III paintings of

Opposite, above: the mosaic fountain in the House of the Large Fountain; below, the fresco with Achilles recognized from the House of the Dioscuri, now in the Museo Nazionale in Naples.

The peristyle of the House of the Gilded Cupids.

mythological subjects: Thetis in Vulcan's workshop acquiring weapons for her son Achilles; Achilles in his tent with Briseis and Patrocles; Jason before Pelias. A series of marble reliefs is set into the south wall of the peristyle: depictions include theater masks and a dancing satyr of neo-attic inspiration. The same side also has a room with wall painting of pictures of various subjects.

The back wing of the peristyle has a triclinium at the center which still shows the damage inflicted by the earthquake of A.D. 62. On either side are two cubicles: the one on the left, perhaps used as a *gynaeceum*, opens onto a small garden and is frescoed with representations of the Seasons; the one on the right is decorated with pictures of amorous subjects, (Diana and Actaeon, Venus Fishing, Leda and the Swan) and portraits of women. Service rooms are situated in the corner across the way. And lastly, on the north side is the double bedroom decorated with cupids in gold leaf and applied on glass disks which give the house its name.

The eclecticism of the owner in the field of religion is witnessed by the presence in the house of a shrine to Isis in the eastern corner of the peristyle and a traditional lararium with figures of the Capitoline triad near the cubicle of the Gilded Cupids.

HOUSE OF THE GREAT FOUNTAIN

This house takes its name from the monumental fountain in a nymphaeum near the back wall of the small garden situated beyond the atrium. The fountain, with a pediment set over a niche, completely faced with mosaic in polychrome glass tesserae, has an opening from which the water gushed and cascaded down steps into a basin below. The rest of the decoration consists of three tragic masks projecting from the jambs of the niche and a bronze statue of a putto with a dolphin set on a base inside the basin, now replaced by a copy.

The facade of the house in rusticated tufa ashlars should also be noted.

HOUSE OF THE DIOSCURI

A painting in the entrance, now in the Museo Nazionale in Naples, of the Dioscuri, Castor and Pollux, sons of Jupiter and Leda, gives the house its name.

This is one of the rare examples in Pompeii of a house with a Corinthian atrium, where the atrium with a central impluvium is surrounded by columns, in this case twelve columns in tufa (the other two alternatives were the Tuscan atrium without columns and the tetrastyle atrium with four columns at the corners of the impluvium). Wall paintings with pictures of mythological subjects were frescoed on the walls of the rooms on either side of the tablinum. Most of them have been detached and are now in the Museo Nazionale in Naples and the British Museum in London.

An initial porticoed courtyard with Doric columns is situated beyond the tablinum and has a temple lararium on

The peristyle of the House of the Vettii.

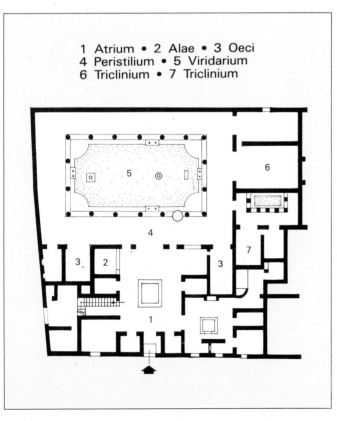

1 Atrium • 2 Alae • 3 Oeci
4 Peristilium • 5 Viridarium
6 Triclinium • 7 Triclinium

the back wall. The second peristyle with a large basin at the center was added later and is reached from the right side of the atrium. Most of the Style IV wall painting is still in place and depicts carpets hung in imaginary architectural surrounds, alternating with panels of still lifes.

HOUSE OF THE VETTII

This luxurious patrician dwelling furnishes us with an important example of what the taste in architecture and decoration was like in the last years of Pompeii, and bears witness to the importance acquired by the merchant classes of *homines novi* who disposed of considerable fortunes. The owners of this house were the affluent freedmen Aulus Vettius Restitutus and Aulus Vettius Conviva, as we know from their bronze seals found in the atrium and the election slogans on the walls outside. The latter figure was *augustale*, that is he belonged to an order nominated by the emperor to qualify for which it was necessary to contribute to costly public works.
The present ground plan is the result of the restructuration of an older house that was effected in the middle of the first cent. A.D. with restoration after A.D. 62.
The entrance portal leads into the vestibule with walls decorated with a cock fight, a sheep with Dionysiac at-

Above the lararium of the same house
and, below, the cubicle with erotic
pictures and a fountain statue.

tributes, and a Priapus who weighs
his gigantic phallus against a bag full
of money on the other scale pan.
The Tuscan atrium with an impluvium in the center has safes on either
side sheathed with iron and bronze
nails, set on masonry bases. The elegant wall painting depicts children
sacrificing to the Penates, putti in
various poses, wagons with the symbols of Bacchus and Mercury, a
scene of sacrifice to Fortuna. The
cubicle to the left of the entrance has
the walls painted with a fish pond
and two panels depicting Leander
swimming across the Hellespont to
reach his beloved Hero and the
awakening of Ariadne after Theseus
had abandoned her on Naxos. In the
adjacent *oecus* there is a picture of
the myth of Cyparissus, the young
hunter transformed into a cypress
for having slain the stag dear to
Apollo, as well as Dionysius and Diana observing the struggle between
Pan and Eros, Jupiter and Danäe,
and Jupiter and Leda. The *alae* are
also frescoed with pictures and
medallions with the heads of Satyr
and Medusa.
From the south side of the atrium a
corridor with steps going to an upper
floor leads to a spacious service entrance on the sides of which are a
stable and a latrine. The north side
opens onto the servants' quarters,
articulated around a secondary atrium with an impluvium in tufa and a
fine aedicule lararium with Corinthian half columns supporting a tri-

Above: a naval battle a theater mask and objects for the cult of Dionysius in the triclinium of the House of the Vettii. Below: the picture with Hercules strangling the serpents, in an oecus in the house.

angular pediment with cult objects in stucco: the Genius in a *toga praetexta* is shown executing a libation between two dancing lares holding the drinking horn while below a crested serpent (a common monster in the lararium) moves towards an altar which holds offerings of food. The kitchen is reached from the west corner where bronze equipment is still in the hearth: a grill, tripods and various utensils. The cubicle behind is decorated with erotic paintings.

In the absence of a tablinum, the back wall of the atrium opens on a large peristyle where numerous marble and bronze fountain statues, circular and rectangular basins, marble tables, two bifrontal herms on columns, are set up as they originally were. The garden beds have also been restored to what they once looked like. At the center of its yellow-ground walls the *oecus* to the left of the entrance to the peristyle has pictures with subjects taken from the Theban myths: Amphion and Zethus bind Dirce to a bull to avenge their mother Antiope, who had been her slave; Pentheus king of Thebes is assaulted and killed by the Bacchantes for not having permitted the introduction of the cult of Dionysius into the city; the infant Hercules strangles the serpents sent by Hera. The panels at the sides are decorated with elegant architectural perspectives.

Above: an oecus in the House of the Vettii with, in the background, the fresco with Pentheus killed by the Bacchantes. Below: Daedalus and Pasiphae in a picture in the triclinium.

The triclinium opens off the northern corner of the peristyle. The walls are frescoed with pictures inserted into an elegant Style IV decoration, with Seasons in frames and perspective architecture, ornamental elements which turn into delicate figurines, small pictures of naval battles set under theater masks and Dionysiac cult objects. Above is a frieze of imaginary architecture and figures of gods, while the dado below is in faux marble. The pictures depict love between the gods and human beings: on the left wall Daedalus shows Pasiphae, the wife of Minos, whom Zeus out of revenge had caused to fall in love with a bull, the model of the wooden cow he had made. The result of the union between Pasiphae and the bull was to be the Minotaur. The myth of Ixion is depicted on the back wall. Zeus had condemned him to be bound with snakes to a wheel made by Hephaestos because he had tried to make love to Hera, whose place was taken at the last minute by a cloud in her form (Nephele) and who was to generate the Centaurs. Hermes, Hera enthroned, and Isis are present while the cloaked woman can be identified as the imploring Nephele. The scene on the right wall shows Ariadne in Naxos, awakened by Dionysius, while Theseus flees with his ship.

A gynaeceum lies on the northwest side of the peristyle, set on a large colonnaded court with cubicle and a triclini-

On both pages, various views of the main triclinium of the House of the Vettii. Above: cupids preparing perfumes. Below: Apollo overcoming Python below a candelabrum. Opposite, above: cupids with wine amphoras and, below, other goldsmith cupids.

um. The pictures in the decoration depict Achilles on the island of Scyros and the drunken Hercules about to seduce Auge who is washing her peplos. The result of their love will be Telephus. The large *oecus* which opens onto the peristyle next to the gynaeceum contains some of the most famous and striking pictorial decoration in Pompeii. Black bands articulate the red walls. The pictures from the central sectors, probably on panels and therefore portable, are no longer extant, while flying mythical couples and ithyphallic Hermaphrodite with Silenus is depicted in the lateral sections. A frieze that runs along over the dado shows cupids and *psychai* busy at work, taking part in sports, or in religious activities. Beginning to the right of the entrance there is first a competition in target shooting, the cupid flower venders transport flowers on a goat and sell garlands. Next comes the preparation and the sale of perfumed oils, a race with chariots drawn by antilopes, and cupid-goldsmiths making and selling precious objects. Next come the activities of the *fullones* cupids, bakers and vintners. The frieze terminates with the triumphal procession of Dionysius on a wagon drawn by goats and followed by an ithyphallic Pan playing the double flute. Some of the friezes on the pilasters below the candelabra depict Agamemnon about to kill the deer sacred to Artemis, Apollo who has defeated the serpent Python.

Above. The principal atrium of the House of the Faun as it is now and, below, the copy of the bronze figurine which gave its name to the house. On the facing page, above, the principal atrium in all its original splendor. Below, the first peristyle of the House of the Faun with the garden at the center, seen from the northern exedra.

HOUSE OF THE FAUN

This imposing private house which belonged to an unknown aristocratic Pompeian family is a fine example of the result of the fusion of the architectural models of the Italic house centered around the atrium and the Hellenistic peristyle dwelling.

The extraordinarily large size of the house is an indication of the wealth accumulated by the Roman-Italic upper classes after the conquests in the east. It occupies an entire *insula* superimposed on an earlier 3rd cent. B.C. dwelling which with its *hortus* was on the site of what is now the first peristyle.

The House of the Faun, discovered and excavated around 1830, was built in two phases, the first dating to the early 2nd cent. B.C. and including the first peristyle, and the second of the late 2nd cent. B.C. in which the second peristyle was added and the final size was established.

The house consists of two quarters which communicate but have independent entrances set in a row of shops. The main quarter, to the west, is reached through a vestibule with a lararium that consists of a temple facade with small Corinthian columns. From here one passes into a large Tuscan atrium with an impluvium paved in a pat-

tern of polychrome rhombs. At the center was a bronze statuette of a dancing faun (now replaced by a copy) after which the house is called. Two series of cubicles and two *alae* are arranged around the long sides, in line with the typical Etrusco-Italic scheme. The one on the right has an *emblema* with a cat attacking a partridge while the one on the left has an *emblema* with three doves taking a jewel from a casket. The back of the atrium consists of a tablinum in the center flanked by two tricliniums.

The tricliniums had *emblemata* depicting fishes and a woman on a panther. The eastern apartment is articulated around a tetrastyle atrium on which various service rooms open.

The first peristyle had Ionic columns in tufa that were stuccoed and was also accessible from one of the tricliniums of the western quarter. An exedra preceded by two columns and two antae piers with stuccoed Corinthian capitals faces onto the north side; on the threshold there is a Nilotic mosaic while on the pavement inside was the famous mosaic of the battle between Alexander the Great and Darius, now in the Museum of Naples.

Various rooms, including an *oecus* decorated in Style II painting, face onto the second peristyle, which is much larger than the first (45 x 40 m.) and with forty-four Doric columns covered with stucco.

TEMPLE OF FORTUNA AUGUSTA

It is situated at the intersection between Via di Nola and Via del Foro. The inscription, originally on the front of the building but found inside the cella, informs us that the temple was built by a private citizen Marcus Tullius on his own property and at his own cost. Under Augustus he held the most important offices in the city (he was *duovir*, augur, military tribune) and obviously the erection of a temple dedicated to Fortuna Augusta was an act of propaganda and political support of his benefactor.

The facade of the Temple of Fortuna Augusta.

The building, which is not very large, had suffered severe damage in the earthquake of A.D. 62 and at the time of the eruption in A.D. 79 restoration was still limited to the cella, which was built in *opus incertum*, originally faced in marble, while the restoration is in brick. The all-over layout is reminiscent of that of the Temple of Jupiter in the Forum: the high podium on which the cella stands, preceded by a pronaos of four columns on the front and two at the sides, was reached by stairs set on the facade, interrupted by a platform where the altar is placed. At the back of the cella a shrine framed by two columns was meant to house the cult statue of the goddess Fortuna.

The side walls have four niches for statues, two of which were found when the excavations were in progress. An inscription found in the alley to the south of the building tells us that this area still belonged to Marcus Tullius. At the back are the dwelling quarters for the temple guardian.

The college of the ministers of the cult was founded by Marcus Tullius himself. Four of their dedicatory inscriptions (plus that of a private individual) refer that they had consecrated in the temple statues of Fortuna or the reigning emperors in a period that ranged from Augustus to Nero.

Above: the Arch of Caligula at the entrance to Via di Mercurio, as it is now. Below, the reconstruction of the arch.

ARCH OF CALIGULA

This arch is set astride Via di Mercurio, of which it marks the beginning, in front of the Forum Baths and the Temple of Fortuna Augusta, near the intersection where Via delle Terme, Via della Fortuna, Via del Foro and Via di Mercurio cross.

This is an honorary arch in brick with a single passageway and its attribution to Caligula is based on an equestrian statue in bronze, found in fragments, which must have originally been set on the attic and which has been identified as Caligula. The arch was built on the same axis as the arch attributed to Tiberius or Germanicus, which constitutes a monumental entrance to the Civil Forum, and which was also topped by an equestrian statue.

Above: the fresco from the House of the Tragic Poet, now in the Museo Nazionale in Naples, with the sacrifice of Iphigenia. Below: the entrance mosaic with the words "beware the dog".

HOUSE OF THE TRAGIC POET

This house is a good example of the Pompeian house in the Imperial age, not overly large, with an underlying architectural concept aimed at a feeling of intimacy, in a climate that was radically opposed to the one in which the large Hellenistic town houses had been created. The same scheme centered around the atrium of Etruscan Italic tradition was maintained in the front part of the building. The entrance is set between two *tabernae* which communicate with the vestibule, a sign of the merchant origins of the owner of the house. A floor mosaic in the entrance depicts a dog with a chain, as if he were a watchdog, together with the warning *cave canem* (beware of the dog). Entrance to the atrium follows, the walls of which are decorated with heroic and mythical scenes inspired by the Iliad. The cubicles and the *alae* face out on the atrium and two staircases originally led to the living quarters on the floor above. At the center is the marble impluvium basin.

VILLA OF MYSTERIES

The large complex of the Villa of Mysteries represents one of the most outstanding examples of suburban patrician villas in antiquity. The square ground plan is laid out on a plot of sloping land so that the western part was realized on an artificial earth fill and supported by a cryptoporticus. In its first phase the villa dates to the first half of the 2nd cent. B.C. but the layout as we know it is the result of remodelling between 70 and 60 B.C., at which time most of the wall painting was also executed. After the earthquake of A.D. 62 the villa underwent a radical transformation from the patrician dwelling it had been to a rustic villa, probably the result of a change in owners. The original entrance of the villa was on Via Superiore, a branch of Via dei Sepolcri, on the opposite side of its current entrance; it leads directly into the area of the peristyle with its sixteen Doric columns. This sector was transformed into servants' quarters with the addition of a series of lodgings on two floors in the space between the original facade of the villa and the Via Superiore. The kitchen courtyard with two ovens is on the south side of the peristyle. Next to it is the small bathing installation comprised of three rooms, including a circular *laconicum* which was no longer used and had been turned into a pantry. A cubicle with two alcoves and an *oecus* decorated in Style II look out on the small tetrastyle atrium

The Villa of Mysteries.

81

Above, the room with the fresco of the Dionysiac mysteries; below, a satyr and a panisca with a fleeing figure.

across the way. Near the northeast corner of the peristyle, two large rooms had been given over to the making of wine and a *torcularium* with two grape presses had been set up, confirming the fact that the villa had at this point been turned into a farm. Next to this is the lararium with an apse, probably where the statue of Livia found in the peristyle was originally located. The owner's living quarters are articulated around a large Tuscan atrium decorated with Nile landscapes. Originally there were also pictures on wooden panels. The cubicle with a double alcove in the north side of the atrium contains one of the most striking examples of Style II wall painting with bold and complex architectural prospects which are illusionistically articulated on various levels until they seem to break through the wall. The tablinum, on the back wall, has an elegant Style III pictorial dècor: Egyptian-style figurines and Dionysiac symbols are painted in miniature on the black-ground walls. Beyond the tablinum is an exedra-like veranda with windows, flanked by hanging gardens and two porticoed wings.

A cubicle with two alcoves situated to the south of the tablinum leads to the salon frescoed with the *megalographia* after which the villa is named, and which can also be reached from the southern portico. This may be the most famous painting of antiquity as a result of the unusual life-size dimensions of the figures and the imposing composition. Traditionally this cycle is interpreted as depicting the rites of initiation into Dionysiac mysteries.

Beginning with the left wall the ritual is read by a nude boy between two matrons; a girl with a tray of offerings moves towards a seated sacrificing figure seen from the back, and assisted by two attendants; next come an old Silenus playing the lyre, a young satyr and a nymph (*panisca*) nursing a kid, a terrorized woman shown shrinking back and about to flee at the sight of the flagellation of one of her companions that is taking place in the opposite corner. The back wall begins with an old Silenus offering a young satire drink, while another satire raises a theater mask over his head; the center of the wall is occupied by Dionysius leaning back on the lap of Ariadne who is seated on a throne, followed by the unveiling of a phallus, symbol of fertility, by a kneeling woman, and a winged female flagellant about to strike. Ideally this is part of the scene on the right wall showing the flagellated woman, perturbed and kneeling with her head in a companion's lap, while a nude maenad dances in an orgy of ecstasy; then comes the preparation of a young bride, as she waits for the initiation rite, assisted by two cupids and a matron, and finally, a seated matron with her head covered, probably the owner of the house, who observes the entire scene.

The fresco must be attributed to a Campanian painter who worked in the villa around 70-60 B.C. and who was inspired by Hellenistic models of the 4th-3rd cent. B.C.

Above: a silenus offering a satyr drink. Below: woman sacrificing with servants and a silenus.

The patrician Deer House flanking Cardo V.

Above, the Large Palaestra; below, Insula III with the House of the Hostel in the foreground.

THE HISTORY OF THE EXCAVATIONS

In 1709 a peasant, digging a well near Resina (a modern town situated where Herculaneum once stood), close to the Barefooted Augustinians' monastery, found some ancient marble tablets which he sold to a marble dealer. These marble pieces captured the attention of Colonel Emanuele Maurizio Lorena, Prince of Elboeuf and head of the Austrian Army in Naples, who bought the field belonging to the peasant and started the excavations. Statues, pillars and commemorative tablets were found in large number. Three beautiful female statues were sent to Vienna as a gift for Eugene of Savoy. After his death they were sent to Dresden. The Prince of Elboeuf excavated, between 1709 and 1716, a large amount of objects and pieces of art, which he kept in his villa in Portici. When he was called back to Vienna, he sold his villa and grounds. Some time later Charles III of the Bourbons, who became king of Naples in 1734, decided to continue excavating in 1738 and the works were carried out under the direction of the engineer Joaquin de Alcubiere. Tunnels and galleries were excavated, sometimes using dynamite. Several statues and pieces of art were excavated but little importance was given to the

architectonic structures and to other remains. In 1738 he started excavating the theatre where a tablet bearing the name of Herculaneum was found for the first time. Several statues were found in the basilica. The architect Carl Weber took part in these excavation works. It was he who made plans of the excavated areas and projected the excavation of the theatre itself. In 1764 Francesco La Vega, an official, took Weber's place and continued the work of documentation of this archeological site.

In 1765 the works were suspended and were not started again until 1828 thanks to King Francis of the Bourbons. The excavations led to rather slight results (only the House of the Genius and the House of Argus were unearthed) and were continued until 1855. In 1869 Giuseppe Fiorelli started the works again, patronized by King Vittorio Emanuele II. The works were again suspended in 1875 because of the opposition of the inhabitants of Resina. In 1927 Amedeo Maiuri started a systematic plan of excavation which is still being carried out in our days. He brought to light large parts of the southern district with several of the Forum structures and the sacred suburban area. Most of the public buildings, temples and the necropolis, in addition to whole districts with houses and shops, are still unexcavated because they lie under the town of Resina.

Above, a picture of Cardo III; below, sewage drain.

THE ROAD NETWORK

Herculaneum, like the neighbouring Neapolis, has a regular urbanistic plan, of Hippodamian type. The thoroughfares cross the town from north to south (Cardines) and from east to west (Decumani), with right angle crossings. Three Cardines have been excavated (III, IV, V) in addition to two Decumani; the main one is the so-called Municipal Forum bed. The roads were paved in the Augustan Age with polygonal lava and limestone stones. All the roads which have been excavated, excluding the lower Decumanus, bear very few traces of waggon wheels; most probably goods to and from the ports along the coast were brought into the city on donkeys or by porters.

As for the water facilities, only Cardo III had a drainage system for the sewage coming from the houses and the Forum; on the other roads the drains flowed onto the road level itself. The water-closet drainage waters were conveyed into special wells. Herculaneum had fewer problems than

Two pictures of the House of Argus with the large peristyle which runs around the garden on three sides.

Pompeii with the drinking water supplies. The water could be found at about eight-ten metres below the ground level. The acqueduct of Serinum *was built during the Augustan period; it solved definitely all water problems.*

HOUSE OF ARGUS

The excavations of this patrician's house, which were carried out only in part of it, date back to the period 1828-65. The main entrance, with its portico, now on Cardo III, was probably the secondary entrance. Several rooms and a triclinial hall open onto a very large peristyle and a garden, surrounded, on three sides, by pillars. The second peristyle has only partially been excavated, whereas the atrium remains unexcavated. The dormitories, the food storage rooms and a large balcony, overlooking the road, are on the second floor. The house takes its name from a painting representing Io and Argus, which no longer exists.

HOUSE OF THE SKELETON

The house takes its name from a skeleton which was found here when the first excavations took place, in 1830-31. The house, originally divided into three separate buildings, has a "testutinate" roofed atrium, with an external water ridge – an architectural solution which is uncommon in the towns of this area. There also were three yards behind the house, one of which was closed at the top by a metal grid. At the entrance, on the left, a two-pool grotto adorns the large triclinium. Behind the tablinum, a large apsidal hall with marble floors overlooks a second grotto with a high podium sacellum.

Two details of the House of the Skeleton: above, a shrine, and below, the remains of a metal grate which covered a courtyard.

SHOP ON CARDO III

The interior of the shop is very spacious: there is a counter walled on three sides, which holds seven amphoras originally used for cereals and legumes. The vaulted niche in the corner bears witness of the existence of a fire-place. Two of the rooms were used as a back-shop. There is reason enough to believe that originally there were some rooms on the second floor, which were probably used to lodge clients.

Above, the sales counter of the Shop of Cardo III; below, a view of Cardo III as it crosses the lower Decumanus.

TWO-ATRIUM HOUSE

This two-storey building has a very original configuration due to the existence of two atriums. Through the vestibule you enter the first atrium, a tetrastyle atrium, which opens onto a tablinum. The room on the right of the vestibule was used as a kitchen and had an oven; the access to the second floor is through the room on the left of the vestibule. The second atrium, with an impluvium, is behind the tablinum. The triclinium, closing the atrium, is decorated with a painting, belonging to the IV style, representing a still-life.

HOUSE WITH THE TUSCAN COLONNADE

The plan is rather classical. It has a vestibule, an atrium and a tablinum, belonging to the 2nd century B.C. The building was altered and restored in the Augustan period, when a peristyle with a Tuscan colonnade was added. On the northern side of the atrium we find the "oecus" with wall paintings of the III style. Most of the other rooms, in particular the triclinium, are decorated with paintings of the IV style. When the house was first excavated 1400 sesterces in gold coins, which had probably been hidden by the owner before his flight, were discovered.

Above, the Two-Atrium House; below, a decorated wall of the House with the Tuscan Colonnade.

Above, the main room of the College of Augustans; below, the cell in which the walls bear paintings depicting Hercules, to be seen on the following pages.

COLLEGE OF AUGUSTANS

This public building was referred to as the College of Augustans because of a memorial tablet which was found in its interior. The tablet was situated three meters above the floor level, therefore it may not belong to the building. Other experts believe that the building was the seat of the Municipal Curia. It consists of a very large hall with four columns supporting a flat roof; it takes as model the Hellenistic hypostyle halls. The walls are decorated with blind arches. A cell was built on the wall at the end of the room, by walling up the space between two columns and the wall. On both sides of the cell there are two paintings which represent Hercules, the city's eponymous hero: *Hercules with Juno and Minerva* and *Hercules with Neptune and Amphitrite*. The floor and wainscot are in marble.

A small room opens into the cell. It was built by means of a partition in "opus craticium". It was the keepers's room and in fact his skeleton was found lying on the bed.

94

Above, the facade of the House with the Wooden Partition; below, the atrium.

HOUSE WITH THE WOODEN PARTITION

The configuration of its plan clearly shows that the house belonged to a noble family and was built in the Samnite style. The alterations, which were carried out after the earthquake in 62 A.D., transformed the rooms, facing the cardo and decumanus, into shops in addition to a second floor with independent entrance. It was to be used as a dwelling place by several families. There is a large Tuscan atrium with a marble impluvium in the centre. The cubiculum, near the entrance, has a beautiful mosaic floor with geometrical patterns and still preserves a marble tablet with support representing the Phrygian divinity Attis. A wood partition (from which the house takes its name), separating the tablinum from the atrium, was found during the excavations. Two double doors, on both ends, which were originally part of it, can still be seen, whereas the middle section no longer exists. Behind the tablinum there is a garden enclosed by a colonnade with an upper gallery, which leads to other cubicula and triclinia.

Above, the double doors of the House with the Wooden Partition; below, the walls with the wooden framework of the Grid House.

HOUSE WITH THE GRID

This house was built using the "opus craticium" technique; a rather cheap but unreliable architectural technique (subject to deterioration and fire). It consisted mainly in building wood-framed walls and walling them up with "opus incertum". The house was inhabited by several families as the three independent entrances leading to the ground floor, the upper floor and the shop and backshop, clearly show.

The facade is embellished by a balcony supported by brick columns. Through the entrance hall you can go to a small inner yard, onto which the dwellings open. Wooden beds and closets with statuettes of the Lares and other divinities, glass objects and several furnishings have been found in some cubicula on the upper floor.

HOUSE WITH THE ALCOVE

The house is made up of two separate buildings with regular plans situated close to one another. The entrance to the transversal vestibule, on the northern side, is through the "fauces". A cubiculum, a kitchen with lavatory and a small courtyard with "exedra" give into the vestibule. From here you pass into a small atrium with a courtyard, onto which several cubicula and an "oecus", with a painting representing a *forsaken Ariadne*, open.

From the vestibule, on the northern side, access is to the southern section of the house. Here we find a second vestibule. A biclinium, with paintings of the IV style, and a large triclinium with marble floors open onto this second vestibule. Through a corridor you enter the dormitories where there can be found an apsidal hall with an alcove preceded by an antechamber.

Above, the window with an iron grate in the House with the Alcove; below, the exterior of the House with the Mosaic Atrium.

HOUSE WITH THE MOSAIC ATRIUM

It is one of the most panoramic houses and is divided into two different sections. The first section has a regular axial plan; that is a vestibule, an atrium with impluvium and a tablinum. The floor in the vestibule and in the atrium are decorated with a black and white mosaic. In the first room there are geometrical patterns enclosed in squares and lined with guilloches, whereas the second room is decorated with a chequered motif. The floor in the atrium is undulated because the ground has subsided due to the weight of the volcanic mud. The tablinum, with an "opus sectile" floor, is divided into a large nave ("oecus aegyptius") and two aisles by columns with stucco work. The second section of the house, which overlooks the sea, is divided into a large garden with a fountain in the centre, enclosed, on three sides, by a colonnade with closed intercolumniations and windows. On the eastern side we find a glazed wall with wooden partition. In the middle of this wall an "exedra" with floor in "opus sectile" and wall paintings of the IV style open onto the garden. The paintings represent: *The Punishment of Dirce* and *Diana and Actaeon*. A large triclinium with other rooms opens onto a covered colonnade and onto a panoramic terrace. On both sides of the colonnade there are two small dwelling rooms.

Two pictures of the House with the Mosaic Atrium: above, a detail of the pavement and below, a view of the interior.

FORUM BATHS

These are the main baths of the town. They are divided
into two sections, one for women and one for men, with
independent entrances on Cardo III and IV. The entrance
to the men's section is through the palaestra which is
surrounded by porticoes. This was the gym place but also
a meeting point. The "apodyterium" (the changing-room)
is a plastered barrel vaulted hall with strigils, podium-like
seats and corbels for clothes. At the end of the room,
which has an apse, we find a "labrum" and a small pool.
The "frigidarium" is a round room with domed vault.
Paintings, representing fishes on a light blue background,
decorate the vault; the pool is also light blue and gives the
impression of bathing in a real sea. The floor in the "tepidarium" is in "suspensurae" and a mosaic represents a
Triton with some dolphins. The "calidarium" has, in addition to a hot water pool, an apse with a "labrum" used
for cold water ablutions.

On entering the women's section we find a large waiting-
room with podium-like seats, which leads to the "apodyterium" with plastered vault and strigils, seats and corbels
along the walls. The mosaic on the floor represents a triton
and a cupid among sea animals. There is also a mosaic in
the "tepidarium" which represents meanders and other
emblems. The "calidarium" has a vault with an opening
right in the centre of it. The floor was raised so that hot air
could pass under it. In this room there is also a marble
pool and a "labrum".

Four pictures of the important complex of the Forum Baths.

Above, still another room of the Forum Baths; below and on the facing page, three views of the lovely Tuscan atrium of the Samnite House.

SAMNITE HOUSE

The house was built at the end of the 2nd century B.C. It is a typical example of Italic pre-Roman style urban architecture. It once occupied the whole western side of the "V insula" and had a garden. The entrance has columns with Corinthian capitals on each side, the "fauces" are decorated with paintings of the I style, in coloured imitation marble and rustic work, the paintings on the upper level belong to the II style and show landscapes. The ceiling is coffered. From this room you enter the large Tuscan atrium with its beautiful floor and its large impluvium in the center. Several other rooms open into this atrium, including a tablinum at the very far end. The atrium, whose plan is typically Italic, has been largely influenced by Hellenistic architecture. In fact there can be found a false arcade with a grid transenna, in addition to columns and semicolumns with closed and fenestrated intercolumniation. The paintings on the walls belong to the IV style.

In the cubiculum we find a painting which represents *The Rape of Europa*. The signinum floor in the tablinum, with a rosette emblem, is a very remarkable piece of art. Later the upper storey was divided into two different flats so that they could be rented.

HOUSE OF NEPTUNE AND AMPHITRITIS

The whole house is built around the atrium. The remains of two decorated marble slabs, one of which has been signed by Alexandros, the artist, have been found in the lararium, inside the atrium. The tablinum opens onto a summer triclinium in which a fountain set on supports can be admired. The grotto, consisting of a central apsidal niche and two smaller lateral niches and decorated by marble theatre masks, is situated on the farthest part of the triclinium. The grotto is decorated with glass mosaics; four "kantharoi" on the jambs of each niche represent flower shoots, whereas the paintings on the lateral niches show scenes of hunting parties with dogs pursuing fleeing deers. The scenes are framed by festoons. The middle apsidal niche probably held a statue. The wall, near the grotto, is adorned with a beautiful glass mosaic. The house is named after this mosaic which portrays Neptune and Amphitritis in a small frame decorated with shells on the upper part.

Above, a view of Cardo IV once lined by numerous shops; below, the facade of the House of Neptune and Amphitritis.

Two pictures of the interior of the shop communicating with the House of Neptune and Amphitritis and large jars on the shelves.

On the following pages, above, the mosaic of Neptune and Amphitritis after which the house where it was found was named; on the facing page, a detail of the mosaic; below, the elegant decorations of the nymphaeum and its niches.

Above, a picture of the Black Hall House; below, the fountain of Venus at the crossing between the Decumanus Maximus and Cardo IV.

Opposite: a view from on high of the Decumanus Maximus.

BLACK HALL HOUSE

The house belonged to L. Venidius Ennychelus, a rich freedman, as some tablets, which were found in the building, inform us. The door-jambs, the architrave and one panel of the main entrance wooden door can still be seen. The plan of the house is classical: a vestibule, an atrium with "alae", a tablinum and a peristyle. A large hall with black walls and paintings, belonging to the IV style, separated by columns and candelabra, opens onto the peristyle. A perfectly preserved small, temple-like aedicula, with small wood pillars and marble capitals was found in this house. The object was probably used as lararium.

DECUMANUS MAXIMUS

It was the main road and crossed the town from east to west. It has not been excavated in all its length. It was the seat of the Municipal Forum and was approximately 12-14 metres wide. Several steps and inscribed pillars at the crossings with cardins testify that the whole area was a pedestrian area. Probably the eastern part was the commercial area. In fact there are several shops along the road and there have been found many cylindrical holes with wood furnishings, used to fit poles in when the covered market was held.

The entrance to the Civil Forum was marked by a large four-faced arch which was originally decorated with marble and statues. Most of the monuments of this area are still to be excavated; they are described in detail in the records which related to the excavation of tunnels and galleries during the 18th century. We know there is a rectangular basilica, divided into a central part and two ambulatories by two rows of pillars. On the farthest end there are three apses with paintings representing *Theseus and the Minotaur*, *Hercules and Telephus* and *Achilles and Chiron*. These paintings are now to the found in the National Museum in Naples. Both the equestrian statues, which portray M. Nonius Balbus, proconsul and first citizen of Herculaneum, together with other statues of his family and of several emperors, were found in this basilica. The sixteenth century plans clearly show that there are two other public buildings in front of the Decumanus. Their function is not known.

FOUNTAIN OF HERCULES

It is situated at the eastern side of the Decumanus Maximus. Originally the water flowed through a fistula from the mouth of a statue which portrayed Hercules. The sculptural style is not one of the best. The rectangular basin is formed by four travertine slabs kept together by cramps. The bottom of the fountain is in signinum.

FOUNTAIN OF VENUS

It is situated at the crossing of the Decumanus Maximus and the Cardo IV and is perpendicular to the street level. The water is supplied by a nearby "castellum aquae". There are two water streams, on both ends of the rectangular basin, which represent Medusa and a bathing Venus. Large limestone slabs, kept together by cramps, form the basin.

The Decumanus Maximus, the main street which cuts the city from west to east.

Opposite: above, the Bicentenary House along the Decumanus Maximus. Below, the Fountain of Hercules.

BICENTENARY HOUSE

The house was so called because it was excavated in 1938, two hundred years after the first excavation works in Herculaneum. The plan is classical: a vestibule, a Tuscan atrium, with black and white panelled mosaic floors, an impluvium, and "alae", a tablinum, a triclinium and a portico. The right wing is separated from the atrium by a wooden gate with two sliding and flexible sections. Most probably worship statuettes of the ancestors were kept in this area. The floor in the tablinum is in "opus sectile". The paintings in this room, belonging to the IVth style, show *Dedalus and Pasiphae* and *Mars and Venus*. The upper storey had probably been let out to a middle-class family. The cross on one of the walls, under which an altar and a wooden prie-dieu were found, seems to indicate that they were Christians.

Above, a wall decorated with red porphyry panels in the Bicentenary House; below, a room where a wooden prie-dieu was found.

*Above, a view of Cardo V; below, the Palaestra,
consisting of various rooms.*

PALAESTRA

The palaestra occupies, in Herculaneum, a whole "insula". The entrance is embellished by a beautiful monumental colonnade. The open-air space is surrounded, on three sides, by Corinthian pillars; whereas on the other side there can be found a cryptoporticus, with a gallery, where the audience sat when sport meetings took place. In the middle of this large space there is a big cross-shaped swimming pool. A trunk-shaped bronze fountain, mounted on a pillar, is situated at the intersection of the arms of the cross. A five-headed Hydra, climbing up the trunk, sprayed water in different directions. On the northern part there is a smaller rectangular swimming pool.
A large apsidal hall with a colonnade, in front of the entrance, with marble floor and wainscot, opens onto the western side of the area. Statues of the emperor's family were probably to be found here. A large marble table, which was used to celebrate the winners of the athletic games has also been found.

Above, the entrance of the House with the Corinthian Atrium; below, one of the bakeries in the city.

PISTRINUM

Two bakeries have been found in Herculaneum, they are both located on Cardo V and are supplied with lava millstones. We know the name of one of these bakers, Sextus Patulcus Felix, thanks to the discovery of his seal. Twenty-five bronze pans, used to bake flat loaves, have also been found. The skeleton of the donkey used for the millstone was found in the other bakery.

HOUSE WITH THE CORINTHIAN ATRIUM

A beautiful small portico with brick columns was built in front of the main entrance. The house takes its name from the Corinthian atrium, with six tufa columns, covered in white and red stucco work. The atrium surrounds an impluvium with a marble fountain and "euripus". The floor in the room on the right of the vestibule is decorated with mosaics. The wall paintings all belong to the IV style.

CORN SHOP

It is the largest shop excavated in Herculaneum. Unfortunately most of the furnishings and the wooden furniture were plundered or destroyed during the first excavation works. Eight amphoras, containing corn and legumes, were walled in a double podium, whereas a very large amphora was placed between two pillars. Probably beverages could also be bought in this shop. Two rooms of the building were used as a back-shop and another room was for the clients. A motto by the cynic philosopher Diogenes had been carved in Greek by a well-educated client.

Two pictures of the Corn Shop, the largest in Herculaneum.

HOUSE WITH THE LARGE PORTAL

The house takes its name from the brick semicolumns which are situated at the main entrance. The columns were originally covered in red stucco; they had tufa Corinthian capitals which portrayed winged Victories supporting the platband architrave and the brick frame. The configuration of this house is rather uncommon: in fact the "fauces" do not lead to the atrium but to a long roofed vestibule, with rooms on each sides, ending in a small courtyard which gives light to the whole area. The large triclinium is also worth seeing. Its paintings, belonging to the IV style, show Dionysius and Ariadne under the watchful eyes of Silenus and two satyrs. Near the triclinium there is an exedra decorated with curtains, flower gardens, birds and cupids. In one of the vestibule wings there can be admired a painting which shows birds pecking at cherries and a butterfly.

Above, the entrance flanked by semicolumns in brick, of the House with the Large Portal; below and on the following page, the elegant decorations of the rooms.

Above, the internal garden of the Deer House; below, a detail of the table outside with griffin-shaped legs.

Opposite: the mosaics on the tympanum of the entrance, with the head of Oceanus at the center.

DEER HOUSE

The house is divided into two different sections: the residential area around the atrium, and a larger area used to entertain guests, with a garden and a panoramic terrace overlooking the sea. The entrance leads to a roofed "testudinate" atrium, with no impluvium. From here you enter the servants' room, through a corridor, the triclinium and the cryptoporticus. The triclinium opens onto the cryptoporticus with a magnificent view over the garden. The paintings on the walls consist of architectonical patterns on a black background and the floors are in coloured marble. Here are exhibited two statues representing two deer pursued by some hunting dogs, which were actually found in the garden and which give the name to the house. In the

"oecus", on the same side of the house and facing the cryptoporticus, there is another very famous statue which portrays a *young satyr with a wineskin*.

The garden, as we have previously mentioned, is surrounded by a columned portico. The walls were originally decorated with more than sixty small panels representing different objects. The paintings are partly preserved on the spot and partly exhibited in the National Museum in Naples. Through the garden (that can still be visited today), in which there were marble tables and several statues, particularly one representing a drunken Hercules,

Two pictures of the "Satyr with a wineskin", to be found inside the Deer House.

you enter the monumental entrance with a beautiful glass mosaic tympanum. Of the mosaic there survives only a head of Oceanus and cupids on sea-horses, which were part of the frieze. On the western part of the garden we find a large "oecus" with marble floor and wainscot, into which two smaller halls open. Proceeding westwards there can be found a pergola with a roof supported by four pillars; two flower beds and two resting rooms are on the sides of the pergola. Both the pergola and the two rooms open into a parapeted terrace with a magnificent view over the sea.

Above, the statue of the "Drunken Hercules", and below, another room in the Deer House.

Above and below, the decoration of the walls with architectonic elements on black ground in the Deer House.

Above, a view of Insula IV with the sacred area in the foreground: above left, the House with the Mosaic Atrium; right, the Deer House. Below, the Suburban Baths seen from above.

Above, the simple facade of the Suburban Baths; below, the atrium with the herm of Apollo which conveyed water into the basin below.

Opposite: above, the neo-attic relief of the myth of Telephus which gave the house its name; below, the columns and walls with red-ground decoration in the portico.

SUBURBAN BATHS

These baths are not divided into two sections, one for women and one for men, as was common practice. Through the semicolumns supporting a tympanum, at the entrance, you enter the atrium with impluvium and a skylight in the vault. The skylight is sustained by four pillars and by a series of superimposed arches. Near the basin there was a marble herm of Apollo on a pillar, which conveyed water into a "labrum". Several bronze fragments of the large boiler have been found in the "praefurnium". There is only one large hall, with paintings and plasters of the IV style, which contains both the "apodyterium" and the "frigidarium" with the pool. There follows the waiting-room with benches along the walls, decorated with relief stuccoes of warriors. This room leads to the "calidarium" in stucco work (the plasters belong to the IV style), with a hot and cold water pool, and to the "tepidarium" with swimming-pool in "suspensurae". The "laconicum" is near the "tepidarium", a round room with four small apses, mainly used for saunas.

HOUSE OF TELEPHUS RELIEF

It is the largest house in Herculaneum and extends on different levels following the conformation of the ground; therefore the plan of this house is rather irregular. The area with the vestibule, the atrium, the "alae" and the tablinum is on the road level. The atrium has a colonnade on three sides which sustains – a rather uncommon architectural solution in these Vesuvian cities – the architraves of the upper storey instead of supporting the four roof slopes, according to the Hellenistic architectural style. The columns and the walls are painted in red; marble "oscilla" hang on the intercolumniation.

The area with the low-parapeted peristyle, which surrounds the garden and a fountain, is on the lower level. Two banquet halls with painted walls open onto it. A corridor leads to the other rooms on the panoramic terrace and in particular to a hall with a magnificent marble-decorated floor and wainscot. The neo-Attic relief, which shows the myth of Telephus, was found in a small room nearby.

On this and the facing page, some of the carbonized furniture found in a house in Herculaneum and after which the house was named.

CONTENTS

OSCEs for Anaesthetists

OSCEs for Anaesthetists

Edited by

A.S. Shambrook FRCA

Senior Registrar,
Department of Anaesthetics and Intensive Care Medicine,
University Hospital of Wales, Cardiff, UK

I.R. Appadurai FRCA

Lecturer/Hon. Senior Registrar,
Department of Anaesthetics and Intensive Care Medicine,
University of Wales College of Medicine, Cardiff, UK

and

M.D. Vickers MBBS, FRCA

Professor of Anaesthetics,
Department of Anaesthetics and Intensive Care Medicine,
University of Wales College of Medicine, Cardiff, UK

CHAPMAN & HALL MEDICAL

London · Glasgow · Weinheim · New York · Tokyo · Melbourne · Madras

Published by Chapman & Hall, 2–6 Boundary Row, London SE1 8HN, UK

Chapman & Hall, 2–6 Boundary Row, London SE1 8HN, UK

Blackie Academic & Professional, Wester Cleddens Road, Bishopbriggs, Glasgow G64 2NZ, UK

Chapman & Hall GmbH, Pappelallee 3, 69469 Weinheim, Germany

Chapman & Hall USA, 115 Fifth Avenue, New York, NY 10003, USA

Chapman & Hall Japan, ITP-Japan, Kyowa Building, 3F, 2-2-1 Hirakawacho, Chiyoda-ku, Tokyo 102, Japan

Chapman & Hall Australia, 102 Dodds Street, South Melbourne, Victoria 3205, Australia

Chapman & Hall India, R. Seshadri, 32 Second Main Road, CIT East, Madras 600 035, India

First edition 1995

© 1995 A.S. Shambrook, I.R. Appadurai and M.D. Vickers

Printed in Great Britain at The Alden Press, Oxford.

ISBN 0 412 618400

∞ Printed on acid-free text paper, manufactured in accordance with ANSI/NISO Z39.48-1992 (Permanence of Paper)

Contents

Colour plates appear between pages 36 and 37

Preface

Objective Structured Clinical Examinations (OSCEs) are a relatively new development on the postgraduate examination scene, although they have been used in undergraduate examinations for many years. The OSCE (as its name indicates) is believed to be Objective and to achieve this it is Structured so that the involvement of the examiner's judgement is at a minimum.

Whether or not it fully achieves this objective, it is undeniable that the format is more appropriate in the examination of anaesthetists than the traditional 'long case' with its emphasis on a detailed history and primary diagnostic ability. Although the format has only recently been introduced in the Final of the Fellowship of the Royal College of Anaesthetists (FRCA), the College has also signalled its intention to use it in the first part of a new two-part examination.

In writing this book we have focused primarily on the OSCE as used in the current final examination and have had to go to press with only very limited experience of it. To what extent the OSCE which is promised for the MRCA will be different or easier cannot yet be predicted.

We hope this book will fulfil several functions. Firstly, it can provide practice for this part of the examination. To facilitate this, the answers are each printed on a single page of the book and can be utilized for practice examinations.

The questions are compiled in sets of twelve, each set providing a balance of topics, usually including at least one question on some aspect of resuscitation and one involving communication skills, thus mimicking the number and format currently used in the final FRCA. The book contains ten such complete examinations.

Knowing whether the answers are right or wrong is of some value in helping candidates assess their preparedness for the examination, but knowing *why* an answer is wrong is even more important. We have therefore combined the answers with a short tutorial on the topic, including a few key references. This has been the most difficult part. It is relatively easy to write an essay on almost any topic: it is infinitely more difficult to restrict it to a single page. However, it was not our aim to write yet another textbook so we have had to be ruthlessly selective.

Finally, we hope this collection of OSCEs will be a general educational tool for those preparing for the final FRCA and be of help to their tutors.

A. S. Shambrook
I. R. Appadurai
M.D. Vickers

Acknowledgements

The responsibility for the accuracy and the content of this book is ours. However, we are deeply indebted to the many people who have been of assistance. We would like to thank Annalisa Page, our Commissioning Editor at Chapman and Hall, for her professional but understanding attitude.

We would like to express our gratitude to several colleagues at the University Hospital of Wales, Cardiff. Mr R.G.S. Mills, Consultant ENT Surgeon and Dr S. Phillips, Registrar in the Department of Radiology kindly provided X-rays. Mr R.G. Williams, Consultant ENT Surgeon, Professor P.S. Harper, Department of Medical Genetics, Professor D.P. Davies, Department of Child Health, and Dr A. Turley, Consultant Anaesthetist, allowed us to use their pictures. Dr S. Maheshwaran, Consultant Radiologist, Mayday Hospital, also provided X-rays for which we are grateful.

We also thank the Department of Medical Illustration, University Hospital of Wales for their excellent photography and Mr C. Juniper, technician in the Department of Anaesthetics, who provided the line diagrams.

We would like to express our great appreciation to Dr J. Mecklenburgh who gave invaluable time, knowledge and effort in the preparation of the camera-ready copy.

We are indebted to the BMJ Publishing Group and the authors for allowing us to use the iso-shunt diagram which was redrawn from:

Benatar SR, Hewlett AM and Nunn JF. The use of iso-shunt lines for control of oxygen therapy. *British Journal of Anaesthesia* 1973; **45**:711.

We are also grateful to the following companies for providing technical data and photographs:

Abbott Laboratories Ltd, Cook Critical Care Ltd, Gambro Ltd, Mallinckrodt Medical (UK) Ltd, Pall Biomedical, and Portex Ltd.

Lastly, but most importantly, we would like to thank our families for their infinite support, encouragement and patience during the creation of this book.

A.S. Shambrook
I.R. Appadurai
M.D. Vickers

Introduction

An OSCE (Objective Structured Clinical Examination) is a clinical examination which aims to test a wider and more relevant range of skills than one involving the traditional 'long and short cases' in a way which is less susceptible to examiner bias.

The examination is conducted at a variable number of 'stations'. A batch of candidates start simultaneously, one at each station. A fixed time is allowed at each station, usually of the order of four to five minutes, and after this time has elapsed, each candidate moves on to the next station. An examiner is present at each station and either marks the candidate whilst he or she is performing the station task or marks written answers whilst the next candidate is at the station. Several studies have reported on the higher reliability of this method of examination of clinical competence, which has been used for many years for undergraduates and has recently been adopted by the Royal College of Anaesthetists.

Examinations are the single most potent influence on teaching and learning, an observation which had been made in several environments. The OSCE in Anaesthesia will be no exception. Whilst one can hope that the influence will be beneficial, the potential always exists for adverse effects. In the case of those parts of an examination which require the recall of knowledge, either the syllabus (if there is one), books of 'typical' questions, or word of mouth determine the topics which students study. The OSCE, which goes beyond factual recall and attempts to evaluate technical expertise and other aspects of professional skills, has the potential to influence professional behaviour as well.

The layout of this book has been deliberately modelled on the initial structure adopted by the College for the OSCE in the Final of the FRCA. The format of the examination can be changed more rapidly than new editions of a book can be produced and this statement may not remain true indefinitely. The complete cycle of the FRCA OSCE is twelve active stations with two rest stations. The book therefore provides 120 stations of OSCEs grouped into ten cycles of twelve questions. We have been told that each examination cycle will always contain at least one station devoted to resuscitation skills and so we have included a resuscitation OSCE in the majority of cycles in this book.

OSCEs fall into one of four broad types which test, respectively

- data interpretation skills,
- technical skills,
- clinical assessment skills,
- communication skills.

Each cycle in this book is a mix of data interpretation, clinical assessment and technical skills. For the reasons given below, we have not attempted to include much in the way of OSCEs devoted to testing communication skills.

Testing data interpretation skills by OSCE need offer few problems. At the simplest level the data (ECG, image, laboratory results) need to be realistic and the candidate asked questions simply requiring a true/false or yes/no answer to a statement such as: 'This ECG shows atrial fibrillation'. More sophisticated is the same ECG but asking the candidate what disorder of rhythm it shows. The marking of the first version is entirely objective. The latter format has to cope with the candidate who writes 'A/F', and who may have meant either atrial fibrillation or atrial flutter. If the question is even less specific, e.g. 'What abnormality is shown on this ECG', subsequent questions such as 'How would you treat it?' may be unanswerable if the candidate cannot answer the first one. Yet he or she may well know the answer to the second and subsequent questions if once told the answer to the first.

There are three possible attitudes to such a situation. One is to avoid using OSCE stations in which being able to answer the first question correctly, influences the candidate's chances in other questions. The second argues that in real life the future practitioner who cannot recognize the condition is unlikely to treat it properly or at all and the marking should fairly reflect that fact. The third attitude is softer and argues that data are not going to be interpreted under examination conditions in real life and that the correct diagnosis may well be reached, perhaps a little more slowly or by discussion. Once that stage has been reached, applying the correct treatment is crucial. Thus, the third attitude is to use such OSCEs but allow the candidate to ask for the diagnosis at a penalty of losing some marks.

Clinical assessment skills are more difficult to test because they crucially involve communication skills. An obviously enlarged thyroid or acromegalic facies may test the observational aspect of data acquisition but testing whether a candidate can identify whether a headache is due to pressure in the pituitary fossa is not so easy. As a consequence, this (or any other) book cannot provide practice for OSCEs testing some aspects of clinical skills.

Technical skills (lumbar puncture, internal jugular cannulation, fibreoptic intubation) may be realistically simulable with a dummy or model or partially simulable on a volunteer but the examiner is now not faced with success or failure in real terms but his or her interpretation of key technical elements. For instance, a successful lumbar puncture depends on good positioning, good local analgesia and correct direction of needle insertion but these alone do not ensure successful puncture. Of these, only the patient's position and initial line of needle can be demonstrated on a volunteer model. Neither is unequivocally right or wrong, merely good or poor.

At the least objective end of the scale are OSCEs which test communication skills. Candidates can best practise these by being in 'exam-mode' when seeing patients routinely and by role playing with a colleague fellow candidate, interchanging the roles of examinee and patient and then discussing performance. This is the area in which professional behaviour is likely to be most influenced. It is not too difficult to imagine marks being deducted for not smiling, not shaking hands or not saying your name, let alone smoking or being inebriated. Some of these 'prejudices' are unexceptionable but what about wearing sandals or not wearing a tie? Whilst forcibly expressed prejudices abound, objective studies have shown that 'real' patients either do not notice, do not remember, or do not care about the dress of the anaesthetist.

Nevertheless, at the risk of encouraging uniform behaviour patterns which may not be in fact universally appropriate, we offer some advice on general behaviour, particularly in the area of communication skills. It seems inevitable that a good deal of folklore will develop around behaviour in the OSCE and we apologize if we are thought guilty of contributing to it by advising on inter-personal behaviour and communication skills.

Standing or sitting? In the days of the 'long case' everyone (candidates and examiners) 'knew' it was important to stand on the right side of the patient. No one ever explained why. It was probably because some procedures such as identifying the apex beat or palpating the abdomen are much better done by a right-handed doctor when standing on the patient's right. There is no logical reason why obtaining essential details at the pre-anaesthetic visit is better done from one side or the other and many patients, sitting beside their bed, actually prefer the anaesthetist to commit the professional solecism of sitting on the bed rather than being interrogated by someone standing looking down at them.

Dress Most candidates automatically 'dress up' for examinations and employment interviews. Despite evidence to the contrary, examiners are likely to believe that patients expect a doctor to look like a doctor, a probably unconscious metonym for 'look like an examiner'.

Demeanour One should use all socially accept-able means of conveying friendliness and sym-pathetic concern. These will include smiling, self-introduction, possibly a handshake and adopting, if possible, an eye level stance. Good eye contact should be made with the 'patient'. If it seems appropriate to sit down (e.g. an empty chair is in the immediate vicinity) ask the patient if they mind. If sitting, don't slouch. It is probably not wise to try to send the examiner to fetch a chair if there isn't one!

Manner If examination of a 'patient' is required, gentleness is desirable, preceded by a full explanation of what you intend to do or want the patient to do. Remember: good communication skills involve listening as well as speaking. Listening is not just the intervals between episodes of speaking. Try and learn the art of controlling the conversation with any patient who has a tendency to irrelevancies, without appearing rude or abrupt.

Body language This may not be consciously noted by the examiner, but both the patient and the examiner will be subconsciously affected by it. Unfortunately, by its very nature, body language is often not consciously appreciated or under conscious control. Do not cross your arms, gaze away for long periods, fidget or show signs of impatience. A simulated relaxed and confident demeanour is therefore a help, despite the alleged objectivity of the examination.

Obtaining a history Always check the name of the patient, what operation they are having done and on which side of the body. Ask specific questions to establish points, such as concurrent drugs, allergies, previous operations, the most recent anaesthetic, any evidence of anaesthetic problems and any serious medical illnesses. Social aspects should include smoking and alcohol intake; take an interest in the home circumstances and transport arrangements if there is a possibility of the operation being done as a day stay procedure. Look out for symptoms of reflux. Always put some open-ended questions to make sure that you have not missed anything: 'Is there anything else of medical significance about you I should know?' This also gives the patient an opportunity to express any anxieties.

Voice Speaking clearly and not too fast, preferably without a pronounced dialect aids communication in any sphere, and certainly applies when trying to take a relevant history within a limited time. To what extent patients or actors (dummy patients) will be instructed to mimic reality is an as yet unanswered question. It is likely that they will be discouraged from volunteering crucial information which has not been directly asked for. The continuous presence of an examiner will act as a regulator of the actor's performance. Nevertheless, the candidate's behaviour is relatively uncontrolled and unrehearsed sequences may lead to unexpected outcomes which the examiner will have to mark using his own judgement.

Attitude Unless the examiner speaks to you we advise you to ignore the examiner's presence. Attempting to assess one's performance from the examiner's facial reactions or body language is likely to be unrewarding.

How to use this book

There are several ways in which this book can be used. By using the twelve grouped questions, ten fairly realistic practice examinations can be conducted. However, we have envisaged the book as being of much more use than this. Published studies have shown that when groups study together, it is more efficient to deal with a single OSCE at a time, and discuss the answer as a group. Many of the OSCEs are more sophisticated than pictorial MCQs which require only true/false responses and will take longer to answer. This makes the book more useful as a revision and learning aid by requiring the retrieval and integration of pieces of information and knowledge. To complement this usage we have included a short discussion about each topic and key references. Used this way, there need be no time constraints and either spoken or written responses can be employed.

There is no need to fear the OSCE. It will favour the well-prepared candidate with both well-rounded knowledge and experience. We may hope to see less of the candidate who keeps failing but whose teachers all believe is a safe and competent practitioner. It will favour the candidate who really has practised the procedure or met the clinical problem over the candidate who has only read it up, and thus encourage students not to try and spend all their time 'bashing the books' but to do as much as possible in the clinical area. This should satisfy those teachers who have long preached the Confucian aphorism:

'I hear and I forget:
I see and I remember:
I do and I understand.'

M.D. Vickers
I.R. Appadurai
A. S. Shambrook

OSCE cycle 1 – questions

Question 1.1

See Plate 1.

1. What is the most likely diagnosis?
2. List ten clinical features associated with this condition.
3. Why might upper airway management prove difficult in this patient?
4. What investigations would be of diagnostic value?
5. List the treatment options for this condition.

Question 1.2

You are asked to review a 60-year-old man on the intensive care unit who has had an elective abdominal aortic aneurysm repaired 48 hours previously. His pre-operative serum urea and electrolytes and urinalysis were normal. Over the last three hours his urine output has fallen from 30 ml/hour to zero.

1. List three intra-operative factors that a review of the case notes would make you suspect intrinsic rather than prerenal failure.

2. Before instituting therapy what simple procedure would you do?

3. Give two causes of prerenal failure. Which of the following would suggest a diagnosis of pre-renal failure?

   (a) urinary sodium of 8 mmol/L
   (b) urinary sodium of 70 mmol/L
   (c) urinary osmolality of 750 mosmol/L
   (d) darkly coloured urine

   Urine to plasma ratios:
   (e) urea 20:1
   (f) creatinine 30:1.
   (g) osmolality 2:1.

4. If you diagnose pre-renal failure which of the following will you do next?
   (h) give noradrenaline;
   (j) give a 500 mL fluid challenge;
   (k) give 500 mg frusemide;
   (l) examine the cardiovascular status.

Question 1.3

Concerning the anaesthetic machine check:

1. What monitor should be calibrated prior to the anaesthetic machine check?
2. Following disconnection of the pipelines you open the valves of all the flowmeters. The bobbins all rest at zero. On opening the reserve oxygen cylinder both the nitrous oxide and oxygen bobbins show a flow of 4 L/minute. Do you discard the machine at this stage?
3. What is a 'fail-safe' valve and is it fail-safe?
4. You occlude the common outlet port while gases are passing through the flowmeters. You hear a hissing sound as a valve opens. At what pressure does this occur and what is the function of this valve? What other reason may explain this hiss?
5. What flow rate is the emergency oxygen flush and why?

Question 1.4

A patient is put on the beginning of your operating session for insertion of Hickman line and he is HIV positive.

Explain to the theatre sister and operating department assistant what precautions you require because of this.

Question 1.5

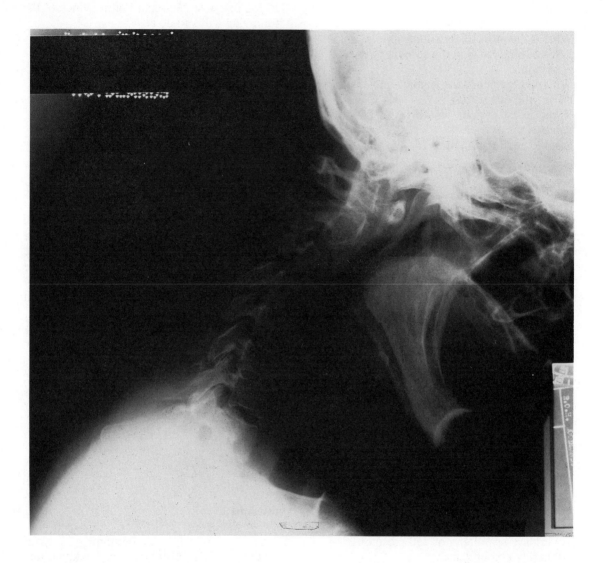

1. (a) What views do the cervical spine radiographs show?
1. (b) What abnormality is seen?

2. List the anatomical abnormalities of the cervical spine that occur with rheumatoid arthritis.

3. How would you assess stability of the cervical spine pre-operatively?

4. Outline the precautions you would take during tracheal intubation in a patient with rheumatoid disease of the cervical spine.

Question 1.5 continued

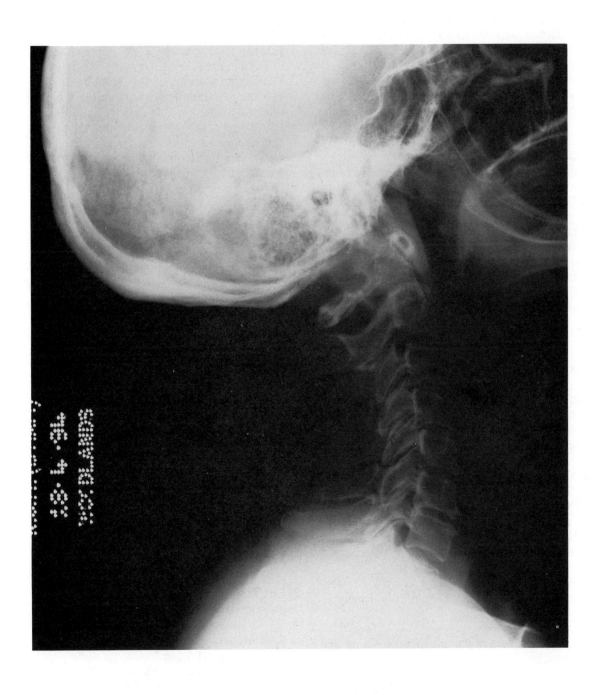

Question 1.6

Concerning brachial plexus block:
1. What two muscles enclose the roots and how can these muscles be demonstrated clinically? If the plexus is blocked at this point is pneumothorax a common complication and what complication is more likely if the needle is used in a cephalad direction?
2. What is the anatomical marking of the subclavian pulse? If you accidentally puncture the subclavian artery in which direction will you redirect the needle in order to approach the plexus?
3. List three end-points that may be used to confirm correct placing of a needle for brachial plexus block.
4. What cutaneous nerve is often missed by an axillary approach resulting in an inadequate block for a Colles' fracture? What nerve is this a branch of and why may the axillary approach miss it?

Question 1.7

You are asked to anaesthetize a 70-year-old man with bronchiectasis for a trabeculectomy. The patient is concerned about the risks of general anaesthesia and expresses a strong preference for the operation to be performed under local anaesthesia (LA).

1. Define bronchiectasis.

2. How would you optimize this patient's medical condition pre-operatively?

3. What factors would you consider when assessing this patient's suitability for local anaesthesia?

4. Outline the role of the anaesthetist during the operation.

5. List the advantages of LA for trabeculectomy.

Question 1.8

A five-year-old boy presents for circumcision in the day surgical unit.
1. List the local anaesthetic techniques that may be used to provide post-operative analgesia.
2. Outline the anatomy of the caudal canal.
3. Outline a technique for performing a caudal epidural block.
4. List the potential side effects/complications of caudal epidural block.
5. Give three reasons for failure of caudal anaesthesia for this procedure.

Question 1.9

A 59-year-old man with long-standing chest disease is scheduled for an elective inguinal hernia repair.

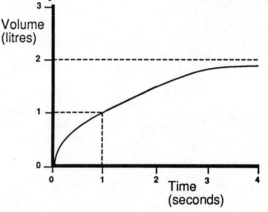

1. What is this graph? What pattern does it show and why?
2. List four types of drugs that might help optimize this patient's respiratory condition prior to anaesthesia.
3. List three nonpharmacological methods that may optimize his respiratory condition.
4. Which of the following is appropriate for this patient's intra-operative management:
   (a) low inspired oxygen concentration;
   (b) short inspiratory phase;
   (c) ventilation to normocapnia i.e $PaCO_2$ of 40 mmHg (5.3 kPa)?

Question 1.10

You notice a neighbour collapse whilst mowing his lawn with an electric lawnmower. You are the first person to arrive on the scene. Demonstrate on a mannikin how you would proceed to institute basic life support.

Question 1.11

Explain to a midwife what cricoid pressure is, why it is important and how it should be performed during induction of general anaesthesia for an emergency Caesarean section.

Question 1.12

A 50-year-old man has chest pain for one week and is admitted to hospital with a suspected myocardial infarction. His ECG is as shown.

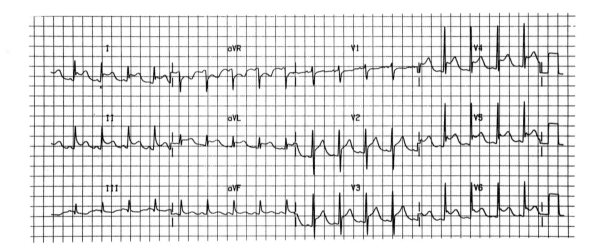

1. What abnormality does the ECG show and what is the primary diagnosis? What clinical sign would support this diagnosis? List the two commonest causes of this condition in the United Kingdom.

He is given heparin and streptokinase and in the following 12 hours his blood pressure falls and he requires inotropic support. Despite a central venous pressure of 20 mmHg he becomes oliguric and is admitted to the intensive care unit.

2. What complication due to the anticoagulation would explain the acute renal failure? Does a normal chest X-ray exclude this complication? List two clinical signs and an investigation that would confirm the diagnosis of this complication.

3. What procedure is the treatment for this complication? In what situation can this be done blindly? What other device can be used at the bedside to aid this procedure?

OSCE cycle 2 – questions

Question 2.1

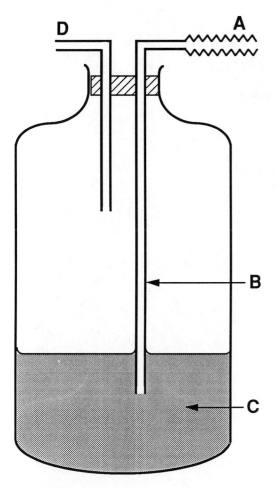

1. Name the parts labelled A – D.
2. What is the purpose of incorporating an underwater seal?
3. Give two disadvantages of the single bottle system.
4. Give three reasons for absence of oscillation of the water level.
5. What is the significance of persistent bubbling?
6. What precautions are necessary before transporting a patient in whom this drainage system is in use?

Question 2.2

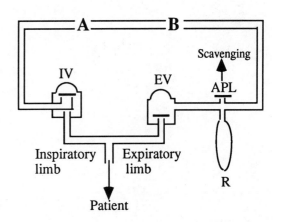

Schematic diagram of a circle breathing system showing inspiratory (IV) and expiratory (EV) one-way valves, adjustable pressure limiting valve (APL) and reservoir bag (R).

1. What two components labelled A and B are missing?

2. List two advantages of this position of the APL valve.

3. How would you check for and quantify a leak?

4. Briefly state what other checks you perform before using a circle system.

5. Theoretically what is the lowest fresh gas flow one could use?

6. What is meant by 'low flow' with respect to the use of circle breathing systems and how may insidious hypoxia occur?

Question 2.3

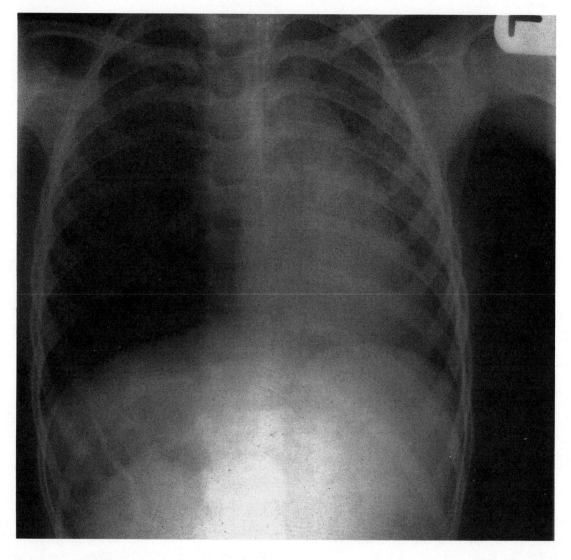

A 2-year-old child presents with a 48 h history of sudden onset of cough.

1. This chest X-ray has been taken in expiration. What abnormality is shown and what is the commonest cause in the United Kingdom? What condition does it cause?
2. What is the definitive treatment for this condition? What is the risk of treating this condition medically with physiotherapy, antibiotics, and bronchodilators?
3. What surgical instrument is used to treat this condition? What are the two types of instrument available?
4. List four reasons why this patient may have arrhythmias during the anaesthetic.

Question 2.4

A 73-year-old woman who is found convulsing in front of her coal fire is admitted to casualty. She is conscious but confused and vomiting. The pulse oximeter shows a saturation of 100% whilst breathing oxygen via an MC mask at 4 L/min.

1. What is the most likely diagnosis and how can it be confirmed?
2. What is your immediate management?
3. What further management may be required?

Question 2.5

A 50-year-old man had a resection of abdominal aortic aneurysm as an emergency. Following this the wound edges oozed and the abdominal drains showed continuing bleeding. A coagulation screen showed:

APTT	100 s (control 40 s)
Prothrombin time	25 s (control 15 s)
Thrombin time	50 s (control 15 s)
Reptilase time	Normal

1. Comment briefly on these results. Why might this result not reflect the coagulation of the patient's blood? What advantage does the activated clotting time have over the standard coagulation tests?

2. State what drug you could give to correct this coagulopathy and give two side effects it may produce.

3. What condition would you suspect if the reptilase test was prolonged and the thrombin time was greater than twice normal? How could you confirm this?

Question 2.6

See Plate 2.

1. (a) Name this piece of equipment.
1. (b) How does it measure blood pressure?

2. What factors may confound blood pressure measurement with this device?

3. What other methods of non-invasive blood pressure measurement may be used in adults?

Question 2.7

Concerning local anaesthesia of the upper airway for an awake intubation:

1. Give two advantages of an anticholinergic premedication for awake intubation.

2. What cranial nerves supply sensation to the nasal cavities? Give one advantage and one disadvantage of using cocaine for anaesthesia of the nasal cavities.

3. What nerves supply general sensation to the tongue? What dose does a 10% lignocaine metered spray deliver per spray?

4. What does the internal laryngeal nerve supply and from which nerve does it derive? What do Krause's forceps hold? Where should they be sited, why and how do you confirm their position?

5. Should an efficient nebulizer be used to deliver local anaesthetic to the airway in order to perform an awake intubation?

Question 2.8

A 28-year-old insulin-dependent diabetic with a two-day history of having been 'unwell' is admitted to hospital with a Glasgow coma score of 10. On examination, he is hyperventilating, dehydrated and has an infected ulcer on his left foot.

1. What is the most likely diagnosis?
2. Outline your initial management.
3. What other types of coma may be encountered in patients with diabetes?
4. (a) Define anion gap.
4. (b) How would you calculate plasma osmolarity?

Question 2.9

You are called to casualty to a cyanosed, apnoeic patient with a known history of asthma. You immediately intubate the patient but are unable to produce chest movement despite applying high pressure to the breathing circuit.

1. Give three possible causes for this inability to ventilate.
2. List three things you could do to help differentiate these causes.
3. Why may aminophylline be a dangerous drug to use in this patient?
4. On ventilation, the abdomen moves but the chest is motionless. Does this guarantee that the tracheal tube is misplaced?

Question 2.10

A 30-year-old man who was involved in a road traffic accident is brought into the casualty department. On admission, his blood pressure is 110/60 mmHg and his Glasgow coma score is 13. After 20 minutes, he suddenly stops breathing, he loses consciousness and his blood pressure becomes unrecordable. The ECG monitor shows the following trace:

1. What is the likely diagnosis?

2. Give three important treatable causes that you would have to exclude.

3. What is the immediate management of this patient?

4. Outline the specific management of each of the three causes listed in (2) above.

Question 2.11

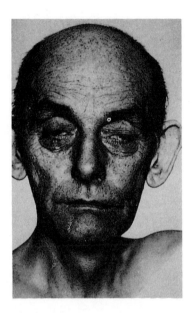

Two years ago this patient had problems after a cataract operation. He presents now for an elective cholecystectomy. Shaking hands with him results in this persistent characteristic grip.

1. What is the diagnosis? What phenomenon is demonstrated and how else can you elicit it in the hand?

2. List three problems this patient may have that increase his anaesthetic risk.

3. List three drugs used in anaesthesia that may produce an abnormal response.

4. Why may operating conditions be imperfect?

Question 2.12

You are asked to discuss Entonox with a student midwife. She asks the following questions:

1. What is 'gas and air'? What is its inherent risk? Is it the same as Entonox?
2. If a mother is having problems holding the mask should I get the husband to hold it to her face?
3. How much Entonox gas does a mother use in labour? How many cylinders should be available for the use of a primiparous mother in labour? What technique should the mother use to gain maximum effect from the Entonox?

4. What is the critical temperature of a gas? What is the critical temperature of Entonox? What are the risks of using cylinders that have been exposed to this temperature? If a cylinder of Entonox has been exposed to this temperature what should I do before I use it?

OSCE cycle 3 – questions

Question 3.1

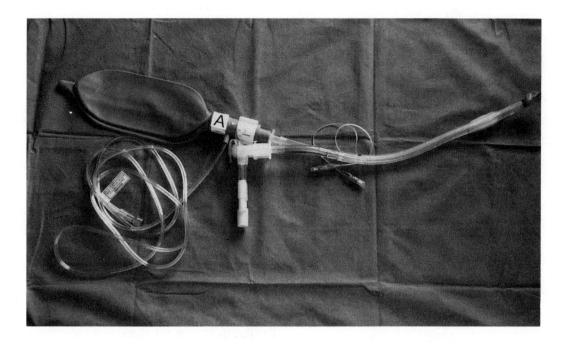

1. What is the device shown in the photograph?

2. How would you confirm the correct placement of this device?

3. What are the absolute indications for the use of this device?

4. List the options available for optimizing oxygenation during one lung ventilation.

Question 3.2

A 50-year-old man with symptomatic oesophageal reflux presents for an elective incisional hernia repair. You decide to do a rapid sequence induction with pre-oxygenation and cricoid pressure.

1. List three pre-operative methods to reduce the acidic content of his stomach. List two factors that may delay emptying of the stomach.

2. What decision concerning laryngoscopy should you make before starting induction?

3. At laryngoscopy you cannot see the epiglottis. What Cormack and Lehane grade of laryngoscopy is this? If you do not manage to intubate the trachea list briefly the first four stages of your failed intubation drill.

4. If you had managed to intubate the trachea, list three features during the operation that would make you suspect the patient had aspirated gastric content.

Question 3.3

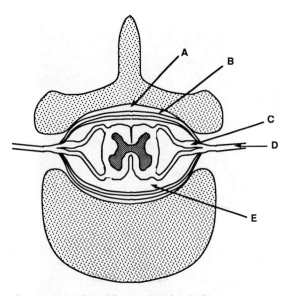

Transverse section of the spinal cord at the level of the sixth thoracic vertebra.

1. What are the parts labelled A – E?

2. a) What structures need to be penetrated when performing an epidural injection using the midline approach?

2. b) What are the boundaries of the epidural space?

3. Why is this not an appropriate level to site an epidural catheter for administering analgesia during labour?

4. List five contraindications to epidural blockade in labour.

5. List five advantages of the paramedian approach.

Question 3.4

See Plate 3.

1. What therapeutic block has been performed on this man's neck? What side effect is shown?

2. List four components of this side effect.

3. Name two complications that can occur with this therapy.

4. Name two other anaesthetic procedures that may cause the side effect shown.

5. If a patient appeared to have this sign bilaterally what disease would you suspect?

Question 3.5

You are asked to anaesthetize for an emergency Caesarean section for foetal distress (meconium stained liquor, foetal blood pH 7.26 and persistent foetal bradycardia). On delivery the paediatrician has not arrived and you are asked to resuscitate the baby. The baby is blue peripherally, and has a poor respiratory effort, decreased tone and a heart rate of 110/min.

1. What should you do before transferring the baby to the resuscitating table?

2. What is the Apgar score and is the foetal scalp pH normal?

3. What is the first thing you will do when the baby is on the resuscitating table?

4. What condition should you suspect if the peripheral cyanosis persists for 24 hours after delivery?

Question 3.6

1. Name the items shown in the photographs.
2. Outline the differences between the two items.

3. List the factors that affect spread of local anaesthetic during subarachnoid block.
4. List the potential complications of subarachnoid anaesthesia.

Question 3.7

A new volatile anaesthetic agent has the following properties:

- Sat. Vapour Pressure at 20°C = 664 mmHg;
- Boiling point = 23.5°C;
- Blood/gas solubility = 0.42;
- MAC = 7.5.

1. Define MAC.

2. How does blood/gas solubility influence the clinical usefulness of a volatile agent?

3. How does oil/gas solubility influence the clinical usefulness of a volatile agent?

4. Outline the attributes of the ideal volatile agent.

5. Based on the physical properties given above, what properties would you predict this new volatile agent to possess?

Question 3.8

Explain briefly to a staff nurse in the recovery unit the factors that have been implicated in the causation of post-operative nausea and vomiting and the measures that can be adopted to minimize this complication.

Question 3.9

See Plate 4.

1. (a) What does this cylinder contain?
1. (b) What features of the cylinder help in its identification?
2. What pressure is shown on the pressure gauge when it is (a) full: (b) half empty?
3. What precautions should be taken when attaching it to the anaesthetic machine?
4. How are these cylinders tested?
5. What other means are available for supplying this medical gas?

Question 3.10

A 50-year-old patient scheduled for an elective laparotomy for excision of a large bowel tumour complained of palpitations. The rhythm strip from a pre-operative ECG is shown below.

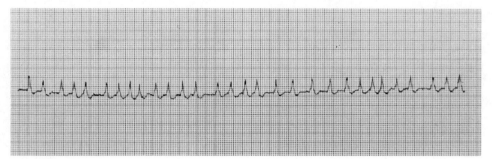

1. What arrhythmia does the ECG show?

2. List the therapeutic options that may be useful in controlling this arrhythmia.

3. Give two important pathophysiological consequences of this arrhythmia that must be considered prior to anaesthesia.

4. List five conditions that could cause this arrhythmia.

Question 3.11

A 68-year-old man with controlled hypertension presents with a three-day history of abdominal pain and intractable vomiting. You are asked to anaesthetize him for a laparotomy for bowel resection. Two strips from his pre-operative 12 lead ECG are shown below.

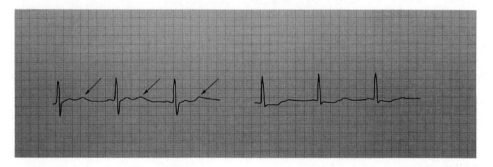

1. (a) What features on this ECG are consistent with hypokalaemia?
1. (b) Why might this patient be hypokalaemic?

2. List the main effects of hypokalaemia on the electrophysiology of the heart.

3. What are the clinical effects of hypokalaemia?

4. What factors would you take into account when considering treatment of hypokalaemia prior to surgery?

Question 3.12

Demonstrate how you would perform a quick neurological examination as part of a pre-operative assessment.

OSCE cycle 4 – questions

Question 4.1

At 20.00 an 8-year-old black Nigerian boy is admitted following a car crash. He has a haemoglobin of 7 g/dl and requires debridement of an ankle wound.

1. Which blood test would you do to exclude which condition? What definitive blood test may confirm this?

If the patient has this disease:

2. List five principles of anaesthetic management to prevent exacerbation of this disease.

3. List one complication of this disease for each of the following organs: lungs, kidneys and spleen.

Question 4.2

See Plate 5.

This patient complains of weight loss and heat intolerance.

1. What disease does this patient have?

2. Name two cardiovascular complications.

3. Name one airway complication.

4. List two other clinical findings that may suggest overactivity of this disease.

5. If this disease is overactive name two types of drugs you may use to prepare the patient prior to surgery.

6. If the disease is not controlled, what life-threatening condition may occur peri-operatively?

Question 4.3

A 20-year-old man was admitted to the casualty department complaining of right-sided chest pain, and breathlessness of sudden onset. His systemic blood pressure was 80/50 mmHg and a chest radiograph taken on admission is shown below.

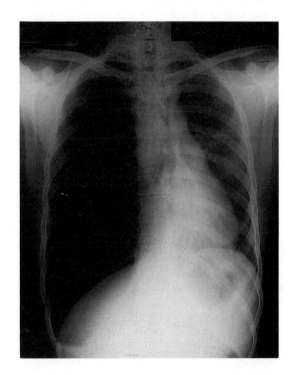

1. What does this chest radiograph show?
2. What is the emergency management of this condition?
3. How would you insert a pleural drain for the management of this condition? (You may be required to demonstrate the landmarks and technique on a mannikin.)
4. List four other indications for pleural drainage.
5. What are the potential complications of chest drain insertion?

Question 4.4

A 40-year-old man is admitted to casualty having been rescued from a fire at a plastics factory. He is conscious and his pulse oximeter oxygen saturation reading is 97%.

1. Having initially assessed his airway, breathing and circulation, what are the next two things you will do to him?

2. List three signs that would make you suspect an inhalation injury.

3. List three advantages that may be gained from intubating this patient.

4. List two advantages of using a fibreoptic bronchoscope in this scenario.

5. List two things that would make you suspect cyanide poisoning in this patient. List two drugs that may be used to treat cyanide poisoning.

Question 4.5

You anaesthetize a 30-year-old man for an elective operation. After giving a long-acting muscle relaxant, laryngoscopy reveals only the tip of the epiglottis but not the cords. You are able to ventilate the patient adequately by mask.

1. You try to pass a gum-elastic bougie (GEB). List two things that would suggest it had passed into the trachea. You try to railroad a tracheal tube over the GEB: should you remove the laryngoscope? What is the best position of the tracheal tube tip to allow it to enter the trachea?

2. You decide to use a Combitube. On insertion, ventilation of the tracheal channel causes gastric bubbling on auscultation. What should you do?

3. If you use a light wand to aid intubation when might you get a false positive result?

4. What size of cuffed endotracheal tube will fit through a size 3 laryngeal mask airway?

5. List briefly five ways of confirming correct placement of a tracheal tube.

Question 4.6

In the following schematic diagrams represents a square-wave, supramaximal stimulus of 0.2 ms duration

(a) Four stimuli at 2 Hz

(b) 1 minute at 1 Hz, 5 s at 50 Hz, a 3 s interval and then 1 Hz stimulation

(c) Three stimuli at 50 Hz followed after 750 ms by a further three stimuli at 50 Hz

1. Name these patterns of stimulation.

2. What advantage has (a) over depression of the first twitch (T1%) when measuring neuro-muscular blockade during surgery?

3. In (a) why are four stimuli used rather than three or five?

4. Under what circumstance is (b) used in preference to (a)?

Question 4.7

See Plate 6.

1. What is this kit? List three indications and three contraindications for siting this device.

2. What are the surface anatomy markings for the ends of the trachea? To what vertebral level do these correspond? What lies over the 2nd to 4th tracheal rings?

3. Where do you make your skin incision? Where should you enter the trachea and why? On entering the trachea what is the next thing you should confirm?

4. List three early complications of siting this device.

5. List two advantages of this technique over the standard surgical technique.

6. How soon does a track form? List two other types of tubes that could be used at this stage to replace the one shown.

Question 4.8

You are asked to anaesthetize a dehydrated seven-week-old boy who presented with regurgitation and projectile vomiting. The results of preliminary investigations are as follows:

Na^+	131 mmol/L
K^+	2.2 mmol/L
Cl^-	84 mmol/L
Urea	6.0 mmol/L
Hb	18 g/dL
pH (arterial)	7.2

1.(a) What is the likely diagnosis?
1.(b) What operation is the surgeon likely to perform?
2. What positive clinical signs would you look for?
3.(a) What are the metabolic consequences of this condition?
3.(b) Does this constitute a surgical emergency?
4. What pre-operative management would you prescribe?
5. Following resuscitation, how might tracheal intubation be achieved in this case?

Question 4.9

A 45-year-old man is anaesthetized for a hernia repair and is allowed to breathe a mixture of isoflurane, nitrous oxide and oxygen, spontaneously through a laryngeal mask airway. Midway through the procedure, the patient becomes apnoeic and the ECG monitor shows the following trace.

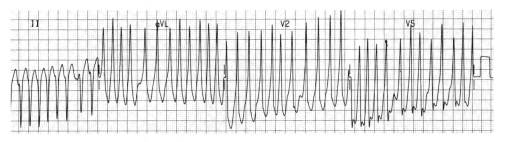

1. What is the diagnosis?
2. List five possible causes for this arrhythmia.

3. What immediate action would you take?
4. Outline the further specific management of this arrhythmia.

Question 4.10

You are asked to visit a pregnant lady in the antenatal clinic and discuss the advantages and disadvantages of epidural analgesia for labour.

Question 4.11

You are asked to see a 30-year-old man who had fractured his wrist eight weeks earlier. The surgeon thinks the patient is developing a reflex sympathetic dystrophy (RSD).

1. List two signs and two symptoms that would support the diagnosis of RSD.

2. You perform an intravenous regional (IVR) sympathetic block with guanethidine. The patient complains of an exacerbation of his pain on injection of guanethidine. List two types of drugs that may be given with the guanethidine to prevent this exacerbation. Is this exacerbation likely to occur with repeat guanethidine blocks?

3. Immediately following injection of the guanethidine the tourniquet cuff fails. What cardiovascular effects might result from systemic guanethidine?

4. If there is no benefit from the block is it worth repeating? Should the arm be immobilized to protect it until the block has worn off?

Question 4.12

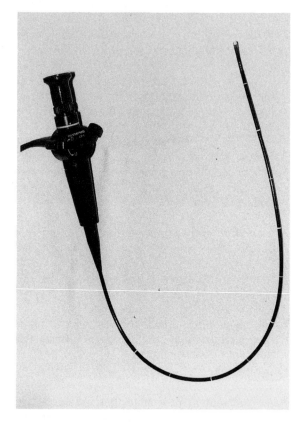

1. What is this object? What components are contained in the shaft?
2. What is the effect of moving the lever on the handle? List two other ways the object can be manipulated.
3. How do you check this instrument before using it?
4. Give two advantages of instilling oxygen down the port on the handle. List three other uses for this channel.
5. On insertion of the object to 15 cm you find the image is unrecognizable. List two possible reasons for this. List two things you may do to improve the image.
6. Why should you check for leaks after use?

OSCE cycle 5 – questions

Question 5.1

A capnogram from a fit 30-year-old woman undergoing laparoscopic sterilization under general anaesthesia is shown below.

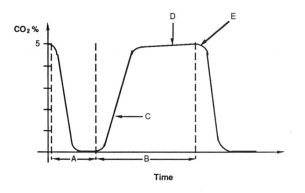

1. What do the parts of the tracing labelled A–E represent?
2. List three differences between mainstream and sidestream capnometers.
3. What are the possible causes for a sudden and sustained decrease in the end-tidal CO_2 concentration?
4. What other methods may be useful in establishing a diagnosis of pulmonary gas embolism?
5. Outline the immediate management of gas embolism in this patient.

Question 5.2

See Plate 7.
1. What is this object?
2. What are the four ports used for?
3. List two drugs that may be added to the system to prolong the object's life and one disadvantage for each.
4. List two nonpharmacological factors that may prolong the life of the object.

Question 5.3

1. What is the incidence of failed intubation? In addition to anatomical features list two other causes of a failed intubation. If one can only see the epiglottis on laryngoscopy what grade is this? What grades are associated with difficult intubation?

2. List two ways that thyroid disease may hinder intubation. If a patient with thyrotoxicosis was not a difficult intubation six months previously does this guarantee they will not be a difficult intubation now?

3. Briefly describe how you would perform the Mallampati test for airway assessment. What muscle is covered by the anterior faucial pillar? How do speech and posture affect the Mallampati test?

4. What are the five components of the Wilson Risk Sum Index for difficult intubation?

5. What thyro-mental and sterno-mental distances suggest intubation may be difficult?

Question 5.4

You are asked to anaesthetize a 70-year-old woman in a casualty unit for closed reduction of a Colles' fracture.

1. List the techniques that may be used to provide anaesthesia for this procedure.
2. List the advantages of intravenous regional anaesthesia (Bier's block).
3. What precautions would you take before performing a Bier's block?
4. List the contraindications to intravenous regional anaesthesia.
5. List the potential complications of intravenous regional anaesthesia.

Question 5.5

You are asked to see a patient in the recovery ward who is shivering and has an axillary temperature of 32°C.

1. What is the first thing you should do?
2. List two differential diagnoses.
3. List the four methods of heat loss and give one example of each that may occur peri-operatively.

4. Give three hazards of post-operative hypo-thermia.

Question 5.6

Discuss the advantages and disadvantages of general and regional anaesthesia with a mother who is due to have an elective Caesarean section for cephalopelvic disproportion.

Question 5.7

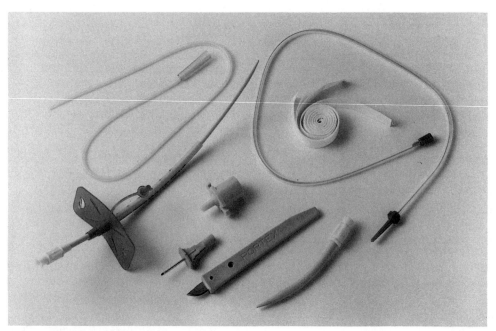

1. What is this kit? How do you position the patient? Where do you make the incision and how deep is it? What is the size of the tracheal cannula? What size suction catheter will pass through this?

2. Define sputum retention. Excluding this device, list three other methods of treating sputum retention.

3. List four advantages of this device.

4. List two immediate complications of siting this device.

5. How long does the wound take to heal on removal of this device? Excluding sputum retention give two other indications for the use of this device.

Question 5.8

A patient presents with bronchial carcinoma for a left pneumonectomy.

1. On examination of the pre-operative arterial blood gases, which is the better predictor of post-pneumonectomy morbidity:
(a) hypoxia or (b) hypercapnia?

2. List two values that can be obtained from a spirometer that predict whether a patient will tolerate a pneumonectomy.

3. Approximately what percentage of pulmonary blood flow goes to the left lung? How could you quantify this more accurately?

4. In patients who have chronic obstructive airways disease what FEV_1 (forced expiratory volume in 1 second) is necessary for an effective cough? How can you predict the post-operative FEV_1?

5. What condition may this patient have that would cause an abnormal response to muscle relaxants? Would they be more or less sensitive to anticholinesterases?

Question 5.9

See Plate 8.

1. What disease is shown?

2. List three reasons why this patient may be anaemic. List two other abnormalities you would look for on this patient's full blood count and one cause for each.

3. List two ways in which this disease may affect the lungs.

4. List two cardiovascular complications of this disease.

5. At what level of proteinuria would you suspect the patient may have nephrotic syndrome? How may you confirm this diagnosis and what may be the cause?

Question 5.10

A man is admitted to the casualty department. He was a passenger in a high speed car chase ending in the car being completely written off as it demolished a brick wall. He was ejected from the car but the driver was killed.

On examination he is agitated, looks pale and is sweating. He has a pulse rate of 130/min, blood pressure of 90/65 mmHg and an oxygen saturation of 96%.

1. List three significant factors in the history and state why they are important.

2. How much blood is he likely to have lost?

3. What three X-rays should be performed urgently?

4. Does pelvic examination by springing exclude major pelvic trauma?

5. What examination should you do before you catheterize the bladder?

Question 5.11

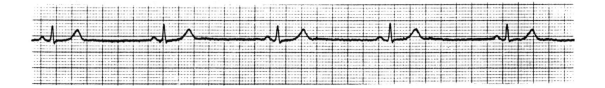

1. What does this ECG rhythm strip show?

2. List the causes of this condition.

3. On what criteria would you decide to treat a bradycardia?

4. Outline the treatment of symptomatic bradycardia.

Question 5.12

A 38-year-old primigravid female who is 40 weeks pregnant collapses suddenly with a cardiorespiratory arrest during a difficult and prolonged second stage of labour. Her lumbar epidural had been topped up a few minutes previously in an attempt to improve the quality of analgesia.

1. List four possible causes of cardiovascular collapse in this situation.
2. What is your immediate management?
3. What difficulties may be encountered when instituting cardiopulmonary resuscitation in advanced pregnancy?
4. List the important causes of *direct* maternal mortality in the United Kingdom.

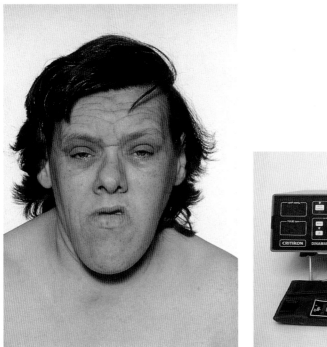

Plate 1

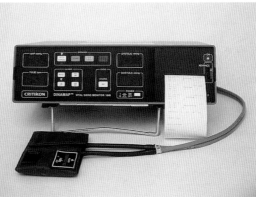

Plate 2

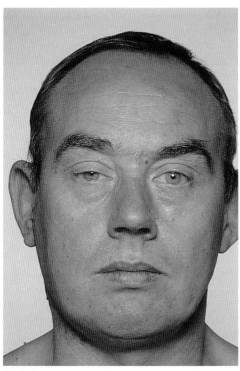

Plate 3

Plate 4

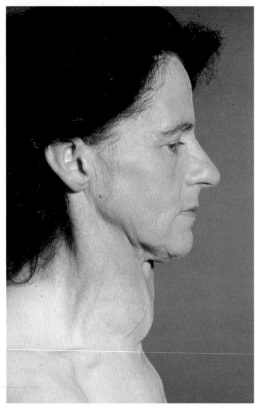

Plate 5

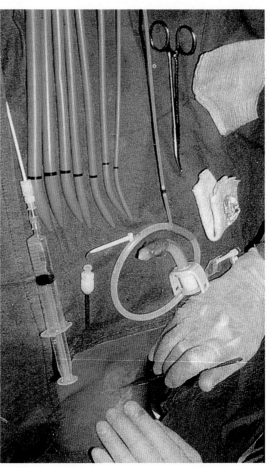

Plate 6

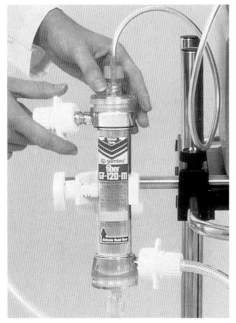

Plate 7

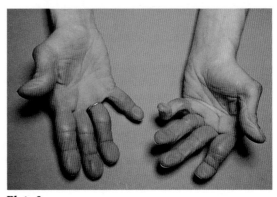

Plate 8

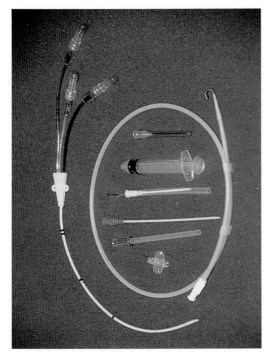

Plate 9

Plate 10

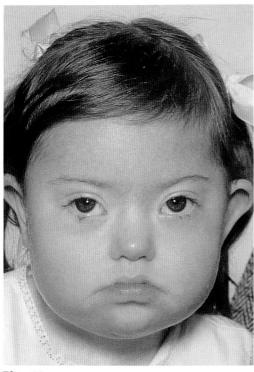

Plate 11

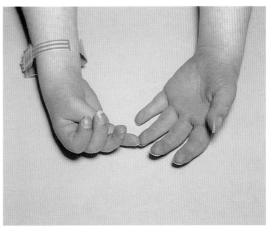

Plate 12

Plate 13

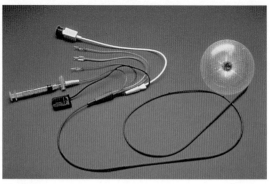

Plate 14

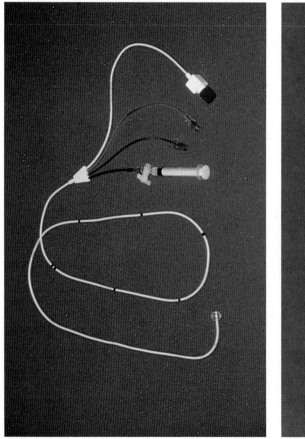

Plate 15

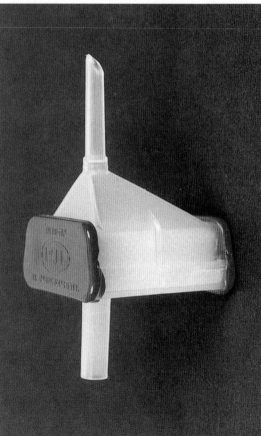

Plate 16

OSCE cycle 6 – questions

Question 6.1

A 50-year-old man is admitted at 14:00 for exploration of a forearm wound. He denies any alcohol intake in the previous six months. He had previously been admitted many times for haematemesis but no cause was found. He has the following blood results:

Hb	11 g/dL
MCV	110 fL
WBC	3600/mm^3
Platelets	50 000/mm^3
Alcohol	200 mg/dL

1. Briefly comment on these results.
2. List two tests that may help confirm the chronicity of this condition.
3. List five associated complications that increase peri-operative risk, if these tests are positive.
4. Why may he be confused post-operatively? Name one drug that may be used in the management.

Question 6.2

You are asked to anaesthetize a 65-year-old man with endogenous depression, in whom drug therapy has failed, for a course of electro-convulsive therapy (ECT).

1. List the reasons for providing general anaesthesia during ECT.

2. List the physiological consequences of ECT.

3. What are the absolute contraindications to ECT?

4. List the important interactions between anti-depressant drugs and drugs that may be used during anaesthesia.

Question 6.3

An 18-year-old youth has an operation on his fractured femur. Ten minutes after intubation he has a pulse of 130/min and is starting to breathe spontaneously despite a relatively large dose of opiate and muscle relaxant.

1. What myopathic condition could account for this? Give three other possible causes for this tachycardia.
2. List three other signs that would support a diagnosis of this myopathic condition.

If you suspect this myopathic condition:

3. What blood tests should be sent?
4. What drug is given to treat this condition, what are its side effects and what else is present in each vial?
5. He has had several previously uneventful anaesthetics. For this operation he has been given total intravenous anaesthesia with no volatile and no depolarizing muscle relaxant. How does this help your diagnosis and management?

Question 6.4

A patient who is 1.7 m tall and weighs 130 kg presents for elective open cholecystectomy.

1. (a) Define body mass index.
1. (b) What is this patient's body mass index?
1. (c) Classify obesity based on body mass index.
2. What are the medical complications of severe obesity?
3. List the causes for pulmonary dysfunction in the severely obese patient.
4. List the problems the anaesthetist may encounter when administering general anaesthesia to this patient.

Question 6.5

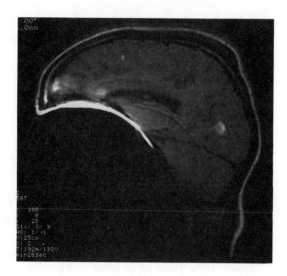 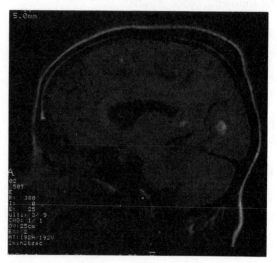

1. What investigation is shown? What artefact is demonstrated? List three problems of anaesthetizing in this environment.

2. List two indications for general anaesthesia during this investigation.

3. Why may there be an oxygen analyser open to room air in the MRI suite? At what percent oxygen level should the alarm be set?

4. List three risks to the patient undergoing this investigation.

Question 6.6

The following questions refer to the use of mechanical devices to provide temporary support in ventricular failure.

1. What options are available for providing temporary mechanical support in ventricular failure?

2. Outline the physiology of intra-aortic balloon counterpulsation.

3. List the indications for intra-aortic balloon counterpulsation.

4. List the complications of intra-aortic balloon counterpulsation.

Question 6.7

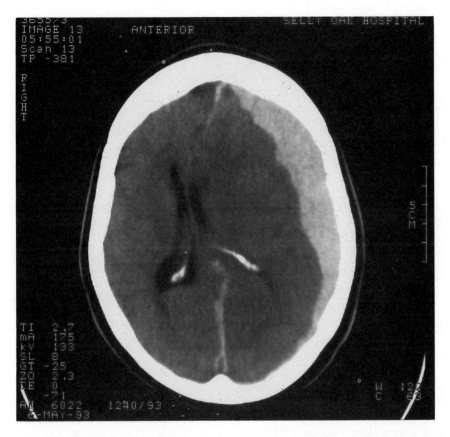

1. What is this investigation and what is the diagnosis?
2. Outline the immediate management of this condition in the casualty unit.
3. What are the aims of surgical management?

4. What physiological variables would you manipulate during anaesthesia and why?
5. List the indications for intracranial pressure monitoring in head injured patients.

Question 6.8

A 4-year-old boy is found unconscious in a swimming pool and admitted to the accident and emergency department. His heart rate is 30/minute and his core temperature 30°C.

1. List two factors that may predispose to drowning.

2. Give two advantages and two risks of tracheal intubation in this patient.
3. List two reasons why this child may be hypoxaemic.
4. Give three methods of increasing his core temperature.
5. What is the immediate risk of core rewarming?

Question 6.9

See Plate 9.

1. What equipment is shown? Where can it be sited?

2. What absolute contraindications are there to the siting of this object?

3. Is it always appropriate to site these cannulae with the patient in the Trendelenberg position?

4. What investigation should be carried out after insertion and why?

5. Why is this an inappropriate cannula for resuscitating a hypovolaemic patient?

Question 6.10

1. What is soda lime?

2. How does it fulfil its role during the administration of anaesthesia?

3. Which volatile agents should not be used with soda lime?

4. List the signs of exhaustion of soda lime.

5. What other methods can be used to eliminate CO_2 from a breathing system?

Question 6.11

The following questions refer to the Bain breathing system.

1. Describe the Bain breathing system.

2. How would you test a Bain breathing system prior to use?

3. How efficient is the Bain breathing system:
   (a) during spontaneous breathing?

   (b) during intermittent positive pressure ventilation?

Question 6.12

You are asked to instruct a junior casualty doctor on the technique of intravenous regional anaesthesia (Bier's block) for surgery of the upper limb.

OSCE cycle 7 – questions

Question 7.1

See Plate 10.

1. (a) What is shown in the picture?

1. (b) How is this gas manufactured?

2. What is the pin index system?

3. Define the term 'filling ratio'.

4. List the problems that may be caused by this gas diffusing into closed spaces.

Question 7.2

You are asked to discuss the use of patient controlled analgesia (PCA) with a ward staff nurse. She asks you the following questions:

1. How common a problem is post-operative pain in Britain? Give me five medical reasons why I should try to provide good post-operative pain relief.

2. Different patients seem to need different amounts of intramuscular morphine for similar operations. Give me two reasons for this variation.

3. When a PCA device is connected with an i.v. drip on which line should the one-way valve be and what is its function? What is the risk of siting the PCA above the level of the patient?

4. Why is a background infusion not used routinely with PCA?

5. What is the risk of using a pethidine PCA without a total dose limit in a patient who is a chronic user of pethidine?

Question 7.3

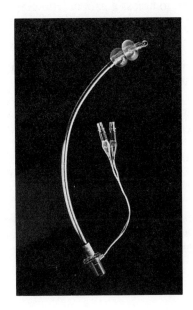

1. What surgical technique is this object used for?

In circumstances when this object is used:

2. List two hazards for the staff and two measures to reduce these risks.

3. List two hazards that might affect the patient.

4. List two ways in which the anaesthetist can reduce these risks.

5. What catastrophe may occur and what are the first three steps in its management?

Question 7.4

You are called to the recovery ward by a junior anaesthetist to assess a patient who at the end of a general anaesthetic is making no respiratory effort.

1. What is the first thing you would do on arriving in the recovery ward?

2. List three pharmacological and three physiological causes for post-operative apnoea.

3. List three monitoring devices and three blood tests that you would use to diagnose the cause of apnoea.

4. List two pharmacological antagonists that may be useful. What is important about their duration of action?

Question 7.5

You are asked to see a 60-year-old male in the pre-operative assessment clinic. He smokes 40 cigarettes a day and is awaiting elective cholecystectomy.

1. List the health risks of tobacco smoking.

2. Outline the effects of smoking on the cardio-vascular system.

3. Outline the effects of smoking on the respiratory system.

4. What are the peri-operative benefits of abstinence from smoking prior to surgery?

5. List your considerations when selecting a technique of general anaesthesia for this patient.

Question 7.6

A 40-year-old woman complains of a headache, vomits and then collapses. On admission to hospital she localizes and opens her eyes in response to pain but does not speak. A lumbar puncture is performed and the sample is reported as containing 200 RBC/mm^3 with no xanthochromia on centrifugation.

1. How can one differentiate this from a traumatic tap? If this is not traumatic what is the diagnosis?

2. What test, if available, should have been done before the lumbar puncture and why?

3. Was the Glasgow coma score on admission 2, 5, 8 or 10?

4. Give two reasons why a central venous catheter would be indicated.

5. Twelve hours after admission she suddenly deteriorates. List two preconditions that must be met before she can be tested for brainstem death. Which of the following is necessary for a diagnosis of brainstem death:

   (a) core temperature of $>35°C$
   (b) apnoea with a $PaCO_2$ >50 mmHg
   (c) absence of seizures

Question 7.7

A five-year-old child presents with a one-day history of sore throat. She looks unwell, won't speak and won't drink. She has signs of upper airway obstruction.

1. List three signs you would look for that suggest upper airway obstruction.

2. What are the two commonest causes of upper airway obstruction in this age group?

3. What is the commonest infecting organism for each?

4. List three factors in the history and three factors in the examination that would favour a bacterial cause for this condition.

5. The child becomes more breathless. Which of the following is part of an appropriate management:
   (a) immediately gaining intravenous access?
   (b) gaseous induction of anaesthesia?
   (c) intravenous rapid sequence induction of anaesthesia to secure the airway?
   (d) gentle inspection of the throat with a tongue spatula?
   (e) lateral neck X-ray?

Question 7.8

1. Sketch an arterial pressure wave, labelling the systolic (SBP) and diastolic (DBP) blood pressures.

2. List three other measurements that can be obtained from it.

3. You accidentally inject thiopentone into an artery. List three ways you may recognize this and three methods of treatment.

4. What solution is used for flushing an arterial line?

Question 7.9

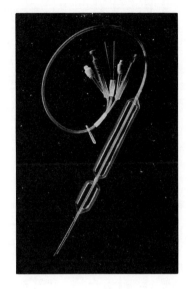

1. (a) What is this device?

1. (b) What are the indications for its use?

2. Outline the method of insertion of this tube.

3. List four potential complications of this procedure.

4. List the causes of oesophageal varices.

5. Outline the treatment of bleeding from oesophageal varices.

Question 7.10

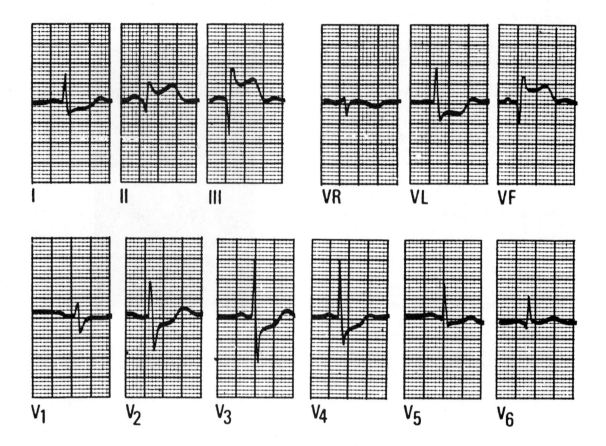

I   II   III   VR   VL   VF

V₁   V₂   V₃   V₄   V₅   V₆

1. (a) What is the diagnosis?
1. (b) What ECG findings support this diagnosis?

2. Outline the immediate treatment of this condition.

3. List the complications that may arise in this condition.

4. How does this diagnosis affect the risk of anaesthesia?

Question 7.11

A 70 kg woman is given 14 units of mainly red cell concentrate during an emergency laparotomy for a ruptured ectopic pregnancy. Post-operatively she continues to ooze from the wound and venepuncture sites.

1. What blood tests would you do to assess her coagulation? What is the likeliest cause of her bleeding?

2. Give two advantages of using whole blood rather than red cell concentrate in this situation.

3. What do the letters SAG-M stand for? Give two advantages and two disadvantages of SAG-M blood over whole blood.

4. By what amount would you expect the platelet count to rise in this patient if given 1 unit of platelets? What else does a unit of platelets contain?

Question 7.12

A 34-year-old lady presents for a trans-sternal thymectomy. She developed an auto-immune disease three years previously and is taking pyridostigmine.

1. What is the disease?

2. List two other nonsurgical treatments for this disease.

3. What two crises of muscle weakness can occur and how can you differentiate them?

4. List two pre-operative abnormalities that increase peri-operative risk.

5. How may the effects of thiopentone, suxamethonium and atracurium be abnormal in this patient?

6. List two factors that might help predict the need for post-operative ventilation?

OSCE cycle 8 – questions

Question 8.1

You are asked to anaesthetize a full-term parturient for an emergency Caesarean section for foetal distress. On questioning she says she is allergic to suxamethonium and can remember waking up in the ITU after her previous Caesarean section. She thinks her mother is also allergic to suxamethonium and has had a blood test to prove it. No notes are available.

1. What is the diagnosis?
2. The patient insists on a general anaesthetic. Would you use suxamethonium?
3. Following the operation the patient's old notes show the following blood results:
   Dibucaine number (DN) - 60
   Fluoride number (FN) - 50
   Is the action of suxamethonium likely to be prolonged in this patient?
4. Give the normal values for DN and FN.
5. Name two alternative methods of anaesthetizing a patient for a Caesarean section without using suxamethonium.

Question 8.2

A 59-year-old man with long-standing chest disease is scheduled for an elective inguinal hernia repair. These are the blood results on air:

Hb	18 g/100 mL
WCC	15 000/mm^3
pH	7.28
PaCO$_2$	12.2 kPa
PaO$_2$	5.0 kPa
Standard bicarbonate	42.0 mmol/L
Base excess	15.2 mmol/L

1. Comment on the haemoglobin and white cell count.
2. Comment on the arterial blood gases.
3. What will happen if he is given a high inspired oxygen concentration?
4. What other tests would you require when assessing this man?

Question 8.3

1. Demonstrate on a 'model patient' how you would examine the jugular venous pulse and assess the jugular venous pressure.
2. How can jugular venous pulsation be distinguished from an arterial pulsation in the neck?
3. Draw and label a normal internal jugular venous pulse waveform.
4. What do the different waves and 'descents' represent?
5. State two causes each for abnormal 'a' and 'v' waveforms.

Question 8.4

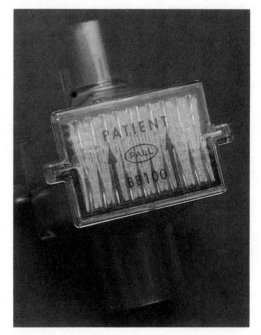

1. What is the device shown in the photograph?
2. Outline the design features of this device.
3. What other types of this device are available?
4. List the potential clinical uses of this device.
5. What other methods have been described for humidifying inspired gases?
6. List the pathophysiological consequences of ventilation with dry gases.

Question 8.5

A 68-year-old man is having a transurethral resection of a large prostate gland under spinal anaesthesia and one hour after the start of surgery he becomes restless and then fits.

1. What is the most probable cause?

2. List two signs and two other symptoms with which this condition may present.

3. List two guidelines that may help prevent this condition.

4. What blood test will confirm the diagnosis and what may be added to the irrigating fluid to monitor the volume absorbed?

Question 8.6

A man is admitted to casualty 1 hour after suffering thermal and acid burns over the whole of his back down to his buttocks. His blood pressure is 80/40 mmHg, his pulse is 120/minute and he has poor peripheral perfusion.

1. What are the first three priorities in the management of this burned patient? What is the most likely cause of his hypotension? What should you put on the acid to neutralize it?

2. What percentage of the body surface area is affected? How do you allow for irregularly shaped burns?

3. What area of burn requires i.v. fluid replacement? What formula gives the exact volume of fluid replacement required for the first 24 hours?

4. List three criteria for assessing the depth of the burns.

5. 24 hours post-burn he is pyrexial. Should you cool him? Should you give prophylactic intravenous antibiotics?

Question 8.7

See Plates 11 and 12.

This child has a low IQ and presents for an elective umbilical hernia repair.

1. What is the diagnosis? What abnormality of the fingers is shown?

2. List four general causes of this finger abnormality. What is the likely cause of this abnormality in this child? Is this finger abnormality present at birth?

3. List two possible intubation problems in this patient.

4. List two possible cardiovascular problems in this patient. Why should you be especially careful not to introduce any air into venous lines?

5. List two post-operative problems in this condition.

Question 8.8

Explain to a newly appointed nurse in the day surgery unit how you would assess a patient's fitness for discharge following inguinal hernia repair under general anaesthesia.

Question 8.9

See Plate 13.

1. (a) What is this piece of equipment?

1. (b) How does it work?

2. List the precautions that should be taken before it is used.

3. If a flat line were to appear on the ECG monitor during resuscitation of a patient, what would you check before making a diagnosis of asystole?

4. Outline the features of an automatic implantable cardioverter-defibrillator.

Question 8.10

You are called to the Casualty department to assess a 4-year-old boy who is thought to have accidentally swallowed some aspirin tablets.

1. Briefly list two abnormalities you may find on arterial blood gas measurement.

2. List three abnormalities you may find on clinical examination.

3. List three causes of dehydration in this patient.

4. List three general contraindications for the use of ipecacuanha syrup.

5. Should gastric lavage be used 12 hours after ingestion of aspirin? List two other methods that may be used to eliminate aspirin from this patient.

Question 8.11

You are asked to see a lady who has developed a headache 24 hours after having had a lumbar epidural catheter inserted for the provision of analgesia during labour.

1. What questions would you ask her?

2. How would you manage her?

3. Describe how you would perform an epidural blood patch.

Question 8.12

You are asked to anaesthetize a 5-year-old boy who is still bleeding on the ward following a tonsillectomy three hours earlier.

1. Estimate his weight, blood volume and likely blood loss.

2. List three signs in this patient that may suggest hypovolaemia. Why may this assessment be difficult?

3. List two problems complicating induction.

4. List two methods of induction of anaesthesia and a disadvantage of each.

OSCE cycle 9 – questions

Question 9.1

You are called to the recovery unit to see a patient who has an oxygen saturation of 90% on air following emergency small bowel resection.

1. What are the causes of early post-operative hypoxia?

2. What methods are useful for assessing hypoxaemia?

3. How would you manage this patient?

4. List the causes of late post-operative hypoxaemia.

Question 9.2

A 50-year-old man presents with abdominal pain and a pulsatile abdominal mass. He has a systolic blood pressure of 70 mmHg and is peripherally vasoconstricted.

1. What is the likely diagnosis?

2. His heart rate is only 80/minute. Does this mean he is normovolaemic? Give one reason why he may not have a tachycardia.

3. Which of the following is appropriate before induction of anaesthesia in theatre?

   (a) Full resuscitation in the admitting department.

   (b) Transfusion of blood pre-operatively until his haemoglobin is 10 g/dL.

   (c) Insertion of a urinary catheter.

   (d) Crystalloids i.v. to maintain a systolic blood pressure of above 80 mmHg.

   (e) Insertion of an arterial line even if it delays surgery.

   (f) Diagnostic peritoneal lavage.

Question 9.3

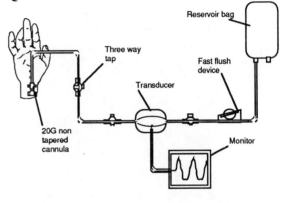

1. Give three indications for the use of this system.

2. List two factors that may overdamp this system.

3. How can you tell if the system is over-damped?

Question 9.4

See Plate 14.

1. What is the object? On which side does the tip normally lie and why?

2. List four channels that may be present.

3. List two variables that can be derived.

4. What measurement is the red light at the tip used for? What variables are assumed to be constant?

Question 9.5

The chest radiograph of a 20-year-old girl scheduled for emergency laparotomy is shown below. She had had an atrioventricular septal defect repaired 2 years previously and had made a good recovery.

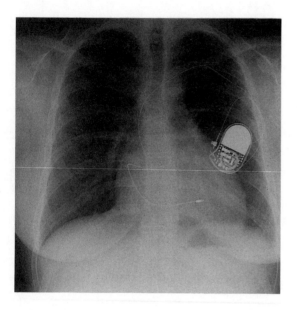

1. (a) What is the most important abnormal feature on this chest radiograph?

1. (b) What other information would be useful pre-operatively?

2. How might the use of diathermy interfere with pacemaker function?

3. What precautions should be taken when using diathermy during surgery on a patient with a permanent pacemaker?

4. List other potential causes of intra-operative interference with pacemaker function.

5. How would you treat intra-operative pacemaker failure?

Question 9.6

What information about the cardiovascular system can be obtained from examining the arterial pulses?

Question 9.7

A 23-year-old man sustains bilateral femoral fractures in a road traffic accident and 18 h later undergoes surgery. Post-operatively you are called to assess him as he is agitated and the nurses think it is due to his anaesthetic. On examination he has a respiratory rate of 35/minute, has a heart rate of 150/minute and is cyanosed.

1. What is your immediate treatment?
2. List three possible causes for this presentation.
3. What rash would you look for?
4. If this rash is present what is the diagnosis and what may you find on examination of the arterial blood gases, ECG and chest X-ray?
5. List three indications for mechanical ventilation in this patient.

Question 9.8

See Plate 15.

1. What is the object?
2. Give three indications for its use?
3. Sketch four pressure waves that are encountered on its insertion.
4. List four complications to this device that are not related to the act of siting it.

Question 9.9

You are called to a delivery room where a baby has just been born at 35 weeks gestation and is on the resuscitation table. The baby is centrally cyanosed, not breathing and not making any spontaneous movements.

1. What is your initial management of the airway?
2. Would you give 100% oxygen to this pre-term baby?
3. What airway pressure would you use?
4. What is the likely range of diameter and length of endotracheal tubes appropriate for this baby?
5. List four normal differences between the neonatal and adult airway that may make intubation or ventilation more difficult.

Question 9.10

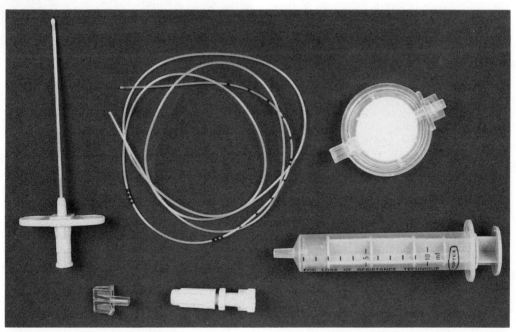

1. Label the items shown in the photograph.
2.(a) What are the contents of the epidural space?
2.(b) What methods may be used for recognizing entry into the epidural space?
3.(a) What are the features of an ideal epidural test dose?
3.(b) What are the manufacturer's current recommendations for epidural test doses using bupivacaine?
4. What other methods are available for confirming correct placement of a catheter within the epidural space?
5. List three immediate complications of epidural anaesthesia that could be life threatening.

(Some epidural simulators are currently being developed and you may be required to demonstrate how you would perform an epidural injection/ catheter insertion.)

Question 9.11

You are called to the recovery ward to see an agitated 55-year-old man who has a blood pressure of 200/120 mmHg and a heart rate of 110 beats/min.

1. List three possible causes of post-operative hypertension and three causes for post-operative agitation.
2. What is the first thing you will do on arrival in the recovery ward?
3. List three risks associated with post-operative hypertension.
4. When might post-operative treatment of high blood pressure be inappropriate?

Question 9.12

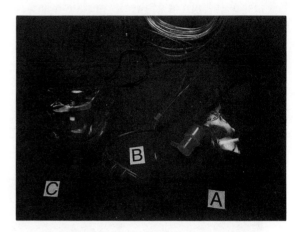

1. List the basic requirements of oxygen therapy systems.
2. How would you classify oxygen delivery systems?
3. (a) What are the devices labelled A, B and C in the picture above?
3. (b) Describe briefly the design features and performance characteristics of each of the devices shown above.
4. List the potential complications of normobaric oxygen therapy.

OSCE cycle 10 – questions

Question 10.1

Immediately following a cholecystectomy, for which you had given a muscle relaxant, the patient is spontaneously breathing 100% oxygen through an endotracheal tube and has an oxygen saturation on pulse oximetry of 100%.

1. If the patient is still anaesthetized give three patterns of ulnar nerve stimulation that indicate residual paralysis.
2. If the patient is swallowing and maintaining normocapnia does this indicate that neuromuscular function is adequate for maintenance of the airway?
3. If the patient is awake what volitional test indicates adequate neuromuscular function for maintenance of the airway?
4. Give four causes of prolongation of non-depolarizing neuromuscular blockade.

Question 10.2

A lady is admitted to the labour ward in the 29th week of her first pregnancy with a blood pressure which is consistently greater than 160/100 mmHg.

1. How would you classify hypertensive disorders of pregnancy?
2. Define pre-eclampsia.
3. Outline how you would manage hypertension in pre-eclampsia.
4. Outline the management of anaesthesia for Caesarean section in this patient.

Question 10.3

The medical houseman asks you to ventilate a 40-year-old man who has suspected pneumonia and the following arterial blood gas values:

pH	7.54
$PaCO_2$	28 mmHg (3.7 kPa)
PaO_2	60 mmHg (8.0 kPa)
Standard bicarbonate	26 mmol/L
Base excess	3 mmol/L

1. What other information would you like to have before you comment on the result?
2. Briefly comment on the blood gases despite this lack of information and give two possible causes other than pneumonia.
3. The houseman has arranged for the nurses to monitor the oxygen saturation overnight and increase the concentration of inspired oxygen to keep saturation levels ≥94%. Why is this management dangerous? When you go to assess him the nurses say he is sleeping and his respiratory rate is down to 10/min. Is this a good sign?
4. What graph helps you predict the inspired oxygen concentration required to maintain a normal arterial oxygenation? Give one other use for this graph.

Question 10.4

You are called to the recovery ward to see a cyanosed patient. She has a thyroidectomy incision and is starting to twitch.

1. What is the first thing you would do?
2. List four causes specific to this patient which could account for her cyanosis.
3. Why may she be twitching?
4. What two signs would you look for to confirm this?
5. What is the treatment?

Question 10.5

A 65-year-old man presents with anorexia, nausea, abdominal pain and a serum Ca^{2+} of 4.2 mmol/L.

1. Which two important causes of hypercalcaemia would need to be considered in this case?

2. What features would help distinguish between the two conditions?
3. List five other causes of hypercalcaemia.
4. What treatment options are available for lowering serum Ca^{2+}?
5. What is the effect of hypercalcaemia on the ECG?

Question 10.6

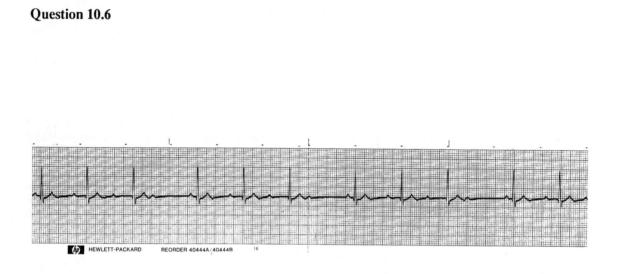

1. What does this ECG rhythm strip show?

2. Classify heart block.

3. What are the causes of heart block?

4. List the principal indications for permanent pacing.

Question 10.7

1. What is the anatomical landmark for the femoral artery? If you attempted to do a femoral artery puncture and entered the femoral vein on which side would you redirect your needle? What are the other contents of the femoral sheath?
2. What are the three nerves of a 3-in-1 block of the lower limb? What area of skin does each supply? When performing this block why is it important to elicit paraesthesiae?
3. What other nerve would you have to block if you wished to fully anaesthetize the lower limb above the knee?
4. Concerning the use of peripheral nerve blocks for orchidopexy, what nerves are blocked 1–2 cm medial to the anterior superior iliac spine? What is their segmental derivation? What area do they innervate? What other nerves should be blocked?

Question 10.8

A 60-year-old woman with chronic bronchitis has become progressively more breathless over the last 10 years. A week before admission she suddenly deteriorated, became orthopnoeic and has since had to sleep in a chair.
On examination, her cheeks are a dusky mauve colour and her blood pressure is 100/80 mmHg. Auscultation at the apex reveals a soft first heart sound, a long, low-pitched, rumbling diastolic murmur and a loud pulmonary second heart sound.

1. What is the diagnosis and probable cause?
2. What other lesion should you attempt to exclude?
3. What is the likely cause of her sudden deterioration?
4. Give three signs that would suggest her lesion is severe.

5. If anaesthesia is necessary for this patient which of the following would be advantageous:
   (a) pulmonary artery flotation catheter?
   (b) routine preloading with colloid?
   (c) tachycardia?
   (d) bradycardia?
   (e) nitrous oxide?
   (f) spontaneous ventilation?

Question 10.9

See Plate 16.

1.(a) What is the device shown in the picture?
1.(b) Give a brief description of its structure.
2.(a) What are the main types of microaggregate filters in clinical use?
2.(b) List the differences between these types.
3. Give three indications for the use of micro-aggregate filters.
4. List the disadvantages of microaggregate filters.

Question 10.10

A fit 45-year-old female presented for elective ovarian cystectomy. She had had one previous uneventful anaesthetic. On induction of anaesthesia with thiopentone she develops a florid urticarial rash and severe bronchospasm and her blood pressure falls to 70/40 mmHg.

1. What is the most likely diagnosis?
2. Outline the immediate management of this condition.
3. List the laboratory tests that may be useful in making the diagnosis.
4. What action would you take with respect to future anaesthesia for this patient, if the diagnosis were to be proven?

Question 10.11

A 60-year-old woman is being ventilated in an intensive care unit following a massive subarachnoid haemorrhage. The results of blood samples on admission and 48 hours later and the urine collected on the second day are:

Table a Serum results

		On admission	At 48 h
Sodium	(mmol/L)	138	171
Potassium	(mmol/L)	3.5	2.8
Glucose	(mmol/L)	7.0	9.4
Creatinine	(μmol/L)	95	113
Urea	(mmol/L)	5.0	7.0

Table b 24-hour urine sample

	Day 2
Volume	3550 mL
Sodium	< 10 mmol/L
Potassium	15 mmol/L
Creatinine	2.3 μmol/L
Urea	85 mmol/L
Osmolality	112 mosm/kg

1. What is the minimum volume of urine a patient must produce in 24 hours to adequately excrete nitrogenous waste?
2. Calculate the serum osmolarity of the two blood samples. Briefly interpret the serum and 24 hour urine results. What is the likely diagnosis? Does this patient's urinary volume confirm that she is not dehydrated?
3. Give two other reasons why the serum sodium may have risen.
4. What is the treatment for this electrolyte imbalance? Give one side effect of this treatment.
5. Why is the treatment of this condition important for kidney donation?

Question 10.12

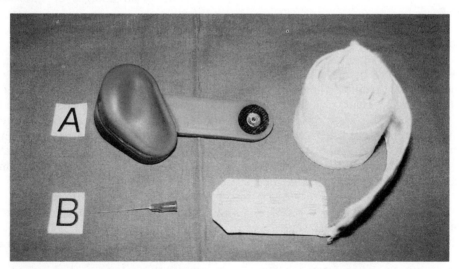

1. (a) What are the items shown in the picture?
1. (b) What are they used for?
2. What techniques of local anaesthesia can be used for eye surgery?
3. What drugs would you choose to perform a peribulbar block?
4. List the main differences between retrobulbar and peribulbar blocks.
5. List the complications of local anaesthesia for cataract surgery.

OSCE cycle 1 – answers

Answers to 1.1

1. Acromegaly. Note the marked prognathism, prominent supra-orbital ridge and rhinophyma.

2. Clinical features develop slowly and presentation is usually in the fourth decade:

- *Local effects*: headaches, visual field defects, evidence of progressive destruction of the sella turcica and increasing intracranial pressure.
- *Direct effects of growth hormone (GH) excess:* overgrowth of bone leads to increase in size of extremities, skull, kyphoscoliosis; overgrowth of connective tissue results in coarsening of skin, formation of skin tags, macroglossia and carpal tunnel syndrome; hyperhydrosis.
- *Cardiovascular effects:* atherosclerosis, hypertension, cardiomegaly and congestive cardiac failure are associated with acromegaly.
- *Other endocrine disturbances:* glucose intolerance, amenorrhoea, impotence, hypothyroidism, galactorrhoea.

3. Altered facial anatomy with overgrowth of the mandible, and enlargement of the lips, tongue and soft tissues of the pharynx may render management of the airway with a facemask difficult. The nasal passages may be obstructed due to hypertrophy of the turbinates and the distance between the incisors and glottis is increased. The glottic aperture may be reduced by connective tissue overgrowth involving the vocal cords, crico-arytenoid joints and recurrent laryngeal nerves. The subglottic diameter may also be decreased.

4. Elevated fasting GH levels combined with the lack of suppression of GH after an oral glucose load are necessary for the diagnosis of excess secretion of GH. Elevated levels of insulin-like growth factor (IGF-I) are uniformly found in acromegaly. Administration of L-dopa, which normally increases GH secretion, decreases GH levels in acromegaly. High resolution computed tomography or magnetic resonance imaging may be used to identify a pituitary adenoma.

5. The aims of therapy are to reduce the size of the pituitary lesion (minimize local effects) and to restore levels of GH to normal.
- *Surgery:* trans-sphenoidal microsurgical resection of the tumour is the preferred option. Trans-frontal surgery may be performed on large tumours.
- *External irradiation:* may be considered as first line therapy or used post-operatively.
- *Bromocriptine:* reserved for use in the elderly. May be used as primary or adjuvant therapy.
- *Octreotide:* this long-acting somatostatin analogue inhibits growth hormone secretion and is of proven value in the treatment of acromegaly. It is increasingly used in preference to bromocriptine.

Notes

Hypersecretion of GH may be due to pituitary tumours, extra-pituitary tumours (breast, ovary, lung, pancreas), and excess growth hormone releasing hormone activity. High GH levels are sometimes found in healthy people and suppression by a glucose load is essential to clinch the diagnosis.

Pre-operative assessment of the glottis by indirect laryngoscopy may be useful. Use a tracheal tube with a smaller diameter than predicted or awake fibreoptic intubation if problems with the airway are anticipated.

Key references:

Melmed S. Acromegaly. *New England Journal of Medicine* 1990; **322:**966–975.

Stoelting RK, Dierdorf SF (eds). *Anaesthesia and Co-existing Disease* 3rd ed. Churchill Livingstone, New York 1993; 369–370.

Answers to 1.2

1. The normal pre-operative serum urea and electrolyte values and urinalysis exclude pre-existing renal failure (RF). They do not exclude renal impairment which is common in these arteriopathic patients. The commonest causes for acute RF in ITU patients are sepsis, hypotension and hypoxia. Intra-operative factors associated with intrinsic RF include:

- periods of hypotension, hypoxia;
- massive blood transfusion;
- suprarenal clamping of the aorta, as this is reflected by a decrease in glomerular filtration rate (GFR) to 60% normal at 24 h;
- cross clamp time >1 h.

2. Examine the abdomen for the presence of a distended bladder which will be dull to percussion. Palpation may be difficult due to its proximity to the wound. Flush the catheter as this may prove both diagnostic and therapeutic. Catheter blockage is the commonest cause for sudden anuria on the ITU.

3. Pre-renal failure is due to a decrease in renal perfusion. This can be secondary to a decrease in cardiac output or hypovolaemia or both. It is differentiated from intrinsic RF by the history, comparison of the urine and blood tests (*see* Table 1.2), the response to therapy and the progress of the renal failure. It should be noted that each test is limited in its specificity and sensitivity and the overall picture should be assessed rather than a single test.

   Items (a) (c) (e) and (g) would support a diagnosis of pre-renal failure. Urine can be darkened by many substances and this bears no relation to the degree of renal failure.

4. (l) Examination of the cardiovascular status. When blood volume or cardiac output falls the blood pressure is maintained by reducing the

Table 1.2 Differential diagnosis of acute renal failure

	Prerenal	Intrinsic
Urinary values		
Specific gravity	> 1020	1010 (fixed)
Osmolality	>400 mosm/L	<300 mosm/L
Sodium	< 10 mmol/L	> 20 mmol/L
Urine/plasma ratios		
Urea	> 20:1	< 15:1
Creatinine	> 100:1	< 40:1
Osmolality	> 2:1	<1.7:1

renal perfusion. Oliguria (<0.5 mL/kg/h) heralds the limit of this compensation. Using inotropes in the face of such hypovolaemia is inappropriate. Specific didactic guidelines are difficult to support as patients may produce urine at different blood pressures. The following basic approach while continuously assessing the response is reasonable:

- Treat any underlying cause, e.g. sepsis and hypoxia.
- Treat hypovolaemia, i.e. optimize the right ventricular preload by fluid challenge until CVP suddenly rises and settles slowly. If appropriate, insert a pulmonary artery flow directed catheter and indirectly measure left ventricular preload.
- Manipulate cardiovascular parameters using drugs to optimize perfusion. For example, if the patient is abnormally vasodilated, nor-adrenaline may improve urinary volume (although the urine quality may not improve).

Adjuncts to this approach include the use of mannitol, which is an osmotic diuretic and free radical scavenger, frusemide and 'renal-dose' dopamine which may increase the chance of progression to polyuric RF, which has a better prognosis than oliguric RF.

Key reference:
Miller RD (ed). *Anesthesia.* 4th ed. Churchill Livingstone, London 1994; 1298–1313.

Answers to 1.3

1. The oxygen (O_2) analyser should be checked and calibrated according to the manufacturer's instructions. In addition to performing the machine check the O_2 analyser may also warn of other problems. It is the responsibility of the engineering and pharmacy departments to ensure the quality of the pipeline gas supply up to the wall connection. The anaesthetist's responsibility is from the wall to the patient. Gas in the pipeline may be faulty, e.g. following installation, maintenance, or when a device for mixing nitrogen and O_2 to produce air fails and the O_2 pipeline fills with nitrogen.

2. No. Disconnection of the pipelines should stop gas supply to the machine. When the flowmeter valves are opened all the bobbins should fall to zero. If a bobbin continues to float check all the cylinders and tighten any that are open. The O_2 and nitrous oxide (N_2O) supplies from the cylinders are then separately and systematically opened to the machine and the movement of the bobbins and the O_2 analyser monitored. First the reserve O_2 cylinder is opened. The O_2 bobbin should float and the N_2O bobbin should stay at zero. If the O_2 bobbin doesn't float, check that the O_2 cylinder isn't empty (the O_2 cylinder manometer pressure is proportional to its content and should read 137 bar when full). If the O_2 cylinder is not empty there is a fault so discard the machine. If the N_2O bobbin continues to float when only the O_2 cylinder is turned on this may be due to an open N_2O cylinder. This could be missed earlier if the machine has a proportioning system or fail-safe valve to prevent delivery of hypoxic mixtures. This becomes evident if closing the N_2O cylinder causes its bobbin to fall to zero.

3. A fail-safe valve is present on all gas supplies except oxygen. If the oxygen pressure upstream from the flowmeter falls then the other gas supplies are reduced or stopped to prevent a hypoxic mixture being delivered. It is not truly fail-safe. If the oxygen flowmeter valve is incorrectly set or there is a cracked flowmeter tube a hypoxic mixture may still be delivered.

4. The machine pressure relief valve, which opens at about 34 kPa (400 cmH$_2$O). The function of this is to protect the machine and specifically its most breakable components, the glass flowmeters. This valve does not protect the patient from barotrauma which becomes likely above 6 kPa. Some ventilators and circuits have low pressure valves to protect the patient which open at 4–6 kPa. The reservoir bag is designed to limit such increases in pressure by distension and may be the only device protecting the patient from barotrauma. The hiss may also be from the connections of the vaporizer or a crack in a flowmeter tube. The flowmeters should always be arranged with the oxygen tube downstream so as to minimize the chance of delivering a hypoxic mixture if one of the glass tubes is cracked. This would be detected by the oxygen analyser which is the only machine safety device that is downstream from the flowmeters.

5. The emergency oxygen flush flow rate is 30–50 litres/min. To ensure that a spontaneously breathing patient inhales 100% oxygen a face-mask must be applied with a gas-tight fit or the patient will entrain air and dilute the oxygen whenever their peak inspiratory flow rate (PIFR~30 litres/minute) exceeds the oxygen flow rate. The oxygen flush exceeds PIFR and in an emergency ensures delivery of 100% oxygen despite a poorly fitting or absent mask.

Key references:

Checklist for Anaesthetic Machines. Association of Anaesthetists, London, 1990.

Miller RD (ed). *Anesthesia* 4th ed. Churchill Livingstone, New York 1994; 188–195.

Answers to 1.4

The aims are:

- a safe anaesthetic for the patient with due care for his associated medical problems;
- protection of the staff and other patients from infection by the patient.

Principles of HIV transmission:

- HIV is transmitted by blood, sexual contact and placentally.
- Amniotic, pericardial, pleural, synovial, cerebrospinal, and peritoneal fluids, semen and vaginal secretions are all high risk fluids.
- Other body fluids are not a significant risk unless they are bloodstained.
- Skin contact with the virus is safe unless the skin is broken.

In practice:

- The patient should be last on the list.
- Inform the minimum number of staff on a need to know basis (patient confidentiality).
- Minimize the number of staff in theatre.
- Staff should wear disposable gowns, gloves, masks and visors until post-operative de-contamination of the theatre is completed.
- Use disposable drapes, instruments, anaes-thetic equipment and bacterial and viral filters.
- Induction of anaesthesia should occur in the operating room.
- Following the siting of lines, induction and, if necessary, intubation the anaesthetist's contaminated gloves should be discarded and should not be used for handling the notes or equipment.
- Needles which have been in contact with the patient should not be resheathed or handed to another person. They should be placed either in a tray or directly into a sharps bin as soon as possible. 40% of needlestick injuries are associated with uncovered sharps.

- Any broken skin must be protected by gloves or a waterproof dressing.
- Blood tests should be kept to a minimum; only experienced staff should take blood and they should not squirt it.
- Blood samples and contaminated material including clothing should be sealed without staples and labelled as infective.
- If inoculation of staff occurs, encourage bleeding from the site and wash with soap and water. Inform the Unit Manager.
- Nondisposable equipment should be auto-claved or washed in detergent and then soaked in fresh 2% glutaraldehyde.
- Surfaces should be washed with hypochlorite and then detergent.

Notes on HIV

Prevalence has a regional variation from 1 in 230 mothers attending a London antenatal clinic to 1 in 16 000 outside London and is 1 in 3500 in the UK as a whole. Following parenteral inoculation with HIV positive blood the risk of transmission is 0.37%. (The risk of transmission of hepatitis B from blood that is 'e' antigen positive is 30% and for hepatitis C is 3%.) Men who are homosexual or bisexual and drug addicts have a higher incidence of HIV infection but about 19% of AIDS patients are heterosexual adults. The size of the epidemic is not known due to under-reporting and one cannot test for HIV without the patient's informed consent. The AAGBI recommends universal precautions, treating **everyone** as HIV positive. Despite this only 16% of anaesthetists wear gloves routinely.

Key references:

HIV and other blood borne viruses – guidance for anaesthetists. Association of Anaesthetists of Great Britain & Ireland, London, December 1992.

Jeffries DJ. HIV and hepatitis – some way to go. *Anaesthesia* 1992; **47:**921–922.

Answers to 1.5

1.(a) Lateral views of the cervical spine taken in flexion and extension.

1.(b) Anterior subluxation of atlantoaxial joint. Subluxation is present when the distance between the atlas and the odontoid process in the lateral flexion view is greater than 3 mm in patients over 44 years of age or greater than 4 mm in younger patients.

2. Anatomical abnormalities:

- Cervical arthropathy occurs in at least 25% of adults with rheumatoid arthritis (RA) and is commoner in males. It is rare in juvenile RA. It may occur without clinical symptoms and signs.
- Atlantoaxial subluxation (AAS) is commoner than subaxial subluxation. AAS can be anterior, posterior, vertical or lateral rotatory.
- Laryngeal and tracheal deviation may occur due to movement of the odontoid peg (the larynx is tipped forward).
- Cervical ankylosis is a late complication.

3. The usual pre-operative physical examination must be carried out. Demonstration of neck flexion and atlanto-occipital extension to predict ease of laryngoscopy must be conducted gently, particularly in patients complaining of symptoms exacerbated by neck movement. At high risk are elderly patients, those with neck symptoms, long-standing and erosive disease and subcutaneous nodules. Lateral cervical spine X-rays must be taken in the neutral position and flexion and extension prior to anaesthesia. Look for evidence of anterior and vertical subluxation and measure the space available for the spinal cord (SAC). The SAC is the anteroposterior luminal diameter of the spinal canal at C1 level that is not occupied by the odontoid process. The SAC in the normal spine is approximately 20 mm. Cord compression will occur if the SAC <14 mm. Review films for the presence of subaxial subluxation and disc space narrowing in the lower cervical spine. The combination of anterior subluxation with either vertical or subaxial subluxations places the patient at high risk of neurological injury.

The Sharp and Purser test: The patient should be in the upright position. The examiner places the index finger of one hand on the spinous process of the C2 vertebra and presses on the patient's forehead with the other hand. A backward gliding movement of the head indicates the presence of AAS.

4. Note that airway management may be further complicated in RA by reduction in mouth opening due to temporomandibular joint involvement, particularly in juvenile RA. Laryngeal obstruction due to crico-arytenoid joint arthritis is a rare complication.

- *Anterior AAS:* Avoid C1–C2 flexion during induction, positioning and transport. Direct laryngoscopy is tolerated as C1–C2 is in extension.
- *Posterior AAS:* C1–C2 extension must be avoided. Direct laryngoscopy is best avoided due to high risk.
- *Vertical AAS:* Neutral head/neck positioning is mandatory throughout the peri-operative period. Avoid direct laryngoscopy.
- *Lateral/rotatory AAS:* Avoid rotation or lateral movement of head during peri-operative period. Nonreducible head tilt may preclude direct laryngoscopy.
- *Subaxial subluxation:* Direct laryngoscopy with neck stabilization in a neutral position should be tolerated.

Key references:

Macarthur A, Kleiman S. Rheumatoid cervical joint disease – a challenge to the anaesthetist. *Canadian Journal of Anaesthesia* 1993; **40**:154–159.

Crosby ET, Lui A. The adult cervical spine: implications for airway management. *Canadian Journal of Anaesthesia* 1990; **37**:77–93.

Answers to 1.6

Several techniques of brachial plexus block have been described. The choice of which to use depends on the particular advantages and risks of each block. The key to these, their performance and their management if not successful is the anatomy. The brachial plexus consists of roots, trunks, divisions and cords. The five roots are formed by the anterior primary rami of the C5-8 and T1 nerves. These pass between scalenus anterior (SA) and scalenus medius and combine to form the trunks as they emerge from behind SA. The upper (C5,6), middle (C7) and lower (C8 and T1) trunks cross the posterior triangle of the neck. At the lateral edge of the first rib and just behind the clavicle, each divides into a posterior and an anterior division. On emerging from behind the clavicle into the axilla, the three anterior divisions form the medial and lateral cords and the three posterior divisions form the posterior cord. The subclavian *a.* is anterior and below the trunks on the first rib. It becomes the axillary *a.* at the lateral edge of the first rib. The axillary *a.* is divided into three parts by pectoralis minor that crosses its second part. The cords approach the first part of the axillary *a.* and are closely applied to its second part, gaining their titles (lateral, posterior and medial) from this relationship. By the third part, the cords have produced all their major branches except the musculocutaneous and axillary branches which have diverged before this. The whole plexus is enclosed from the vertebra to the distal axilla by an extension of the prevertebral fascia. Whatever technique is used, brachial plexus block involves entering this sheath and injecting local anaesthetic (LA) to fill it. The extent of the block will depend on which part of the sheath is entered, the volume of LA injected and whether pressure is used to direct the LA. A volume of ≥40 mL is required to block an adult arm effectively.

1. Scalenus anterior and medius bound the interscalene groove. This is demonstrated by the patient sniffing or taking a maximal inspiration. It is entered at right angles at the level of C5,6 above the level of Sibson's fascia so pneumothorax is rare. The roots emerge from the intervertebral foramina in a caudad direction. A needle that points cephalad may enter these and result in a subarachnoid or epidural block or vertebral artery injection.

2. The subclavian pulse can be palpated directly under or directly behind the midpoint of the clavicle. The plexus is at its most compact here and lends itself to an effective block. Supraclavicular and infraclavicular approaches have been described. Supraclavicular approaches may enter the skin at the inferior part of the interscalene groove behind the subclavian pulse. The sheath is pierced near the first rib. If the subclavian *a.* is entered the needle is withdrawn and then directed posterior to the artery. Pneumothorax occurs in up to 5% and phrenic *n.* block in 50%.

3. The needle position can be confirmed by arterial puncture, paraesthesiae, peripheral nerve stimulation (distal muscle contractions at <1 mA), loss of resistance to saline, a 'pop' as fascia is pierced or pulsation of the needle. Monitoring nerve potentials generated at the wrist with the block needle and ultrasound methods have also been described.

4. The lateral cutaneous *n.* of the forearm is a branch of the musculocutaneous *n.* which leaves the plexus proximally at the level of the first rib and enters coracobrachialis. It can be blocked by injecting 10 mL of LA into this muscle just superior to the plexus in the axilla. The muscle's fascia limits the spread of the LA.

Key reference:

Brockway MS, Wildsmith JA. Axillary brachial plexus block: method of choice? *British Journal of Anaesthesia* 1990; 64:224–231.

Answers to 1.7

1. Bronchiectasis is an abnormal and irreversible dilatation of the bronchi which may be localized or widespread, and is caused by destruction of the elastic and muscular layers of the bronchial walls.

2. Treatment is symptomatic as specific therapy directed at the underlying pathophysiological mechanisms is not available.

Regular chest physiotherapy with percussion and postural drainage of excessive bronchial secretions is of value in reducing cough and sputum and in preventing recurrent infection.

Antibiotics to control infection: *Haemophilus influenzae* and *Pseudomonas aeruginosa* are common infections. Continuous antibiotic therapy may be necessary if recurrences are frequent.

Bronchodilator drugs (methylxanthines, ß₂-agonists and anticholinergics) to reduce airway tone. In this context, anti-inflammatory drugs may also prove to be beneficial.

Controlled oxygen therapy may be required to treat hypoxaemia.

General measures should include cessation of smoking and adequate hydration to mobilize secretions. There is no evidence for the efficacy of nebulized saline, mucolytics or enzymes.

3. The treatment of the bronchiectasis must be optimized and any acute exacerbations dealt with effectively prior to surgery. For trabeculectomy to be performed under local anaesthesia the patient should be able to lie flat with 1–2 pillows and remain still for 20–30 minutes. Dyspnoea at rest or uncontrolled coughing would preclude local anaesthesia. The ability to lie flat comfortably for periods up to 30 min must be assessed pre-operatively, on the ward. Other contraindications to local anaesthesia include lack of comprehension or co-operation, severe anxiety or claustrophobia and involuntary movements.

4. A full clinical pre-operative evaluation must be carried out and special investigations (e.g. ECG, chest X-ray) requested when indicated, irrespective of whether local or general anaesthesia is to be used. Patients presenting for eye surgery are often elderly and treatment of co-existing medical conditions must be optimized. Following full explanation and informed consent, LA of the eye may be instituted by either the surgeon or the anaesthetist. Intravenous access must be established (for resuscitation/sedation/rapid lowering of IOP) and supplementary oxygen is provided underneath the drapes. Verbal contact should be maintained throughout and monitoring should include blood pressure measurement, ECG and pulse oximetry.

Sedation with its potential for respiratory depression is best avoided in this patient. It also decreases patient co-operation during surgery and is unnecessary when painless local anaesthetic techniques are used. It is useful to hold the patient's hand during the procedure so that the patient can indicate the need to speak or cough by squeezing the anaesthetist's/nurse's hand. The surgeon can then be forewarned of imminent movement. The anaesthetist should also be responsible for supervision of post-operative recovery.

5. Safety and simplicity of providing anaesthesia, akinesia and low IOP necessary for the procedure. LA avoids interference with the respiratory system and possible exacerbation of symptoms. Endocrine and metabolic responses are attenuated and elderly patients tolerate surgery under LA very well. The shortening of hospital stay is economically advantageous.

Key references:
Royal College of Anaesthetists/College of Ophthalmologists. *Report of the joint working party on anaesthesia in ophthalmic surgery*, 1993.

Wyngaarden JB, Smith LH Jr, Bennett JC (eds). *Cecil Textbook of Medicine* 19th ed. WB Saunders Company, Philadelphia 1992; 415–418.

Answers to 1.8

1. Caudal epidural block; dorsal nerve of penis block; subcutaneous ring block; topical anaesthesia with lignocaine gel, ointment and spray (EMLA cream is not as effective as dorsal nerve of penis block).

2. The caudal space is a continuation of the spinal canal. The roof is formed by the fused posterior laminae of the sacral vertebrae. The failure of development and fusion of the laminae of the S5 vertebra produces the sacral hiatus, marked laterally by the sacral cornua which are the remnants of the articular processes. The sacral hiatus extends from the sacrococcygeal joint to the fused arch of S4 and is covered by the sacrococcygeal membrane which is the continuation of the ligamentum flavum. The canal is bounded anteriorly by the vertebral bodies and laterally by the modified intervertebral foramina through which the sacral nerve roots emerge. The caudal canal contains the dural sac, nerve roots, valveless veins, fat and areolar tissue. The dural sac terminates at S2 in adults, but extends to the S3-S4 vertebral level in children.

3. *Preliminaries:* Obtain informed consent from parents; observe strict aseptic precautions.
Position: Prone, knee-chest or lateral positions may be used. The lateral position is most convenient in a child of this size. Flexing the hips to 90° optimizes access.
Location of sacral hiatus: It is easily felt between the sacral cornua in children. A triangle, the apices of which are the posterior superior iliac spines and the sacral hiatus, is usually equilateral.
Needle insertion: A variety of needles, cannulae with hollow stylets, and angles of entry have been recommended; a 21 gauge needle is a popular choice. Advance needle at 20° to 30° to skin until a 'give' is felt as the sacrococcygeal membrane is pierced. Entry into the epidural space can be confirmed by negative aspiration tests for blood and CSF and loss of resistance to saline or air injection (NB: injection of air has been associated with significant venous air embolism in infants). A test dose may be used. The needle should not be inserted beyond a depth of 2–3 mm once the sacrococcygeal membrane is pierced.
Dosage: Various dosage regimens have been suggested. A useful formula is 0.5 mL/kg of 0.25% plain bupivacaine which reliably provides a high sacral block.

4. *Accidental intravascular injection:* This can be a serious problem because of the vascularity of the region and the large volumes of local anaesthetic used. The use of blunt short bevelled needles and plastic cannulae will help reduce the incidence.
Motor blockade: Weakness of the muscles of the legs is minimal when concentrations ≤0.25% bupivacaine are used.
Delayed micturition: True retention is rare.
Nausea and vomiting: An incidence of up to 30% has been reported after caudal anaesthesia with local anaesthetics.
Other: All of the undermentioned problems are rare: accidental dural puncture and spinal anaesthesia; intraosseous injection with systemic toxicity; penetration of pelvic organs, infection (the anus is in close proximity).

5. There is considerable anatomical variation in both the sacral hiatus and the caudal canal; the sacral hiatus may be difficult to locate. Spread of local anaesthetic may be uneven or unilateral, particularly in older children, due to dense areolar tissue. Leakage through the intervertebral foramina may render a predetermined dose inadequate.

Key references:

Gregory GA (ed). *Pediatric Anesthesia* 3rd ed. Churchill Livingstone, New York 1994; 290–294.

Wildsmith JAW, Armitage EN (eds). *Principles and Practice of Regional Anaesthesia* 2nd ed. Churchill Livingstone, Edinburgh 1993; 224–227.

Answers to 1.9

1. Spirogram. An obstructive pattern of lung disease as FEV_1/FVC is less than 70%. This patient's FEV_1, the forced expiratory volume in the first second of expiration, is 1 L and the FVC, the forced vital capacity is 2 L. A restrictive pattern has an FVC lower than predicted and a ratio of FEV_1 to FVC >70%. The FVC in a normal pattern is within normal predicted limits for that population's age, sex and size and the ratio FEV_1/FVC is greater than 75%.

2. Patients with Chronic Obstructive Airways Disease (COAD) are twice as likely to suffer post-operative respiratory problems as a normal patient. The key to pre-operative management is accurate assessment allowing appropriate optimization of the patient's condition. The effect of drugs should be monitored as it is difficult to predict how much benefit each will have. The following may be used:

- ß2-agonists (e.g. salbutamol) should be given even if initial spirometry does not show benefit, as this can occur later.
- Anticholinergic drugs, e.g. ipratropium bromide, have a more prolonged duration of action than the ß2-agonists.
- Aminophylline has a narrow therapeutic–toxic window. Blood levels are affected by many drugs and diseases and so must be monitored. It may also improve pulmonary function by inotropy of the diaphragm.
- Inhaled corticosteroids (e.g. beclomethasone dipropionate) work by decreasing bronchial mucosal inflammation, so reducing bronchial oedema and secretions.
- Disodium cromoglycate is a mast cell stabilizer and is used for asthma prophylaxis.
- Diuretics may improve right ventricular failure but thicker secretions may impair expectoration.
- Antibiotics are only indicated when an acute respiratory infection is diagnosed. Specific therapy is guided by sputum cultures.

3. Physiotherapy, including deep breathing exercises to prevent basal atelectasis and postural drainage and percussion to facilitate coughing of trapped secretions. Nutrition is important if a patient is debilitated. Delaying a case from winter to summer may be appropriate for a patient with chronic bronchitis. If obese, reducing weight will:

- increase FRC so reducing basal atelectasis;
- reduce the work of breathing;
- reduce the risk of upper airway obstruction.

Stopping smoking will decrease carboxy-haemoglobin levels within 24 hours. Improvement in ciliary function and excessive mucus production takes six weeks. Raised pulmonary and systemic vascular resistance due to nicotine may improve on withdrawal.

4. None. Intra-operative management of ventilation includes:

- a high inspired oxygen concentration to maintain a PaO_2 of >75 mmHg (10 kPa);
- a long inspiratory time allowing adequate ventilation of underventilated alveoli;
- a long expiratory phase to prevent gas trapping by the obstructed airways;
- a minute volume that maintains the pre-operative $PaCO_2$ level without barotrauma;
- aspiration of sputum.

Inevitably, one must use a low respiratory rate and a tidal volume which produces peak airway pressures unlikely to cause a pneumothorax.

Key reference:

Clague JE, Calverley PMA. Management of chronic obstructive pulmonary disease. *Hospital Update* January 1990; 20–32.

Answers to 1.10

First make sure that you and the casualty are safe. Turn off the power to the mower. Check responsiveness by shaking the casualty and shouting 'Are you all right?' If the casualty is unconscious, shout for help. Open the airway. Manoeuvres that help are flexing the neck, extending the head at the atlanto-occipital joint, chin lift, jaw thrust and clearing the mouth of any obvious obstruction. Check breathing. Look for chest excursions, listen at the mouth for breath sounds and feel for expired air for 5 s. If absent, check pulse. Palpate a carotid artery for 5 s. If absent, cardiac arrest is established. Go and dial 999 for an ambulance before commencing basic life support (BLS). Open airway and give two inflations of expired air. Pinch nose, obtain a good seal around the lips and deliver a tidal volume of 800–1200 mL which is needed to cause visible rising of the chest. Allow chest to fall before giving second inflation. Start external chest compressions at a mean rate of 80/min. Loosen any tight clothing and locate the middle of the lower half of the sternum (one finger's breadth above the point at which the costal margins meet in the midline). With the heels of the hands placed one above the other and the elbows locked, compress the chest vertically downwards, depressing the sternum 4–5 cm. Allow equal time for both compression and release phases. Ensure that the casualty is on a firm, flat surface and that pressure is not applied over the ribs. Continue compressions and ventilations at a ratio of 15:2 until help arrives. Do not interrupt BLS for pulse checks unless casualty responds.

Notes

The guidelines for basic life support issued by the European Resuscitation Council (ERC) in 1992 are currently applicable. It is vitally important to practise basic life support skills under supervision regularly. Mannikins that incorporate skill meters are available for objective assessment of performance. The ERC recommends that hospitals should provide compulsory training/retraining in CPR skills for all staff involved in direct patient care. BLS refers to maintaining an airway and supporting breathing and the circulation without the use of equipment other than a simple airway device or protective shield (e.g. pocket facemask and one-way valve).

The precordial thump is included in the advanced life support guidelines in the event of a witnessed cardiac arrest but it is *not* recommended for lay rescuers.

It is unlikely that effective cardiac activity will be restored by BLS alone without the institution of ALS. Yet, it is important to continue BLS as it delays further deterioration of the internal milieu. Survival is greatest when the heart arrests in ventricular fibrillation, the arrest is witnessed and resuscitation is started immediately with early defibrillation.

If the casualty is responsive at initial assessment, check for injuries, send for help and reassess at regular intervals.

If, on clearing the airway, the casualty is breathing spontaneously, place in the recovery position unless this might aggravate an injury, observe closely and seek help.

If a pulse is present with no ventilatory effort, give 10 breaths of expired air. This sequence of 10 inflations should take about 1 minute. Seek help, reassess and observe closely.

When injuries to the cervical spine are suspected, care must be taken to ensure that the head and neck are in the neutral position during airway manoeuvres.

The Advanced Life Support Group (UK) recommends the **SAFE ABC** approach: **S**hout for help, **A**pproach with care, **F**ree from danger, **E**valuate **A**irway, **B**reathing, **C**irculation.

Key reference:

Basic Life Support Working Party of the European Resuscitation Council. *Resuscitation* 1992; **24**:103–110.

Answer to 1.11

Cricoid pressure refers to the simple manoeuvre whereby firm pressure applied to the cricoid cartilage results in temporary occlusion of the upper oesophagus between the cricoid cartilage and the cervical vertebrae. This manoeuvre is performed by an assistant during the rapid sequence induction of general anaesthesia. A cricoid force of 44 N has been shown to be effective in preventing regurgitation of gastric contents in the majority of patients. Cricoid pressure has been shown to withstand oesophageal pressures up to 100 cmH$_2$O and also prevents inflation of the stomach during positive pressure ventilation. A large survey by Olsson in 1986 reported the incidence of pulmonary aspiration as a consequence of regurgitation to be 4.7 per 10 000 anaesthetics with a mortality of 5%. The value of cricoid pressure is in preventing this potentially fatal complication.

During induction of anaesthesia the patient lies supine with a left lateral tilt or pelvic wedge. The head and neck are extended which increases the anterior convexity of the cervical spine, stretches the oesophagus and minimizes lateral displacement. The anatomy of the neck must be examined and the cricoid cartilage identified by the assistant prior to the induction of anaesthesia. The cricoid cartilage is stabilized between the thumb and middle fingers to prevent lateral displacement and firm downward pressure is applied with the index finger to occlude the oesophagus between the cricoid cartilage and the cervical vertebrae. This should be started at the beginning of induction (following pre-oxygenation) as it is probably safest, although it may be briefly unpleasant for the patient. Cricoid pressure must *not* be released until the trachea has been safely intubated, the cuff inflated, a seal ensured and correct placement of the tracheal tube confirmed. Cricoid pressure must be maintained until the anaesthetist indicates that it is safe to release it. It must be remembered that improper application is ineffective and places the patient at increased risk of regurgitation and aspiration. It also renders visualization of the larynx and tracheal intubation difficult.

Notes

Bimanual cricoid pressure confers some advantages. The assistant's other hand is placed underneath the neck, supporting it and providing counterpressure which helps maintain the integrity of the arch of the vertebral column. This prevents collapse of the arch downwards with cricoid pressure and affords the best view of the glottis. The bimanual technique has the advantage that it can be applied in the supine, lateral or any other position. Further precautions must be taken in those in whom the cervical spine is 'at risk'.

Contrary to Sellick's view, recent evidence suggests that a nasogastric tube (NG tube), introduced pre-operatively to reduce the volume of gastric contents, does not interfere with the effective application of cricoid pressure and may even improve it. Thus a NG tube need not be removed prior to rapid sequence induction of anaesthesia.

It has been suggested that application of cricoid pressure from the right-hand side of the patient may further impede difficult laryngoscopy because the hand of the assistant can interfere with positioning of the laryngoscope handle. It is claimed that this contact does not occur when cricoid pressure is applied with the left hand from the left side of the patient.

Key references:

Sellick BA. Cricoid pressure to control regurgitation of stomach contents during induction of anaesthesia. *Lancet* 1961; 2:404–406.

Vanner RG, Pryle BJ. Regurgitation and oesophageal rupture with cricoid pressure: a cadaver study. *Anaesthesia* 1992; 47:732–735.

Crowley DS, Giesecke AH. Bimanual cricoid pressure. *Anaesthesia* 1990; 45:588–599.

Answers to 1.12

1. The ECG shows elevated ST segments that are concave upwards in leads I, II, aVL, aVF, and V_2–V_6. The diagnosis is acute pericarditis. In myocardial infarction (MI) the ST elevation is convex upwards. Days later the ST segments may return to normal with inverted T waves but Q waves do not occur. At this later stage differentiation from MI is more difficult but serial ECGs and cardiac enzymes help. Clinical symptoms of pericarditis include chest pain, malaise, fever, myalgia and cough. The pain is retrosternal and sharp or aching. It may radiate to the shoulder, neck or abdomen. It may be exacerbated by lying flat, movement or inspiration and relieved by sitting up or leaning forward. Though not always present, a pericardial rub confirms the diagnosis. It is affected by respiration so the patient should stop breathing during auscultation. It is described as a superficial, scratchy noise that is unrelated to murmurs and has up to three parts, i.e. atrial and ventricular contraction and ventricular relaxation. The site at which it is best heard may change. If it disappears a pericardial effusion should be suspected. In the United Kingdom, of the many causes, the commonest are Coxsackie A or B viruses and as an early complication in 15% of patients with MI.

2. Cardiac tamponade secondary to a haemorrhagic pericardial effusion. Anticoagulation is contraindicated in the presence of acute pericarditis for this reason. Small effusions may produce no specific symptoms or signs. The heart sounds and the rub may become quiet. The ECG may show small complexes. When the effusion volume reaches the elbow of the pericardium compliance curve the pressure rises steeply. When this pressure exceeds the right atrial and right ventricular pressures it limits filling and the diagnosis becomes cardiac tamponade as characterized by Beck's triad: low arterial pressure, high venous pressure and an absent apex beat. Clinical signs include:

- distress, tachypnoea and tachycardia secondary to the fall in cardiac output;
- raised JVP which increases during inspiration (Kussmaul's sign);
- hypotension and pulsus paradoxus.

CXR may be normal or show a large globular heart shadow with sharp cardiophrenic angles or a pleural effusion. This is not diagnostic and may signify heart enlargement instead. Pulmonary venous congestion favours left ventricular failure. Pericardial effusion can be confirmed by CT or MRI scan but echocardiography is the most convenient method.

3. The treatment for pericardial tamponade is pericardial drainage. Post-cardiac surgery, sternal wires are cut and the pericardium opened surgically. In other situations pericardiocentesis (PC) is performed. PC, if required for electromechanical dissociation, may be done blindly. Less urgent bedside PC can be aided by ECG or echocardiography. The patient is sat up so the effusion collects antero-inferiorly. The needle ($\geq$18 gauge) has a sterile electrode clip attached from its base to the V lead of the ECG. Using a 10 mL syringe of local anaesthetic the needle is advanced with alternate infiltration and aspiration. The subxiphoid approach is safer than the parasternal or apical approach. The skin is entered on the left of the xiphoid process. It passes deep to the left costal margin and is then aimed at a 15° dorsal tilt towards the left shoulder. On entry, blood is aspirated that does not clot on standing. If the myocardium is touched the ECG shows raised ST or PR segments. A Seldinger technique can be utilized to insert a 5 FG catheter.

Key reference:

John RM, Treasure T. How to aspirate the pericardium. *British Journal of Hospital Medicine* 1990; **43**:21–223.

OSCE cycle 2 – answers

Answers to 2.1

1. A = Pleural drainage tube from patient .
   B = Underwater seal tube.
   C = Collection chamber containing sterile
       water.
   D = Vent to atmosphere or attachment to
       suction.

2. The underwater seal acts as a one-way valve through which air is expelled from the pleural space and prevented from re-entering during the next inspiration. The distal end of the drainage tube is placed 2 cm below the surface of the sterile water, providing minimal resistance to the escape of air.

3. When large volumes of blood or fluid are drained, a greater length of tube is submerged resulting in an increased resistance to drainage. Retrograde flow of fluid into the patient's pleural space may occur if the collection chamber is raised above the level of the patient. Frothing in the chamber may make the measurement of volume of drainage difficult.

4. Absence of oscillations may indicate obstruction of the drainage system by clots or kinks, loss of subatmospheric pressure or complete re-expansion of the lung.

5. Persistent bubbling would indicate a continuing bronchopleural air leak. Massive or continuous inspiratory and expiratory leaks may suggest intra-parenchymal chest drain placement.

6. The collection chamber should be kept below the level of the patient at all times to prevent fluid being siphoned into the pleural space. During the brief period when the chamber has to be raised above the level of the chest, the chest drain should be clamped. Clamping a pleural drain in the presence of a continuing air leak may result in a tension pneumothorax.

Notes

The effective drainage of air, blood or fluids from the pleural space requires an airtight system to maintain subatmospheric intrapleural pressure. This allows re-expansion of the lung and restores haemodynamic stability by minimizing mediastinal shift. The basic requirements are a suitable chest drain with minimal resistance, an underwater seal and a collection chamber. The drainage tube is submerged to a depth of 1–2 cm in a collection chamber of approximately 20 cm diameter. This provides minimal resistance to drainage of air and maintains the underwater seal even in the face of a large inspiratory effort. It is recommended that the collection chamber is placed 100 cm below the chest as subatmospheric pressures up to -80 cmH$_2$O may be produced during obstructed inspiration. Drainage can be allowed to occur under gravity or suction may be applied. Suction is limited to about -20 cmH$_2$O in clinical practice. A suction system with a high volume displacement is needed if the air leak is large. It is important to note that wall-mounted suction systems do not provide an outlet when they are turned off. Suction of pleural drains is contraindicated in patients who have had a pneumonectomy, as it may result in mediastinal shift and haemodynamic instability. Efforts to improve pleural drainage systems have resulted in the two and three bottle modifications of the basic underwater seal system. In the three bottle system the proximal bottle traps drainage, the middle bottle provides the water seal and the distal bottle regulates the level of suction.

Key references:

Kam AC, O'Brien M, Kam PAC. Pleural drainage systems. *Anaesthesia* 1993; **48**:154–161.

Kaplan JA (ed). *Thoracic Anesthesia* 2nd ed. Churchill Livingstone, New York ,1991; 611–613.

Answers to 2.2

1. Many configurations are possible for circle systems. The diagram shows the most commonly used layout with A as the fresh gas flow (FGF) port and B as the CO_2 absorber. The other components of a basic circle are the adjustable pressure limiting valve (APL or pop-off valve), inspiratory (IV) and expiratory (EV) one-way valves, reservoir bag and the patient connection. The FGF port should be in the inspiratory limb to minimize the number of connections between it and the patient and to ensure minimal mixing of FGF with circle gas before inhalation. The FGF should enter before the IV so that it is not wasted during expiration. The site of the reservoir bag is less important. During IPPV it can be replaced by a bag-in-bottle ventilator. If a Nuffield Penlon type ventilator is used it must be connected to the circle by a tube of ≥ tidal volume to stop driving gas entering the circle and risking awareness.

2. Advantages of siting the APL valve in the expiratory limb between the EV and the CO_2 absorber include:

- it will exhaust the maximum amount of CO_2 containing gas before it reaches the absorber so as to preserve the absorbent;
- during induction it exhausts gas that contains low concentrations of volatile;
- during recovery it exhausts gas that contains large amounts of volatile.

3. Circle leak test:

- manually check all connections and close the APL valve (closed system);
- open fresh gas flowmeter until manometer reads 30 cmH_2O and then turn off FGF;
- if the pressure falls there is a leak which can be quantified by increasing the FGF until the pressure is just maintained;
- a leak of <100 mL/min is acceptable.

4. The following should also be checked:

- leak test with absorber in and out of circuit;
- the configuration of parts;
- check the absorber on/off control and condition of absorbent;
- check mobility and functioning of the inspiratory, expiratory and APL valves.

5. With a closed circle the theoretical minimum FGF possible is the patient's oxygen consumption of ≅225 mL/min. Initially a high flow must be used to stop nitrogen exhaled into the circle causing hypoxia. With both IPPV and spontaneous ventilation if the FGF ≥ the patient's minute volume no rebreathing occurs and the CO_2 absorber is not needed.

6. 'Low flow' anaesthesia is a technique in which a FGF of ≤3 L/min is used in an adult. A CO_2 absorber must be used and methods include circles and the to-and-fro circuit with a Waters' canister. The gas composition in the circle depends on the composition and flow of the gas entering and leaving the circle. Fresh gas and exhaled patient gas enter the circle, some gas is absorbed by the patient, some is scavenged through the APL valve and CO_2 is taken up by the CO_2 absorber. The patient's uptake of oxygen is constant at about 225 mL/min. However, the uptake of N_2O decreases exponentially from 500 mL/min to 100 mL/min at 60 minutes. If the composition of the fresh gas flow is constant then after about 30 minutes more oxygen than N_2O starts to be absorbed and the proportion of N_2O in the circle will increase and the proportion of oxygen will decrease. This risk of giving the patient a hypoxic mixture can be avoided by maintaining a FGF of 50% oxygen.

Key reference:

White DC. Closed and low flow system anaesthesia. *Current Anaesthesia and Critical Care* 1992; **3**:98–107.

Answers to 2.3

1. The chest X-ray shows air trapping in the right lower zone. The diagnosis is foreign body aspiration (FBA). Despite children's bronchi deviating from the trachea at similar angles, more foreign bodies (FB) lodge in the right than the left and some lodge in the trachea. About 10% have a normal chest X-ray. Ninety per cent of FB are radiolucent but can produce a variety of X-ray features. Absorption atelectasis with collapse distal to the FB and compensatory emphysema of the remaining lung may occur. Distal air trapping due to a ball-valve effect may show up on an expiratory film. Fluoroscopy may show abnormal mediastinal movement with respiration. Pneumothorax and lung abscess are uncommon. The peak incidence of FBA is 6 months to 3 years. In the United Kingdom a peanut is the commonest cause. Its oil causes a chemical pneumonitis. An organic FB will absorb water, swell and putrefy. Sweets may dissolve in secretions, producing viscous solutions. Older children tend to aspirate objects, e.g. toys, rather than organic matter.

2. The management of FBA depends on the clinical presentation. Acute airway obstruction with respiratory distress or cyanosis is treated with artificial expulsive manoeuvres appropriate for the child's age, e.g. Heimlich's. The definitive treatment for less severe presentations is urgent removal of the FB by bronchoscopy. Antibiotics and steroids may be used but in addition to bronchoscopy and not as an alternative. Any delay in performing the bronchoscopy may result in movement of the FB and complete airway obstruction. A history suspicious of FBA warrants a diagnostic bronchoscopy even if clinical examination and chest X-ray are normal. Up to a third present more than 3 days after aspiration, usually with a persistent cough or pneumonia. Most cases of FBA have positive clinical signs, e.g. stridor, tachypnoea, nasal flaring, cyanosis, the use of accessory muscles, tachycardia, monophonic wheezing (partial bronchial obstruction) or signs of pneumonia or lobar collapse. The child may be toxic with general malaise, pyrexia or leucocytosis. Children tend to swallow sputum rather than cough it up. Haemoptysis is uncommon.

3. In children the rigid bronchoscope is used for FB removal. The fibreoptic bronchoscope (FOB) limits ventilation as it occludes most of the lumen of the paediatric tracheal tube. It tends to remove the FB piecemeal and its aspiration port is only 1–2 mm so aspiration of blood and secretions is not as effective. The rigid type allows ventilation along its lumen. It is more likely to remove the FB whole and allows the use of larger suckers and forceps. Rigid bronchoscopes include the open-ended type, e.g. Negus, or the ventilating type, e.g. Storz. The open-ended type require a Sanders Venturi injector or high-frequency jet ventilator, both of which risk barotrauma in a child. The ventilating type (smallest external diameter 4 mm) has a side port for connection to an anaesthetic circuit. A hinge or slide attachment with a window can close the proximal end, allowing IPPV or spontaneous ventilation with scavenging. It can be opened intermittently, allowing the use of forceps and suction.

4. Arrhythmias may occur due to hypoxia, hypercarbia, direct surgical stimulation of the heart or deep or light anaesthesia. If there is any risk that IPPV may further impact or push the FB further into the bronchial tree then the child should have a gaseous induction with halothane and 100% oxygen. If the FB is in a stable peripheral situation, relaxants can be used: this has the advantage of preventing coughing during removal of the FB.

Key reference:

Steen KH, Zimmermann T. Tracheobronchial aspiration of foreign bodies in children: a study of 94 cases. *Laryngoscope* 1990; **100**:525–530.

Answers to 2.4

1. Carbon monoxide (CO) poisoning. The history is strongly suggestive, particularly if the fire was used continuously for a long period with inadequate ventilation in the house. Acute CO poisoning may cause convulsions and coma and prove fatal if resuscitation is not immediate. Pallor of the skin is commoner than the classical cherry red coloration. Skin necrosis occurs at pressure points. Carboxyhaemoglobin (COHb) causes overestimation of oxygen saturation by pulse oximetry. A tachycardia and ECG evidence of myocardial ischaemia/infarction may be present. The measurement of COHb content in a heparinized blood sample may confirm the diagnosis. Note that blood COHb levels are of limited value in assessing the severity of exposure, particularly after O_2 therapy.

2. 100% oxygen should be administered via a tight fitting facemask. Variable performance plastic masks deliver only 60–80% oxygen even at high flow rates. If the level of consciousness deteriorates or the patient is uncooperative, tracheal intubation and positive pressure ventilation with 100% oxygen must be instituted. In addition to general supportive measures, specific treatment may be required for convulsions, cerebral oedema and metabolic acidosis. Useful tests include: arterial blood gases, electrolytes (hypokalaemia), cardiac enzymes and baseline chest X-ray.

3. If the COHb level is greater than 40% she should be referred for hyperbaric oxygen (HBO) therapy. HBO therapy is recommended at this level even when symptoms are absent. Posthypoxic diffuse cerebral demyelination warrants long term follow up. Neuro-psychiatric sequelae include headaches, irritability, confusion, parkinsonism, memory loss and personality changes.

Notes

1. CO is formed when carbon-containing materials, particularly solid and liquid fuels, undergo incomplete combustion. The poor and elderly are at increased risk in the winter when fires are used for long periods with poorly maintained flues and chimneys and inadequate ventilation. Chronic exposure to CO causes non-specific influenza-like symptoms including fatigue, confusion, nausea, vomiting, dizziness and abdominal pain.

2. The affinity of CO for Hb is 250 times that of oxygen. CO binds avidly to Hb resulting in decreased O_2 carriage. Shift of the oxyhaemoglobin dissociation curve to the left inhibits O_2 release from Hb. Tissue hypoxia is made worse by inhibition of cellular respiration due to CO binding to haem-containing enzymes cytochrome oxidase and P450. It also binds to myoglobin. COHb concentration correlates poorly with clinical symptoms and has little prognostic significance. The elimination half time of CO from COHb is 2–5 h when breathing air, 80 min when breathing 100% O_2 at 1 bar and about 20 min when breathing 100% O_2 at 3 bar. 100% O_2 at 3 bar optimizes CO release from Hb and provides enough dissolved O_2 to meet tissue needs. HBO is used at 2–3 bar for the treatment of CO poisoning and the duration of treatment varies with the severity of symptoms and response to treatment. HBO also minimizes cerebral oedema that may result from cerebral hypoxia.

3. Others who should be considered for HBO therapy include those who have been unconscious, pregnant women (foetus has increased risk) and those with cardiac, neurological and psychiatric complications.

Key references:
Cross M. Carbon monoxide poisoning. Guidelines for the referral of cases to the South Western Hyperbaric Medical Centre, Plymouth, September 1993.

Broome JR, Pearson RR. Carbon monoxide poisoning: forgotten not gone! *British Journal of Hospital Medicine* 1988; **39**:298–305.

Answers to 2.5

1. This shows a heparin effect. Table 2.5a summarizes the basic coagulation tests and Table 2.5b the results in some coagulopathies. Heparin potentiates (x2000) antithrombin III which neutralizes the activated factors XIIa, XIa, IXa, Xa, IIa and XIIIa. It causes an increase in the prothrombin time (PT) and larger increases in the activated partial thromboplastin time (APTT) and the thrombin time (TT). The reptilase test is similar to the TT but is not affected by heparin and this supports a diagnosis of heparin coagulopathy. The blood sample may have been contaminated by heparin flush in the line. The duration of the coagulant effect of heparin is dose dependent but 100 mg/kg has a half-life of 1 h. If the dose and timing of heparin given intra-operatively correlate with the coagulation result, it should be treated but if not, suspect contamination and send another sample. The activated clotting time can be performed in theatre or at the bedside: 3 mL of blood is agitated with 12 mg of diatomaceous earth in a tube which is rotated at 37°C. A metal bar in the tube moves freely until the blood clots. The bar then rotates with the tube and a magnetic sensor stops the timer. It reflects the intrinsic system and is normally <135 s.

2. Protamine is a basic protein which reacts with heparin to form a stable compound with no anticoagulant effect. It is produced from salmon and may cause systemic hypotension, pulmonary hypertension, bronchospasm, bradycardia and anaphylaxis, especially in patients who are allergic to fish. It should be given slowly. By itself it can cause bleeding by an effect on platelets and fibrinogen.

3. Disseminated intravascular coagulopathy (DIC): a pathological condition involving increased coagulation causing microvascular ischaemia and consumption of coagulation factors and platelets leading to increased bleeding.

Table 2.5a Coagulation tests

Name	Pathways tested	Factors tested
PT	Extrinsic and common	VII, X, V, II and I
APTT	Intrinsic and common	VIII, IX, XI, XII X, V, II and I
TT	Common	X, V, II and I

Table 2.5b Some examples of coagulopathy

	PT	APTT	TT
Normal (s)	10 – 14	30 – 40	10 – 12
Warfarin	+++	+	Normal
Heparin	+	+++	++
Dilution	+	+	Normal
Acute DIC	+	+	> 2 x normal

+ = prolonged
DIC = disseminated intravascular coagulopathy

The diagnosis would be supported by a platelet count of <150 000/μL with a prolonged APTT and PT and fibrinogen levels <1.6 g/L (normal 2–4 g/L). DIC would be confirmed by fibrinolysis tests, e.g.

- Increased fibrinogen (and fibrin) degradation products (FDPs) which reflect plasmin activity. Dilutions of serum are added to a combination of fibrinogen-coated latex particles and antifibrinogen antibodies. FDPs inhibit the agglutination. The highest dilution at which agglutination occurs is reported: more dilute than 1 in 16 suggests DIC.
- Euglobulin lysis time <120 minutes.

The FDP titre and the TT are both affected by heparin but the reptilase test is then normal. The treatment of DIC is that of the underlying cause and replacement of coagulation factors and platelets. Cryoprecipitate is given to replace factors I and VIII. The use of heparin is controversial and a haematologist should be consulted.

Key reference:

Kaufman L (ed). *Anaesthesia Review 6*. Churchill Livingstone, London 1989; 89–116.

Answers to 2.6

1. (a) Critikon Dinamap 1846 (<u>D</u>evice for <u>I</u>ndirect <u>N</u>on-inv<u>a</u>sive <u>M</u>ean <u>A</u>rterial <u>P</u>ressure).

1. (b) This device is based on the oscillometric method for measuring blood pressure non-invasively. It uses a single cuff which is initially inflated to a preset level for adults. If oscillations are detected at this point there is a further increase in cuff pressure. A stepped deflation procedure starts once no oscillations are detected. The pressure is decreased by 7 mmHg each time two equal pulsations are detected, or after a preset time lag, whichever comes first. The cuff pressure and oscillations at each step are stored electronically. As the cuff pressure decreases, systolic pressure is taken when the oscillations rapidly increase. Mean arterial pressure is taken as the lowest pressure at which the oscillations are maximal and diastolic pressure is taken when the oscillations rapidly decrease.

2. *Cuff size.* The standard cuff is 5 in wide and is designed for use on an average adult arm. If used on a large arm (circumference >35 cm) or on an adult thigh the reading will be spuriously high. The American Heart Association recommends that the cuff width should be 40% of the midcircumference of the limb: the length should be twice this width. The cuff width should be 3.5 cm in infants and small children and 7 cm in children from 2 to 5 years.

Air leaks. Leaks from the cuff or the connecting tubes may cause spuriously low readings due to faster stepped deflation.

Arrhythmias/bradycardia. If two oscillations of equal amplitude are not detected before the preset time lag, further deflation will occur.

Other. Movement (tremors/fasciculations), external pressure on the cuff may be interpreted as oscillations.

3. *Manual sphygmomanometer.* The arm should be at heart level and the cuff inflated to 30 mmHg above the expected systolic pressure. The cuff is then deflated slowly (3 mmHg/s) and the blood flowing past the constricting cuff gives rise to five phases of Korotkoff sounds. Phase I (the first appearance of sound) = systolic pressure. Diastolic pressure is taken at phase IV = muffling of sound, or at phase V = disappearance of sound. Phase V correlates better with intra-arterial diastolic pressure but there is greater inter-observer variation.

Von Recklinghausen's Oscillotonometer. The double cuff incorporates an upper occluding cuff and a distal sensing cuff. The cuffs are inflated above the anticipated systolic pressure and a slow leak is then obtained. A mechanical amplification system allows the pressure waves sensed by the distal cuff to be displayed as oscillations of a needle.

Ultrasound. Arteriosonde uses a Doppler signal to identify resumption of arterial wall movement under the cuff whilst Infrasonde uses microphones to identify Korotkoff sounds. Both are subject to error from dislodgement and motion artefact.

Finapres. This allows *continuous* noninvasive monitoring. A small cuff which contains a light emitting diode and a photodiode detector is wrapped around a finger. The photo-plethysmograph, which continuously measures digital arterial diameter by transillumination, is connected to a pressure transducer by an electromechanical servo system. Operation of the device is in two phases. Initially the cuff pressure is varied to establish the vessel size at which oscillometric swings are maximal. The external pressure applied to the cuff is then varied by the servo system to keep the vessel size constant. The arterial pressure is monitored throughout the cardiac cycle, the waveform is displayed, and systolic, mean and diastolic pressures are computed.

The APM 770 uses a standard arm cuff and produces an arterial pressure waveform in addition to measuring systolic, mean and diastolic pressures.

Key references:
Hutton P, Prys-Roberts C (eds). *Monitoring in Anaesthesia and Intensive Care* 1st ed. WB Saunders, London 1994;105–120.
Miller RD (ed). *Anesthesia* 4th ed. Churchill Livingstone, New York 1994; 1163–1165.

Answers to 2.7

1. Advantages of an anticholinergic premedication for awake intubation include:

- reduction in secretions gives a better view with the laryngoscope/fibrescope;
- reduction in secretions that would dilute and wash away local anaesthetic (LA);
- prophylaxis against bradycardias and bronchospasm due to airway stimulation.

2. General sensation of the upper airway from the nose and mouth to the larynx is by the trigeminal (V), glossopharyngeal (IX) and vagus (X) cranial nerves. The nasal cavities are the beginning of the airway. They extend from the anterior nares to the nasopharynx. The olfactory (I) *n.* supplies the special sensory olfactory area in the upper part of the nose. The V *n.* supplies general sensation to the remaining mucosa by:

- the anterior ethmoidal branch of the ophthalmic (V^I) *n;*
- branches of the maxillary (V^{II}) *n.* via the pterygopalatine (sphenopalatine) ganglion.

Anaesthesia of the nasal mucosa can be achieved by topical application of LA or siting LA in the upper nose (by the anterior ethmoidal *n.*) and along the floor behind the middle meatus (by the sphenopalatine ganglion). For topical anaesthesia, sprays, pastes, packs and soaked pledgets or cotton wool on probes may be used. If LA solution is instilled into the patient's nose, the patient kept supine but placed head down, the solution collects next to the sphenopalatine ganglion. Cocaine is the only local anaesthetic to cause vasoconstriction due to its inhibition of noradrenaline re-uptake. This reduces haemorrhage from the nasal mucosa which is otherwise common and can impair the view or cause airway obstruction. The main disadvantage of cocaine is the risk of myocardial ischaemia and cardiac arrhythmias. It is a potent central nervous system stimulant and may cause fits. It is available in 4–10% preparations. The recommended maximum nasal dose for a fit adult is 1.5 mg/kg.

3. The general sensation of the posterior one-third of the tongue is supplied by the IX *n.* The anterior two-thirds is by the lingual *n.* (branch of the mandibular *n.*). The IX *n.* supply to the tongue can be blocked directly by injecting 2 ml of LA at the base of each palatoglossal arch. The 10% lignocaine metered spray delivers 10 mg per spray.

4. The X *n.* supplies sensation to the larynx. The superior laryngeal (SL) *n.* leaves the X *n.* just below the inferior ganglion and passes down and forwards over the greater cornu of the hyoid. It passes around the outside of the thyrohyoid membrane where it gives off the internal (IL) and external laryngeal nerves. The IL *n.* pierces the thyrohyoid membrane to provide sensation to the laryngeal mucosa above the cords. Krause's forceps hold a pledget soaked in LA. They are passed over the back of the tongue and sited in each piriform fossa (this can be checked by palpation externally just above and lateral to the thyroid cartilage). Here the SL *n.* is anaesthetized as it lies in the submucosa. The inferior laryngeal *n.* is a terminal branch of the recurrent laryngeal *n.* It is motor to all the laryngeal muscles except cricothyroid and sensory to the laryngeal mucosa below the cords.

5. A relatively inefficient nebulizer should be used to produce 'rain out', i.e. deposition of LA in the proximal airways, not in the alveoli.

Key references:

Telford RJ, Liban JB. Awake fibreoptic intubation. *British Journal of Hospital Medicine* 1991; **46**:182–184.

Ellis H, Feldman S. *Anatomy for Anaesthetists* 5th ed. Blackwell Scientific Publications, Oxford, 1988; 40–41.

Answers to 2.8

1. Diabetic ketoacidosis.
The history is strongly suggestive; he may also not have taken his insulin as prescribed. The diagnosis is confirmed by demonstrating hyperglycaemia and ketonaemia/ketonuria together with acidosis shown by arterial blood gas analysis.

2. Initial management includes:

- *Replacement of fluid and electrolyte losses:* Give consecutive 1 L bags of 0.9% NaCl over 30 min, 60 min, 1, 2, 4, and 6-hour periods. Add 20 mmol KCl to each bag. CVP monitoring is useful to monitor the haemodynamic effects.
- *Replacement of insulin:* Give insulin 6 units i.v. *stat* followed by 6 u/hour by i.v. infusion.
- *Restore acid–base and electrolyte balance:* Monitor blood glucose and electrolytes hourly. Adjust K^+ replacement according to results. Bicarbonate should not be given to correct acidosis unless the pH is ≤7.0. When blood glucose falls to 12 mmol/L replace saline infusion with 5% dextrose infusion with K^+ (1 L six-hourly) and change insulin dosage to sliding scale regimen.

Other investigations should include FBC, ECG, chest X-ray, and blood and urine cultures. Catheterize if urine output is poor and pass naso-gastric tube to prevent acute gastric dilatation. Intravenous fluids and insulin are continued until the patient is able to eat and drink. The maintenance regimen of subcutaneous insulin can then be restored.

3. Other types of coma in diabetes include:

- *Hyperosmolar non-ketoacidotic coma:* This accounts for 5–15% of diabetic hyper-glycaemic emergencies. The patient is usually elderly, often with previously undiagnosed diabetes. There is usually a long history, and profound dehydration, with plasma glucose >35 mmol/L and osmolality >340 mmol/kg. Focal neurological signs and disseminated intravascular coagulation may be present. Common precipitating factors are intercurrent illnesses and consumption of glucose rich drinks. Treatment is as for ketoacidosis. Use 0.45% NaCl if serum Na >150 mmol/L. Anticoagulate as risk of DVT is high.

- *Hypoglycaemic coma:* Usually a consequence of inadequate calorie intake or insulin overdose. Presents with behavioural change, sweating, tachycardia, fits and coma of rapid onset. A rapid response is usually seen when 50 mL of 50% dextrose is given i.v. If i.v. access is difficult, 1–2 mg of glucagon may be given i.m.

4. (a) The anion gap is calculated as $(Na^+ + K^+)$ minus $(Cl^- + HCO_3^-)$. The normal anion gap is <17. The anion gap is helpful in the differential diagnosis of metabolic acidosis. If the anion gap is normal in the presence of acidosis, it is likely that H^+ and Cl^- is being retained or $NaHCO_3$ is being lost. An increased anion gap reflects an increase in unmeasured anion which could be endogenous or exogenous. Causes of metabolic acidosis with an increased anion gap include lactic acidosis, ketoacidosis and salicylate toxicity.

4. (b) The osmolarity of a solution is the number of osmoles of solute per litre of a solution and is therefore dependent on temperature. Approximate plasma osmolarity can be calculated as $2[Na^+] + [urea] + [glucose]$ mosmol/L. This may be taken to reflect osmotic pressure (usually measured by depression of freezing point of solution) and will be increased in dehydration and decreased in fluid overload.

Key references:

Kumar P, Clark M (eds). *Clinical Medicine* 3rd ed. Bailliere Tindall, London 1994; 841–844.

Oh TE (ed). *Intensive Care Manual* 3rd ed. Butterworths, Sydney 1990; 326–330.

Answers to 2.9

1. Causes of difficult ventilation include:

- blocked tracheal tube lumen by blood, tissue, tumour, secretions or foreign body;
- kinking or external pressure on the tracheal tube, e.g. teeth biting;
- cuff herniation;
- blocked breathing circuit;
- pneumothorax;
- bronchospasm;
- pulmonary oedema.

2. The golden rule when ventilation is difficult following intubation is 'If in doubt, take it out', i.e. remove the tracheal tube.

Methods for the differentiation of causes of difficult ventilation include:

- Disconnect the taper mount from the breathing circuit and check the pressure of gas at the patient end of the breathing circuit. If there is no gas pressure at the circuit end, change the circuit. Remove the tracheal tube and ventilate by mask. If ventilation using a mask is easy the tracheal tube is at fault.
- Auscultate the lungs. Breath sounds may be absent in severe bronchospasm. Unilateral breath sounds suggest endobronchial intubation or pneumothorax. Spontaneous pneumothoraces are more common in asthmatic patients. If there is a possibility of a pneumothorax, insert an intravenous cannula in the midclavicular line in the second intercostal space. If there is a release of air under pressure your diagnosis is confirmed and ventilation should improve. Leave the cannula in place and site a chest drain.
- Pass an endobronchial sucker down the tracheal tube. If it does not pass easily suspect kinking, external compression or blockage of the lumen. Deflate the cuff and if the sucker suddenly passes through, the diagnosis is herniation of the cuff. Examine the tracheal tube in the oropharynx to exclude kinking. The commonest misdiagnosis of an obstructed tracheal tube is bronchospasm.
- Aspirate the endobronchial sucker. Frothy pink secretions suggest pulmonary oedema, purulent secretions suggest a chest infection and a dry aspirate suggests bronchospasm. In practice, the diagnosis by tracheal aspiration may not be clear cut.
- Fibreoptic examination through the tracheal tube may show malposition, deformation due to external pressure, cuff herniation, intraluminal obstructions and the presence of secretions.

3. The difference between therapeutic and toxic levels of aminophylline is small. If the patient has taken aminophylline recently any further administration may lead to toxic levels. This may manifest as vomiting, haematemesis, sinus tachycardia, ventricular or supraventricular arrhythmias, profound hypokalaemia, or convulsions. The usual treatment for aminophylline toxicity is a ß-blocker but this is contraindicated in asthmatic patients.

4. No. Abdominal movement without chest movement can occur when the tracheal tube is correctly placed and the lungs are being ventilated normally. This happens if the chest wall is fixed because expansion of the lungs is then solely dependent on diaphragmatic movement, e.g. in ankylosing spondylitis. It is therefore mandatory in such circumstances to be absolutely certain of the tracheal tube position.

Key reference:

Stoetling RK. Asthma. *Current Anaesthesia and Critical Care* 1989; **1**: 47–53.

Answers to 2.10

1. Electromechanical dissociation (EMD). There is continued electrical activity of the heart despite absent or undetectable contraction. EMD has a poor prognosis except when treatable causes are recognized and dealt with early.

2. Tension pneumothorax, hypovolaemia, cardiac tamponade.

3. Send for help, ensure the safety of both patient and resuscitators and evaluate the airway, breathing and circulation to confirm the diagnosis of cardiac arrest in EMD. Initiate basic life support (see OSCE 1.10).
A history must be obtained and a rapid but systematic examination must be performed bearing in mind the correctable causes of EMD following trauma. Consider the possibility of trauma to the cervical spine.
The European Resuscitation Council (ERC) 1992 guidelines for EMD must be followed. This includes tracheal intubation, establishment of vascular access, administration of 1 mg of adrenaline followed by ten sequences of compression:ventilation at the rate of 5:1 (two operators).
If there is no evidence for a specific cause of EMD, a further dose of 1 mg of adrenaline is given and the cycle repeated. After three unsuccessful cycles the higher dose of adrenaline 5 mg i.v. may be tried. Other drugs that may be considered in EMD are pressor agents, alkalinizing agents and calcium chloride. The ERC does not recommend the routine use of these drugs in EMD.

4. *Hypovolaemia:* External haemorrhage must be controlled with direct compression. Bleeding may be profuse yet covert (e.g. intra-abdominal bleeding with fractured lower ribs). Treat initially with colloid infusion i.v. through wide bore cannulae. External cardiac compression may be ineffective in hypovolaemia.

Tension pneumothorax: Unilateral absence of breath sounds, hyper-resonance on percussion and tracheal deviation to the opposite side clinch the diagnosis, which is clinical, not radiological. Immediate decompression by needle thoraco-centesis (see OSCE 4.3) must be followed later by insertion of a pleural drain.
Cardiac tamponade: May be caused by direct injury to the heart or deceleration as occurs with steering wheel impact. The classical triad of raised JVP, soft heart sounds and low arterial pressure will be masked by the cardiac arrest. Emergency treatment is pericardiocentesis with a long, 16 gauge needle.

Notes
The expression 'pulseless electrical activity' (PEA) refers to pulselessness in the presence of electrical activity other than VT or VF. PEA includes EMD and the recently described pseudo-EMD. Other causes of EMD include:
Pulmonary embolism: A history suggestive of increased risk of thromboembolism must be sought. External cardiac compression may disrupt/dislodge smaller clots. Embolectomy, where facilities exist, may be life saving.
Electrolyte imbalance: Calcium has been implicated in ischaemic tissue injury and its use has been restricted to hypocalcaemia, hyper-kalaemia or where there is a history of calcium antagonist intake.
Hypothermia: Advanced life support must not be interrupted until the core temperature is above 32°C. Below this temperature, defibrillation is unlikely to be effective.
Drug overdose: Specific antidotes need to be considered. In poisoning with tricyclic anti-depressants, early administration of sodium bicarbonate is recommended.

Key references:
Advanced Life Support Working Party of the European Resuscitation Council. Guidelines for advanced life support. *Resuscitation* 1992; **24**:111–121.

The Advanced Life Support Group. *Advanced Cardiac Life Support* 1st ed. Chapman & Hall, London 1993; 101–103.

Answers to 2.11

1. Dystrophia myotonica and myotonia. Dystrophia myotonica is classified as a myopathy but affects multiple systems. Although rare, it is the commonest cause of myotonia. Other causes (myotonia congenita and hereditary paramyotonia) are rarer still. Myotonia is the inability of muscles to relax after a contraction. It is due to a defect in chloride ion movement across the muscle membrane. This results in difficulty in relaxing the grip and the characteristic hand shape shown. Patients may develop ways to disguise this, e.g. only using a loose grip. Myotonia can be elicited by asking patients to make a fist or screw up their eyes and then relax. It may be improved by exercise and precipitated by cold. Percussion myotonia is elicited by tapping the thenar eminence firmly with a patellar hammer. This causes opposition of the thumb across the palm which then takes several seconds to recover its position. Dystrophia myotonica is diagnosed by:

- the presence of myotonia clinically and the characteristic 'dive-bomber' effect on audio-electromyogram;
- clinical history and examination of the patient and family for features of the syndrome.

2. The variation in genetic expression, the slow progression of the disease and the patients' somnolence, low IQ and stoic nature often results in these patients presenting for surgery before the diagnosis is known. Their lack of symptoms belies underlying pathology that increases anaesthetic risk. They have:

- restrictive pulmonary function from atrophy and myotonia of the respiratory muscles and so may require post-operative ventilation and physiotherapy;
- cardiomyopathy, conduction defects and arrhythmias and so may require pacing;
- post-operative airway obstruction due to upper airway muscle involvement;

- pharyngeal and oesophageal involvement causing dysphagia and regurgitation which predisposes to pulmonary aspiration.

Other features of the disease include frontal balding, cataracts, gonadal atrophy and diabetes mellitus. Atrophy of the temporalis and facial muscles gives an expressionless, triangular face, ptosis and the risk of peri-operative temporomandibular dislocation. Sternocleidomastoid atrophy causes neck flexion. Distal limb muscles may also be affected. Pre-operative tests should include arterial blood gases, blood sugar, ECG, chest X-ray and an echocardiogram.

3. Even asymptomatic patients may show the following abnormal drug reactions:

- prolonged apnoea following benzodiazepines, opiates, volatiles or thiopentone (consider no premedication and reduce all doses);
- prolonged myotonia due to suxamethonium which may make intubation impossible;
- prolonged muscle weakness due to anticholinesterases (avoid by using a short-acting muscle relaxant and be prepared to ventilate until full muscle power has returned).

4. Operating conditions may be poor due to myotonia produced by surgical stimulation, diathermy, potassium or cold. The defect is in the muscle so neuromuscular blocking agents and neural blockade have no effect. Ensuring a warm theatre may prevent the onset of myotonia. Topical bupivacaine has been reported as reducing uterine myotonia. Post-operative shivering may cause myotonia and should be avoided.

Key reference:

Aldridge LM. Anaesthetic problems in Myotonic Dystrophy. *British Journal of Anaesthesia* 1985; 57:1119–1130.

Answers to 2.12

1. 'Gas and air' is a mixture of nitrous oxide (N_2O) and air rather than N_2O and oxygen. In 1934 Dr R.J. Minnitt described his gas–air analgesia apparatus for use in labour. In 1949 it was shown to deliver potentially dangerous hypoxic mixtures. At high flow rates some gas–air machines gave only 8% oxygen. They were replaced by gas–oxygen machines. This allowed greater concentrations of N_2O to be used safely. N_2O is a strong analgesic. 20% N_2O is equivalent to 15 mg of subcutaneous morphine. The optimal analgesic concentration was found to be 70% N_2O but some mothers became unconscious so it could not be used safely by unsupervised midwives. 50% N_2O in oxygen is safer and has become the standard. Initially it was delivered by mixing the two gases at the time of use. This was superseded by the more convenient pre-mixed cylinders. Entonox is the BOC trade name for this gas mixture.

2. The Minnitt apparatus has a valve that has to be held open while inhaling. The Pneupac Analgesia Valve and BOC Entonox system have demand valves that open on active inhalation. A safety feature is that the mother controls administration. If she loses consciousness her hand will fall and she will stop inhaling the gas. No-one else should hold the mask or this safety factor is lost and she may become anaesthetized with all its risks.

3. Labouring mothers may have tidal volumes of 2.25 L, minute volumes of up to 90 L/min and peak inspiratory flow rates of 300 L/min. Primiparous mothers use on average 764 L (multiparous ~ 292 L). 2580 L have been used in one labour. Three full 500 L (D) cylinders should be available for a primiparous mother. Entonox reaches its full effect after 30 s or 6 breaths. For optimum effect inhalation should start when the contraction tightens to co-ordinate the maximal effect with the central painful

part of the contraction. Inhalation should stop as the contraction eases or the mother will feel light-headed and be unable to co-ordinate the next inhalation with the next contraction.

4. The critical temperature (CT) of a gas is the maximum temperature at which compression can cause liquefaction. Mixing gases may change their CTs (see Table 2.12). If pressurized oxygen is bubbled through liquid N_2O it dissolves in the N_2O. The N_2O evaporates and a 50:50 mixture of the two gases forms (Poynting effect). This reduces the CT of the N_2O so Entonox has a pseudocritical temperature of – 6 °C. If a cylinder cools below this temperature N_2O will condense and the two gases will separate (laminate). Initially the mother will breathe mainly O_2 and have poor analgesia. When the oxygen is exhausted she will breathe a hypoxic mixture of mainly N_2O. If a cylinder has been exposed to cold below – 6 °C it should be warmed for 5 min in a 37°C water bath or for 2 h in a room at 15°C. It should then be inverted three times before use. Hospital pipeline supplies are from a manifold of 5000 L cylinders each containing a pipe that delivers gas from within 10 cm of its base. If lamination occurs this pipe ensures that the initial gas is derived from the liquid N_2O at the base which contains 20% dissolved oxygen.

Table 2.12. Physical data of gases

	Oxygen	N_2O	Entonox
Critical temperature (°C)	– 118	36	– 6
Physical state at 15 °C	Gas	Liquid	Gas
Cylinder pressure (atm) at 15°C	135	43	135

Key reference:

Nimmo WS, Rowbotham DJ, Smith G (eds). *Anaesthesia* 2nd ed. Blackwell Scientific Publications, London 1994; 79–80, 1006–1007.

OSCE cycle 3 – answers

Answers to 3.1

1. Plastic disposable Mallinckrodt double lumen endobronchial tube with CPAP attachment. The advantages of these modern tubes include:

- Provision of flexible stylet to aid intubation.
- Provision of endobronchial suction catheters.
- The clear plastic allows observation of condensation within the tube during ventilation.
- High volume low pressure cuffs.
- The blue coloured endobronchial cuffs are easily seen during fibreoptic bronchoscopy.
- Contoured right endobronchial cuffs allow ventilation through right upper lobe bronchus.

2. Once the tube has been positioned manual ventilation is commenced with the tracheal cuff inflated. Air entry should be equal on both sides, breath sounds should be heard in both axillae and there should be no leak around the tracheal cuff. The tracheal side of the adapter is then clamped and the tracheal port is opened distal to the clamp. The bronchial cuff is inflated so as to just eliminate air leak from the tracheal lumen. Breath sounds should be heard only on the side of the endobronchial intubation. The tracheal limb is then unclamped, the tracheal port closed and the bronchial limb of the adapter is clamped and the bronchial port opened to air. Breath sounds should only be heard on the contralateral side. Fibreoptic bronchoscopy down the tracheal lumen should reveal the carina and the top edge of the blue bronchial cuff should be just visible in the main stem bronchus. When a right-sided tube is used the fibrescope should be used to visualize the orifice of the right upper lobe bronchus.

3. Absolute indications for double lumen tube intubation (separation of the lungs) are:

- Isolation of a lung to prevent spillage of infected material or blood into it, from the other lung.

- Selective ventilation of one lung. Bronchopleural or bronchopleurocutaneous fistula (eliminates risk of gas flow along the path of least resistance); giant lung cyst or bulla (eliminates risk of rupture and consequent pneumothorax/pneumomediastinum); surgery of major conducting airway; tracheobronchial tree disruption;unilateral bronchopulmonary lavage (e.g. pulmonary alveolar proteinosis).

Relative indications include the facilitation of surgical exposure for operations on the lungs, oesophagus, thoracic aorta and thoracic spine.

4. Manoeuvres are directed at minimizing atelectasis in the ventilated lung and shunt in the nonventilated lung.

Ensure proper tube position; suction at intervals. Set initial tidal volume at 10 mL/kg and adjust respiratory rate to keep $PaCO_2$ at 40 mmHg. Use FIO_2 of 1.0.

PEEP applied to the ventilated lung will reduce atelectasis but oxygenation may deteriorate due to increase in shunt through the other lung.

CPAP to the nonventilated lung to expand it just enough so as not to interfere with the surgery will help reduce shunt.

Oxygen can be insufflated into the nonventilated lung via a suction catheter. Alternatively, the nonventilated lung can be inflated briefly with 100% O_2 at intervals.

Persistent hypoxia that does not respond to combinations of the above manoeuvres and differential lung PEEP/CPAP must be treated with resumption of two-lung ventilation with 100% O_2. Failing this, clamping of the pulmonary artery of the surgical lung should improve oxygenation.

Key references:

Benumof JL. Management of the respiratory system during pulmonary surgery. *Refresher Courses in Anesthesiology* The American Society of Anesthesiologists, Inc. Philadelphia 1992; 1–14.

Benumof JL (ed). *Clinical Procedures in Anesthesia and Intensive Care*. J B Lippincott Co., Philadelphia 1992; 227–251.

Answers to 3.2

1. "The minimum gastric content in humans that may result in aspiration pneumonitis is 25 mL (0.4 mL/kg) of pH <2.5" provides the basis for prophylaxis for aspiration pneumonitis. The pH value bears scrutiny but the volume value is overcautious. These levels are exceeded by up to 60% of all patients. The incidence of aspiration pneumonitis is of the order 0.1–0.01%. Food can cause airway obstruction and should be restricted for 6 h pre-operatively. Clear fluids given up to 2 hours pre-operatively do not increase gastric content. Cisapride, metoclopramide and nasogastric aspiration reduce gastric volume. Gastric acid production is normally 1 mL/kg/h. Production is reduced by omeprazole which inhibits the hydrogen-potassium-ATP pump (proton pump) and H_2 receptor antagonists, e.g. ranitidine or cimetidine. These should be given from 6 h pre-operatively as they only stop production of acid and time must be allowed for emptying of any acid already present. Sodium citrate is given just before induction to neutralize the acid already present. *Mist. Mag. Trisil.* is not used as it is particulate and can itself cause aspiration pneumonitis. Causes of delayed stomach emptying include trauma, pain, autonomic neuropathy (e.g. diabetes mellitus), labour, opiates, achalasia, pyloric stenosis, small bowel obstruction, ileus and peritonitis. No method reduces the gastric acidity and volume to a level that guarantees 100% safety from aspiration pneumonitis.

2. You should have already decided what management you would take if you could not intubate the trachea. If you are suddenly in a situation of a failed intubation you will not have the time to ponder over what to do next. You should have a management scheme already decided; e.g. for a Caesarean section whether you will wake up the mother and do a regional technique or an awake fibreoptic intubation, or continue the anaesthetic with a mask and spontaneous breathing.

3. Cormack and Lehane Grade 4. The first part of the failed intubation drill is to make the conscious decision that you cannot intubate the patient. The following steps should then be taken:

- give 100% oxygen and call for help;
- maintain cricoid pressure and turn the patient head down into the lateral position;
- maintain airway patency (± oropharyngeal airway) and apply gentle IPPV to maintain oxygen saturation;
- allow the patient to wake up and breathe spontaneously.

The problems and controversy occur when one cannot maintain the airway and the patient becomes cyanosed. Alternatives then include:

- removing cricoid pressure;
- nasopharyngeal or laryngeal mask airway;
- turning the patient supine which may make airway control more familiar and easier;
- cricothyroid puncture, cricothyrotomy;
- oesophageal obturator airway.

4. Features which suggest aspiration include:

- visual presence of acid in the pharynx or on suction of the endotracheal tube (use litmus paper to check pH);
- difficulty in ventilating if solids aspirated;
- presence of shunt, recognized by decreased saturations or PaO_2 despite an increased inspired oxygen concentration;
- presence of wheezes or coarse crepitations generally or localized to the right lower lobe (may present as bronchospasm).

Key reference:

Atkinson RS, Adams AP (eds). *Recent Advances in Anaesthesia and Analgesia 18*, Churchill Livingstone, Edinburgh 1994; 59–73.

Answers to 3.3

1. A= epidural space. B= dura mater. C= dorsal root ganglion. D= mixed spinal nerve. E= subarachnoid space.

2. (a) Skin, subcutaneous tisssue, supraspinous ligament, interspinous ligament and the ligamentum flavum.

2. (b) Posterior = vertebral laminae, and ligamenta flava which extend laterally to the capsules of the articular processes and intervertebral foramina. Lateral = pedicles and intervertebral foramina. Anterior = posterior longitudinal ligament. Superior = foramen magnum where the periosteal and spinal layers of dura fuse. Inferior = sacro-coccygeal membrane.

3. Labour pain is transmitted by two pathways. During the first stage of labour, pain from the cervix and uterus is transmitted by fibres that accompany sympathetic fibres via the pelvic, inferior, middle and superior hypogastric plexuses to enter the spinal cord at T10–T12 and L1. During the late first and second stages perineal pain is transmitted via the afferent somatic pudendal nerves to S2–S4. Thus an epidural catheter would be optimally sited in the lumbar region to provide analgesia during labour. This also avoids direct trauma to the thoracic spinal cord.

4. Contraindications include:

- patient refusal;
- patient mentally unsuitable/unable to co-operate during procedure;
- absence of adequate numbers of trained staff;
- absence of resuscitation facilities;
- anticoagulant therapy or established coagulopathy;
- local or systemic sepsis;
- severe anatomical abnormality of the spine;
- major haemorrhage/hypovolaemia;
- raised intracranial pressure.

5. (a) There is a relevant deep bony landmark.

(b) Catheter insertion is easier and inadvertent dural puncture is less likely as the convex Huber tip of the epidural needle pushes the dura away.

(c) Avoids the interspinous ligament which may be calcified, particularly in the elderly. Also, the false positive loss of resistance sometimes obtained with the needle in the interspinous ligament is avoided.

(d) Extreme flexion of the spine is not necessary.

(e) Useful in the thoracic region as it avoids the long, down-sloping spinous processes.

Notes

1. The dura is lined by the thin arachnoid mater. Between these layers is a potential space, the subdural space, which contains a film of serous fluid. The subdural space does not communicate directly with the subarachnoid space which is found between the arachnoid and pia mater.

2. The supraspinous ligament links the tips of the vertebral spines and continues rostrally to the external occipital protuberance as the ligamentum nuchae. The interspinous ligament runs obliquely between the vertebral spines and merges anteriorly with the ligamentum flavum. Both supraspinous and interspinous ligaments are thickest in the lumbar region. The fibres of the 3 mm thick elastic ligamentum flavum run vertically joining the lower half of the anterior surface of the lamina above to the upper half of the posterior surface of the lamina below.

4. Contraindications are present in approximately 10% of patients but not all are absolute.

Key references:

Reynolds F (ed). *Epidural and Spinal Blockade in Obstetrics.* Baillière Tindall, London 1990; 19–32.

Morgan M (ed). *Foundations of Obstetric Anaesthesia.* Farrand Press, London 1987; 19–33.

Answers to 3.4

1. Stellate ganglion block and a Horner's syndrome.

2. Components of Horner's syndrome are:

- miosis;
- enophthalmos;
- partial ptosis (sympathetic nerves only supply one third of levator palpebrae superioris);
- ipsilateral anhydrosis;
- vasodilatation of the head, neck and arm: so the patient may complain of a unilateral blocked nose.

3. Complications of stellate ganglion block include:

- pneumothorax due to puncture of Sibson's fascia;
- intra-arterial injection of a relatively small dose of local anaesthetic into the vertebral artery may cause direct cranial neurotoxicity;
- intravenous injection may cause systemic local anaesthetic toxicity;
- brachial plexus block or damage;
- hoarse voice due to recurrent laryngeal nerve block;
- vasovagal syncope.

4. Other anaesthetic causes of Horner's syndrome include:

- brachial plexus block;
- spinal anaesthesia;
- epidural anaesthesia;
- cervical plexus block.

5. Dystrophia myotonica – but also:

- myasthenia gravis;
- myopathy, e.g. ocular myopathy;
- tabes dorsalis;
- syringomyelia (true bilateral Horner's).

Notes on the administration of local anaesthetic blocks

When asked how you would do a particular local anaesthetic block, start at the pre-operative assessment, *not* with 'I would insert the needle here...' If the examiner does require only the performance of the block, this will be made clear to you.

Assess and prepare the patient as for a general anaesthetic, i.e. history, physical examination and relevant tests. Explain the procedure and its risks and benefits to the patient and obtain consent. The patient should be fasted as for a general anaesthetic.

In theatre, prepare and check all the drugs and equipment necessary for performing the block and for resuscitation. An adequately trained assistant should be present. Explain what you are doing so that the patient is not suddenly startled. This reduces the chance of them moving, makes the procedure less frightening and also monitors the level of consciousness. All blocks can then be described by the mnemonic: **I AM PRACTICAL.**

- **I**ntravenous **A**ccess,
- **M**onitoring,
- **P**osition of the patient,
- **R**egional **A**natomy,
- **C**lean skin and drape,
- **T**echnique including end-point criteria,
- **I**njection – drug, volume and concentration,
- **C**omplications during block,
- **A**ftercare,
- **L**ate complications.

Aftercare includes specific positioning, monitoring and instructions to the patient and the nursing staff.

Key reference:
Miller RD (ed). *Anesthesia* 4th ed. Churchill Livingstone, London 1994; 2356.

Answers to 3.5

1. The surgeon should maintain circumferential chest compression to stop the baby from inspiring meconium and you should suck out any meconium from the oropharynx and nasopharynx.

2. The Apgar score is 5 to 7 as only four of the five variables are given. The foetal pH is normal.

3. Intubate and perform tracheal suction.

4. This is normal.

Notes on meconium aspiration (MA)

Meconium is a mixture of amniotic fluid, intestinal cells and secretions. It is a sterile, chemical irritant. After 37 weeks gestation perinatal hypoxia can cause mesenteric vasoconstriction, vagally stimulated peristalsis and anal sphincter relaxation resulting in meconium staining of the liquor. Meconium stained liquor occurs in 10% of deliveries and half of these babies will have meconium in the trachea. Meconium stained liquor is a poor predictor of foetal outcome but it should alert the anaesthetist to the risk of MA. The hypoxia also causes foetal gasping and the meconium is then aspirated. This may lead to:

- complete physical obstruction of the airway causing lobar or lung collapse;
- partial obstruction with a ball-valve effect causing air trapping and pneumothorax;
- chemical pneumonitis.

Following birth, the initiation of spontaneous breathing can exacerbate the condition by moving meconium distally from the oropharynx into the peripheral lung tissue. At delivery, management is aimed at preventing this exacerbation.

- During vaginal delivery the oropharynx and nasopharynx are aspirated before the chest is delivered. At Caesarean section the surgeon should maintain circumferential chest compression while the oropharynx and nasopharynx are aspirated. Suction should not exceed 100 mmHg. A trap is used to allow examination of aspirate.
- Chest compression is continued and the baby is transferred in the Trendelenberg lateral decubitus position to the resuscitation table. The radiant heater is on.
- An assistant should palpate the umbilical pulse as bradycardias are common with intubation and suction due to vagal dominance. Basic resuscitation of the newborn is part of the management of MA and if the HR falls below 80/min for more than 30 s then IPPV with 100% oxygen and chest compressions should be started.
- Avoid stimulating respiration. Intubate and pass a suction catheter through the endotracheal tube. Remove the endotracheal tube with the catheter *in situ* as the meconium may be particulate.
- Allow spontaneous ventilation or gently assist for 20 – 30 s.
- Repeat the intubation, suction and ventilation until the aspirate is nearly free of meconium.
- Dry vigorously and stimulate by gently slapping the feet. If respiratory effort is still poor, consider naloxone.
- Empty the stomach before extubating.

Following MA the baby should be monitored for the development of respiratory distress and should have chest physiotherapy including postural drainage and suction. Routine prophylactic antibiotic cover is not indicated.

Key reference:

Advanced Life Support Group. *Advanced Paediatric Life Support*. BMJ Publishing Group, 1993; Ch. 7.

Answers to 3.6

1. (a) Quincke spinal needle
1. (b) Whitacre spinal needle

2. The Quincke needle has a sharp point and a cutting bevel with an end hole. The bevel cuts through the fibres of the dura which are orientated longitudinally.

The Whitacre pencil point needle has a solid tip, a completely rounded non-cutting bevel and a side hole. It is designed to spread the dural fibres rather than cut them and the residual hole in the dura upon removal of the needle is thought to be smaller.

The diameter of the needle and the design of its tip are important factors that influence the incidence of post-dural puncture headache (PDPH). In one large study of pregnant patients who underwent spinal anaesthesia for Caesarean section or vaginal delivery the rates of PDPH were as follows: Quincke needle 26 G – 5.4%; Quincke needle 27 G – 2.5%; Whitacre needle 25 G – 1.1%. A low incidence of PDPH has also been reported with the Sprotte 24 G needle. The longer side hole in the Sprotte needle may lead to an increased incidence of failed blocks (some of the calculated dose of drug may be deposited outside the CSF) and may weaken the tip, resulting in bending on contact with bone. An introducer helps to direct the smaller spinal needles (≥25 G), and facilitates penetration of the tough supraspinous ligament.

3. Patient factors:
Age: Spread is greater in the elderly, probably related to the decrease in volume of the spinal canal and CSF.
Anatomy: Posture and height influence spread of LA. Kyphoscoliosis may affect spread and careful positioning may be necessary.
Abdominal pressure: Increased intra-abdominal pressure (e.g. pregnancy, tumour) increases spread. Reduced inferior vena caval blood flow results in the opening of collateral channels in the epidural space. This produces a decrease in the volume of CSF.
Drug factors:
Baricity of solution, dose, volume, speed of injection and barbotage may influence height of block.

4. Hypotension, bradycardia, nausea and post-operative urinary retention are common accompaniments of spinal anaesthesia.

- *Total spinal:* the consequences of an excessively high block that ascends to and beyond the cervical region are profound bradycardia, hypotension, loss of consciousness and cardiorespiratory arrest. Treatment is symptomatic and supportive (including tracheal intubation and ventilation).
- *Post-dural puncture headache:* (*see* OSCE 8.11 for details of treatment).
- *Backache:* Associated with 25% of procedures performed under spinal anaesthesia. This may be due to periosteal trauma from the needle or stretching of the ligaments of the back.
- *Neurological complications:* Nerve damage is possible from needle trauma, intraneural injection or contamination of injectate. Anterior spinal artery syndrome may follow prolonged hypotension. Cauda equina syndrome has been reported after continuous spinal anaesthesia.
- *Spinal/epidural haematoma:* Exceedingly rare but the resulting prolonged nerve compression can cause permanent nerve damage. Early surgical decompression, following confirmation of diagnosis by CT scan, is the only available treatment.

Key references:

Wildsmith JAW, Armitage EN (eds). *Principles and Practice of Regional Anaesthesia* 2nd ed. Churchill Livingstone, Edinburgh 1993; 87–99.

Mulroy MF. *Regional anesthesia (An illustrated Procedural Guide).* Little Brown, Boston 1989; 65–87.

Answers to 3.7

1. Minimum Alveolar Concentration (MAC) is a standard index of the potency of volatile anaesthetic agents. MAC is defined as the concentration of volatile anaesthetic (at 1 atmosphere) measured in end-tidal gas that prevents a response (gross muscular movement) to a standard painful stimulus (surgical incision) in 50% of subjects.

MAC_{95} is the concentration of anaesthetic which prevents response to a supramaximal stimulus in 95% of subjects. MAC_{95} is 1.3–1.5 times MAC and is probably more useful in terms of achieving clinical anaesthesia.

'MAC_{awake}' has been defined as the alveolar anaesthetic concentration at the first response to command.

'MAC_{aware}', which is a measure of awareness, is the alveolar concentration of volatile anaesthetic at which 50% of subjects are aware and 50% are not. MAC_{aware} is approximately 40% of the MAC value of an anaesthetic agent.

2. Blood/gas solubility is an important determinant of the rate of rise of alveolar partial pressure of an anaesthetic agent when the inspired partial pressure is held constant. With agents with high blood/gas solubility, equilibrium between the inspired and alveolar partial pressures is reached slowly. The lower the blood/gas solubility of an agent the more quickly the alveolar–blood–brain equilibrium of volatile agent concentration will be achieved. The blood/gas solubility, therefore, has an inverse relationship to the speed of induction.

3. Meyer and Overton found that hypnotic potency of volatile anaesthetic agents is proportional to their oil/water partition coefficients. Better correlation is found between hypnotic activity and the oil/gas partition coefficient. The product of the oil/gas partition coefficient of an anaesthetic agent and its MAC is approximately constant. The oil/gas partition coefficient reflects the avidity with which a volatile agent is taken up by neuronal tissue and is directly proportional to the potency of a volatile anaesthetic agent.

4 The attributes of an 'ideal' volatile agent are given below:

- cheap;
- chemically stable;
- nonflammable, not irritant or pungent;
- minimal autonomic effects;
- low blood/gas solubility;
- high oil/gas solubility, i.e. low MAC;
- minimal metabolism ;
- minimal cardiovascular depressant effects;
- dose dependent/predictable side effects;
- environmentally friendly;
- no teratogenicity.

5. This drug has a relatively high MAC which implies that it is of low potency. Large quantities of the agent would therefore have to be administered, which could prove expensive. It has a high saturated vapour pressure at 20°C, i.e. it is almost boiling. This will result in the production of large volumes of vapour and excessive cooling unless the vaporizer is provided with an external heat source. The inability to administer this agent from a standard vaporizer would mean additional capital expenditure. An advantage of the drug is its low blood/gas solubility. This should ensure rapid onset of inhalational anaesthesia unless the drug possessed irritant qualities. The low blood/gas solubility should also facilitate precise control of the depth of anaesthesia and rapid recovery.

Key references:

Stoelting RK. *Pharmacology and Physiology in Anesthetic Practice* 2nd ed. JB Lippincott Company, Pennsylvania 1991; 20–32.

Nimmo WS, Rowbotham DJ, Smith G (eds). *Anaesthesia* 2nd ed. Blackwell Scientific Publications, Oxford 1994; 43–55.

Answers to 3.8

The aetiology of post-operative nausea and vomiting (PONV) is multifactorial and its pathophysiology is not completely understood. Contributory factors can be classified into pre-, intra- and post-operative ones.

Pre-operative factors:

Anxiety and stress can cause an endocrine response (secretion of ACTH, GH and prolactin) and together with aerophagy and gastrointestinal distension may increase the risk of PONV. A previous history of PONV is a known risk factor and may be related to anxiety and fear of this unpleasant complication recurring. Adult women are up to three times more likely to suffer PONV, particularly in the luteal phase of the menstrual cycle. Obesity, conditions that delay gastric emptying (e.g. diabetes, pregnancy), emergency surgery (full stomach) and motion sickness are associated with PONV. Premedication with opioids and/or anticholinergics increases the incidence of PONV.

Intra-operative factors:

Some types of surgery (abdominal, gynaecological, laparoscopic and adenotonsillectomy or strabismus surgery in children) increase the risk of PONV. A higher incidence of PONV has been reported with inexperienced anaesthetists (more gastric inflation with manual ventilation and deeper planes of anaesthesia) and prolonged surgery associated with greater exposure to anaesthetic agents and increased pain. Opioids as part of a balanced anaesthetic technique, nitrous oxide, the volatile anaesthetics, and some i.v. induction agents such as thiopentone, etomidate and ketamine, have all been implicated in PONV. Neostigmine has significant emetic properties. A higher incidence of nausea and vomiting is seen with those who develop hypotension and high blocks during central neural blockade.

Post-operative factors:

Pain *per se* is associated with nausea and vomiting although emesis can be provoked by excessive doses of opioids. Hypotension, hypoxia, early intake of food, positional changes, movement and early ambulation may all trigger PONV.

Pre-operative counselling and preparation may be combined with anxiolytic premedication such as lorazepam. Prophylaxis with antiemetics is not a routine practice in anaesthesia because of the side effects of the drugs available. Not all patients experience PONV. Prophylaxis must be considered for those at high risk and ondansetron is effective with minimal side effects. A regional technique may be considered with careful avoidance of hypotension and a high block. PONV can be minimized by the choice of drugs and techniques if general anaesthesia is used (careful airway management at induction and emergence, gastric suction, provided the tube is inserted after induction and removed prior to emergence to minimize pharyngeal stimulation, use of TIVA and avoidance of nitrous oxide). Pain, hypotension and abrupt positional changes must be avoided post-operatively. Drugs used include the 5-HT$_3$ antagonists (e.g. ondansetron, side effects–headache, flushing, arrhythmias), antidopaminergic drugs (e.g. metoclopramide, side effects–extrapyramidal reactions), phenothiazines (e.g. prochlorperazine, side effects–sedation, acute dystonias, hypotension), butyrophenones (e.g. droperidol, side effects–delayed recovery, extrapyramidal reactions), antihistamines (e.g. cyclizine, side effects–sedation, dry mouth) and anticholinergics (eg: hyoscine, side effects–somnolence, mydriasis, dry mouth).

Key references:
Smith G, Rowbotham DJ (eds). Supplement on postoperative nausea and vomiting. *British Journal of Anaesthesia* 1992; **69** (Suppl. 1).

Harmer M (ed). Ondansetron – a new concept in antiemetic therapy for postoperative nausea and vomiting. *Anaesthesia* 1994; **49** (Supplement).

Answers to 3.9

1. (a) Oxygen. (b) Colour code – black body with white shoulder (varies from country to country). Labelling – on shoulder. The name of the gas contained is stencilled both on the shoulder and the valve block. The pin index system – holes at 2 and 5 positions. Each cylinder has a unique serial number. (The plastic test disc indicates the quarter and the year in which the cylinder was last tested.)

2. The pressure within a full 'E' size cylinder (size used with standard anaesthetic machine) is 1987 psi (137 bar). It is capable of supplying 680 L at room temperature. When a non-liquefied gas such as oxygen is discharged the pressure within the cylinder declines steadily. When the cylinder is half full, the pressure gauge will read approximately 990 psi.

With gases that are stored partially in liquid form, the pressure gauge will show a constant pressure (at constant temperature) until all the liquid has evaporated. After this, there is a rapid decline in pressure as the gas is used up. The gauge pressure cannot be used to estimate the contents of a N_2O cylinder but the weight of the cylinder will decline steadily during use. N_2O pressure gauges are marked 'full at varying temperatures'.

3. Confirm identity of cylinder, inspect it for damage and ensure it has not come into contact with dirt or grease. Remove plastic dust cover from valve block. The outlet must be cleared of dust by briefly opening the valve before mounting the cylinder. A single Bodok seal must be used and the cylinder attached so that the pins on the machine yoke and the holes on the valve block are perfectly matched. Connections should not be forced and only appropriate spanners should be used for tightening. The cylinder valve should be opened slowly initially and once the pressure gauge has stabilized it can be opened fully. Ensure that the gauge pressure is appropriate and there are no leaks.

4. *Hydraulic pressure tests* – carried out every five years. The cylinders are subjected to pressures considerably greater than would be required in clinical use. The test pressure is stencilled on the valve block of the cylinder.
Tensile test – one out of every 100 cylinders manufactured is tested. Strips are cut from the body and stretched to assess yield point.
Other tests include *Flattening, Impact* and *Bend tests*. Endoscopic examination of the interior of cylinders is performed to detect flaws in the molybdenum steel walls.

5. *Vacuum-Insulated Evaporators (VIE):* These consist of an inner shell of stainless steel and an outer shell of carbon steel between which a vacuum is maintained. The temperature is kept between –150°C and –175°C (the critical temperature of O_2 is –118.4°C and the temperature must be kept below this to store it in liquid form). O_2 is supplied in gaseous form through a dedicated copper pipeline network leading to Schraeder wall outlets which accept non-interchangeable Schraeder probes that are attached to named and colour coded gas hoses.
O_2 concentrators: These devices separate oxygen from air and produce O_2 concentrations >90% at flow rates of 3–5 L/min. An air compressor drives filtered air through zeolite columns (hydrated aluminium silicate which acts as a molecular sieve) which adsorb N_2. The N_2 is later purged. A solenoid switching device which alternates between zeolite columns, a reservoir and a flow control mechanism are usually incorporated. Concentrators require only electricity and minimal servicing, are reliable and provide a continuous supply of oxygen. Disadvantages are capital expense, size, limited flow rates and noise when in use.

Key reference:

Dorsch JA, Dorsch SE. *Understanding Anaesthesia Equipment* 3rd ed. Williams & Wilkins, Maryland 1994; 1–23.

Answers to 3.10

1. Atrial fibrillation with a ventricular response of 180 beats/minute.

2. DC cardioversion, digitalization, treatment with ß-adrenoceptor antagonists (esmolol), calcium channel blockers (verapamil), or class 1 anti-arrhythmic drugs (quinidine, procainamide). Anticoagulation may be indicated. It is important to treat any precipitating cause appropriately.

3. Atrial fibrillation is often associated with clinically significant cardiac disease. The loss of the atrial boost to ventricular filling consequent upon the irregular beating of the atria may significantly decrease cardiac output. Atrial fibrillation, particularly when associated with mitral valve disease, could result in the formation of atrial thrombi which may lead to systemic embolization.

4. Causes of atrial fibrillation include ischaemic heart disease, hypertensive heart disease, rheumatic heart disease with involvement of the mitral valve, heart failure, cardiomyopathy, constrictive pericarditis, sick sinus syndrome, atrial myxoma, endocarditis and thyrotoxicosis. It is often seen after cardiac and thoracic surgery.

Notes

Atrial fibrillation is an irregularly irregular rhythm characterized by uncoordinated atrial activity and lack of effective atrial contraction. P waves are absent on the ECG and are replaced by f-waves which represent chaotic baseline activity of varying amplitude. The atrial rate is usually between 350 and 500 beats/min and the ventricular response is between 100 and 170 beats/min in the untreated patient with normal A–V conduction. The QRS complex is normal.

Physical findings include a pulse deficit, an irregular ventricular rhythm, absent 'a' waves in the jugular venous pulse and a first heart sound of varying intensity.

If atrial fibrillation results in acute haemodynamic compromise, DC cardioversion with 100–200 J should be used. Anticoagulation with warfarin is necessary prior to cardioversion to reduce the incidence of embolization in those at risk. Antiplatelet drugs may be used if warfarin is contraindicated. The main disadvantage of cardioversion is the need for general anaesthesia. In the absence of acute cardiovascular decompensation the patient should be treated with digoxin to maintain a resting ventricular rate of 60–80 beats/min. Digoxin slows anterograde conduction of impulses through the A–V node. Quinidine and procainamide can be used both to restore sinus rhythm and to maintain it. Verapamil is effective but the effect is transient and its negative inotropism may worsen borderline cardiac failure. Esmolol is effective in the peri-operative period and is likely to be additive with digoxin. Amiodarone has been used in the treatment of paroxysmal atrial fibrillation. Atrial fibrillation that is refractory to drug treatment can be controlled by surgical or radio-frequency ablation of the A–V node. These procedures are irreversible and necessitate permanent cardiac pacing.

Key references:

Andreoli TE, Bennett JC, Carpenter CCJ, Plum F, Smith Jr LH (eds). *Cecil Essentials of Medicine* 3rd ed. WB Saunders, Philadelphia 1993; 94–97.

Stoelting RK, Dierdorf SF. *Anesthesia and Co-Existing Disease* 3rd ed. Churchill Livingstone, New York 1993; 70–71.

Answers to 3.11

1. (a) Flattened T waves; ST segment depression; prominent U waves (marked with arrows); prolonged QT interval. Even with low normal serum K^+ (3.5 mmol/L) there may be a decrease in T wave amplitude and prolongation of the QT interval. A further decrease in serum K^+ results in flattened and inverted T waves, prominent U waves, depressed ST segments and large P waves. Arrhythmias commonly associated with hypokalaemia include:
- sinus, atrial and nodal tachycardia;
- ventricular extrasystoles, tachycardia and fibrillation;
- second and third degree heart block.

1. (b) Poor oral intake. Vomiting over a 3-day period can result in acute hypokalaemia due to fluid loss from the GI tract. This may be worsened by the metabolic alkalosis which will move K^+ into the intracellular space. Large amounts of K^+ can be lost from villous adenomas. This patient's hypertension may be under treatment with a diuretic resulting in a chronic component to the hypokalaemia. Consider Conn's syndrome in a person who is hypertensive, is <u>not</u> on diuretics, and has a hypokalaemic alkalosis.

2. The main electrophysiological changes are:

- Automaticity – increased;
- Duration of action potential – increased;
- Refractory period – increased;
- Resting membrane potential – increased;
- Threshold potential – increased;
- Conduction velocity – decreased.

3. Clinical features include:

- Cardiac muscle – arrhythmias.
- Skeletal muscle - weakness, hypotonia, cramps, tetany, ascending paralysis.
- Smooth muscle – constipation, ileus.
- CNS – depression, coma.

- Other – glucose intolerance, nephrogenic diabetes insipidus, metabolic alkalosis.

4. *Is the hypokalaemia acute or chronic?* The rapidity with which hypokalaemia develops is important. In chronic hypokalaemia the ratio between ICF and ECF concentrations of K^+ (40:1) is maintained, and even serum K^+ levels of 2 mmol/L may be well tolerated. Acute hypokalaemia causes arrhythmias.

What medication is the patient taking? With concurrent digoxin therapy a serum level of 3.5 mmol/L should be aimed for as hypokalaemia precipitates digoxin toxicity. Hypoxia, hypercarbia, catecholamines and anticholinergics are more likely to provoke arrhythmias intra-operatively in the presence of hypokalaemia.

Is there evidence of ischaemic heart disease? Hypokalaemia is more likely to precipitate ventricular arrhythmias in these patients.

Nature and urgency of surgery? If surgery is being undertaken to correct the cause of the hypokalaemia or is so urgent that it cannot be postponed, i.v. K^+ therapy will need to be undertaken simultaneously with the surgery. The urgency of intravenous K^+ replacement depends on the rapidity with which the hypokalaemia develops and the clinical effects and ECG changes, not necessarily on the level of serum K^+. Moderate to severe hypokalaemia (K^+ $\leq$2.9 mmol/L) with evidence of ECG changes should be treated with an i.v. infusion of K^+; the infusion rate should not normally exceed 40 mmol/h. Continuous ECG monitoring is important during treatment and serum K^+ should be measured frequently. Acute i.v. infusion of K^+ can cause cardiac standstill by altering the K^+ gradient across myocardial cell membranes.

Key references:
Wong KC, Schafer PG, Schultz JR. Hypokalemia and anesthetic implications. *Anesthesia and Analgesia* 1993; 77:1238–1260.

Miller RD (ed). *Anesthesia* 4th ed. Churchill Livingstone, New York 1994; 974–976.

Answers to 3.12

General observation of the patient may yield useful clues to underlying neurological disease that may have implications for the anaesthetist.

Observe the face:
• *Myasthenia gravis:* Facial weakness and ptosis may develop during the course of the interview and examination.
• *Cranial nerve palsies:* Squint, facial weakness or asymmetry, ptosis.
• *Epilepsy:* Pigmented papules of adenoma sebaceum suggest a diagnosis of tuberous sclerosis.
• *Parkinsonism:* Mask like facies and associated features (e.g. pill rolling tremor, bradykinesis, festinant gait). Extrapyramidal signs may be produced by drugs such as the butyrophenones and phenothiazines (anti-dopaminergic agents).
• *Myopathic facies:* Pouting lips and transverse smile.
• *Chorea:* Facial grimacing is associated with the abnormal movements.

Test higher mental function: Level of consciousness, orientation in time, place and person. Speech impediments may be discovered at this time (dysphasia, dysarthria, dysphonia).

Examine cranial nerves:
I – ability of each nostril to identify smells, not routinely tested.
II – Visual acuity; gross assessment on patient's ability to read newspaper. Visual fields; sit opposite patient, test one eye at a time with the other one covered. Check fields in all four quadrants for each eye and note field loss or sensory inattention. Ophthalmoscopy completes examination but is not routinely performed.
III, IV and VI – These nerves supply the extrinsic ocular muscles. Test for pursuit movements and nystagmus at end of range of movement. (III palsy – ptosis, eye looking down and out, large pupil; IV palsy – diplopia on looking down or in; VI palsy – diplopia on lateral gaze).

Pupils – check size, shape, symmetry, reaction to light (direct and consensual) and accommodation.
V – Test sensation in all three areas of distribution. Test corneal reflex. Motor palsy results in wasting of the muscles of mastication. Jaw deviates to side of lesion on opening mouth.
VII – Ask patient to show teeth and raise eyebrows. Palsy causes facial weakness and drooping; LMN lesion affects whole of one side of face, UMN lesion usually affects lower 2/3rds only.
VIII – Test by blocking one ear, and asking patient to repeat number whispered in the other.
IX, X – Gag reflex. Ask patient to say 'Ah' and observe uvula – it deviates to the normal side, if there is a lesion of the Xth nerve.
XI – Test the trapezius and sternomastoid muscles against resistance.
XII – Observe tongue for atrophy and fibrillation. It protrudes to the side of the lesion, on extrusion.

Motor system: Test tone, power and reflexes in both upper and lower limbs. Co-ordination can be tested using the finger–nose and heel–shin tests. Observe muscle wasting, abnormal posture, gait and movements.

Sensory system: Test for light touch, pinprick and proprioception.

Miscellaneous: Delayed relaxation of grip on initial handshake is characteristic of dystrophia myotonica. Romberg's sign is +ve in sensory ataxia (balance is worse on shutting eyes). Test for neck stiffness.

Key references:

Munro J, Edwards C (eds). *Macleod's Clinical Examination* 8th ed. Churchill Livingstone, Edinburgh 1990; 187–254.

Hope RA, Longmore JM, Hodgetts TJ, Ramrakha PS. *Oxford Handbook of Clinical Medicine* 3rd ed. Oxford University Press, Oxford 1993; 32–33.

OSCE cycle 4 – answers

Answers to 4.1

1. Sickle cell disease should be excluded. This includes the homozygous (HbSS) sickle cell anaemia (SCA) and the heterozygous (HbAS) sickle cell trait (SCT). Although commonest in black Africans this genetically determined haemoglobinopathy can occur in other ethnic groups and Caucasians. When sickle cell haemoglobin (HbS) is deoxygenated it starts to polymerize and after a delay forms a gel that is insoluble. This process is enhanced by acidity, hypothermia, infection, low 2,3-DPG levels, high % HbS and a high mean corpuscular haemoglobin concentration (MCHC). It is inhibited by the presence of other haemoglobins e.g. foetal HbF, which is present up to six months of age. Polymerization occurs at differing levels of hypoxia that are dependent on these factors and causes the red blood cells to become sickle shaped. The homozygous state, SCA, is symptomatic as sickling starts at a PaO_2 of 40 mmHg which occurs in normal venous blood. The severity of SCA varies from mild rare crises to those needing 40 admissions a year or childhood death. In the heterozygous state, SCT, sickling only occurs below a PaO_2 of 30 mmHg so symptoms only occur under severe physiological stress. Sickling causes an increase in blood viscosity resulting in vessel occlusion and infarction of potentially all tissues. The severe ischaemic pain produced by these vaso-occlusive crises contrasts with the minimal clinical findings. HbS releases oxygen to the tissues more easily so between crises these patients feel well. The life span of sickle cells may be reduced by 85% (normal is 120 days) due to increased fragility. The haemolytic anaemia that results may cause hepatomegaly, jaundice or frontal bossing. Outside daytime hours a sickle solubility test will show the presence of HbS in patients over 2 years of age: a reductant, e.g. sodium metabisulphite causes blood with HbS to become turbid or show sickling under microscopy. This does not distinguish SCA from SCT. In SCA the Hb concentration is usually 6 – 8 g/dL and the reticulocyte count is 10 – 20%. In SCT the Hb concentration and the film are normal. During daytime hours the definitive diagnosis can be made by Hb electrophoresis.

2. The aims of anaesthesia in SCA are to prevent sickling and to monitor and treat complications over the whole peri-operative period. Patients with SCT are less susceptible to sickling but should be treated similarly:

- avoid hypoxia, acidosis and hypothermia;
- ensure hydration as this decreases MCHC; hyponatraemia may reduce sickling;
- maintain cardiac output and avoid stasis, e.g. due to aortocaval compression or positioning of the patient; if a tourniquet is absolutely necessary then exsanguinate the limb fully and minimize the duration;
- peri-operative analgesia and oxygen;
- consider antibiotic cover and transfusion.

3. Complications of SCA include:

- *Lungs:* pulmonary infarcts can result in ARDS or pulmonary hypertension and cor pulmonale.
- *Kidneys:* papillary necrosis and tubular acidosis can cause hyposthenuria (inability to concentrate urine); this predisposes to dehydration and impaired excretion of alkaline compounds, e.g. norpethidine.
- *Spleen:* multiple infarcts cause regression (auto-splenectomy), making these patients susceptible to streptococcal and *Haemophilus influenzae* infections, so prophylactic penicillin and vaccines are given. Sequestration of blood into both the spleen and liver can cause sudden hypovolaemic shock, severe anaemia and possible death.

Key reference:

Esseltine DW. Sickle cell states and the anaesthetist. *Canadian Journal of Anaesthesia* 1988; **35**:385–403.

Answers to 4.2

1. Graves' disease or thyrotoxicosis. Eye signs are caused by infiltration of the orbital contents outside the globe and include:

- Exophthalmos – forward displacement of the eyeball. While staring forwards the sclera is visible above the lower eyelid. The eyeball is visible anterior to the orbital margin when looked at from directly above the patient.
- Lid retraction – sclera visible below upper eyelid.
- Lid lag – on following your finger slowly downward the upper lid lags behind the eyeball.
- Ophthalmoplegia – especially diplopia on upward gaze.
- Conjunctival injection and oedema.

2. Cardiovascular complications include:

- sinus tachycardia even during sleep;
- atrial fibrillation diagnosed clinically by an irregularly irregular pulse and on the ECG by an absence of P waves. This is best seen in lead II as irregularly spaced QRS complexes in the rhythm strip;
- congestive cardiac failure due to a hyperdynamic circulation secondary to the increased metabolic rate.

3. Airway complications include:

- tracheal deviation diagnosed clinically by gently placing one's finger in the suprasternal notch or from a plain chest X-ray;
- stridor due to tracheal compression or laryngeal nerve palsy;
- retrosternal goitre which may require thoracotomy, and may be shown by a Valsalva manoeuvre or thoracic inlet chest X-ray.

4. Hot, moist palms, tremor, nervous facies, tachycardia, atrial fibrillation, thyroid bruit, rapid ankle reflex, lid lag and lid retraction.

Eye signs usually persist after treatment and do not correlate well with the other clinical and biochemical assessments of thyroid activity.

5. Thiouracils, e.g. carbimazole, block the synthesis of thyroxine, start to work in one hour but take 4–8 weeks to make the patient euthyroid. Oral iodine works immediately, inhibiting the release of thyroxine, and reduces the thyroid size and vascularity. Its effect diminishes after 14 days so it should only be started a week preoperatively. Thyroxine increases the number of ß-adrenoreceptors on the myocardium, which becomes more sensitive to catecholamines. ß-blockers have no effect on thyroxine production but will stop the catecholamine-mediated symptoms.

6. Thyrotoxic crisis or storm.

Notes on thyrotoxicosis

It is important to recognize undiagnosed and undertreated thyrotoxicosis as any acute medical intervention or trauma may precipitate thyrotoxic crisis. Thyrotoxicosis may present as irritability, heat intolerance, weight loss despite increased appetite, diarrhoea, exertional dyspnoea, palpitations or fatigue. It may be misdiagnosed as anxiety, depression or cardiac failure. The signs and symptoms may be less florid in the elderly or masked by ß-blockers. Thyroxine increases metabolic rate, oxygen consumption, carbon dioxide and heat production, leading to vasodilatation, tachycardia and an increased cardiac output. Elective surgery should be cancelled until the patient is euthyroid. Urgent surgery should be delayed until some control of the metabolic state has been initiated.

Key reference:

Vickers MD, Jones RM (eds). *Medicine for Anaesthetists* 3rd ed. Blackwell Scientific Publications 1989; Ch. 13.

Answers to 4.3

1. Frontal chest radiograph taken in expiration, showing right-sided tension pneumothorax. Note flattened right hemidiaphragm and mediastinal shift to the left side.

2. The tension pneumothorax has to be relieved immediately to prevent further respiratory and haemodynamic embarrassment. A wide bore (14 gauge) intravenous cannula should be inserted into the pleural space, preferably through the 2nd intercostal space in the mid-clavicular line on the affected side. A three-way tap and syringe system can then be attached to the cannula to allow aspiration of air and to promote re-expansion of the collapsed lung. This should be followed by insertion of a standard chest drain.

3. Maintain strict asepsis. Choose the 5th or 6th intercostal space and enter the pleural space in the mid-axillary line. Generous infiltration with lignocaine 1% makes the procedure more tolerable for the patient and easier for the operator. A chest drain with a minimum internal diameter of 6 mm (26 FG) is required to drain a pneumothorax effectively. Make the incision above the lower rib of the chosen intercostal space. This avoids damage to the neurovascular bundle which runs inferior to its corresponding rib in the subcostal groove. Clear the pleural space by sweeping the index finger within it. Ensure the lung is not adherent to the thoracic wall. Insert the chest drain having withdrawn the trocar. Do not push the chest drain with trocar in place blindly into the chest. Connect the chest drain to the underwater seal drainage system and ensure that the system is working. Use a purse string suture which helps to seal the hole in the chest wall when the chest drain is removed. Request another chest radiograph and ensure that the end hole and side holes of the drain are within the pleural space (PVC pleural drains have a radio-opaque stripe). If re-expansion of the lung is incomplete, negative pressure of up to – 20 cmH$_2$O may be applied to the underwater seal drainage system.

4. Drainage of fluid collections in the pleural space: effusions, empyema, haemothoraces. Management of bronchopleural fistulae.
Pre-operatively: prior to anaesthesia and positive pressure ventilation in patients with multiple fractured ribs even when no significant pneumothorax is diagnosed initially.
Post-operatively: post-thoracotomy.

5. Complications include infection (empyema), haemorrhage from damage to intercostal blood vessels, subcutaneous emphysema, and injuries to the heart, lungs, diaphragm and sometimes even to intra-abdominal viscera. Intra-abdominal or extra-pleural placement of chest drains is potentially fatal.

Notes
Apical drains allow drainage of air and basal drains allow drainage of fluid with the patient sitting up. Milking or stripping of pleural drains with rollers can be used to clear obstructions and create a negative pressure within the tubing. The use of these techniques is controversial and may generate large negative pressures which could result in lung trauma. When a chest drain is being removed, the patient must be instructed to perform a Valsalva manoeuvre, the purse string suture must be pulled tight and a sterile occlusive dressing applied over the area. This will help prevent the pneumothorax recurring.

The loss of lung volume due to pneumothorax predicted on the basis of an anteroposterior chest X-ray will be an underestimate because of the cylindrical shape of the pleural cavity.

Key references:
Kam AC, O'Brien M, Kam PAC. Pleural drainage systems. *Anaesthesia* 1993; 48:154–161.

Andreoli TE, Bennett JC, Carpenter CCJ, Plum F, Smith Jr LH (eds). *Cecil Essentials of Medicine* 3rd ed. WB Saunders, Philadelphia 1993;173–174.

Answers to 4.4

1. A pulse oximeter reading of 97% and consciousness does not exclude cyanide (CN) or carbon monoxide (CO) poisoning. Give 100% oxygen until these are excluded. Remove clothing and contaminated material as hot plastic may continue to burn the skin.

2. Inhalation injury is clinically significant damage to the airway or lungs caused by hot or noxious gases or smoke. This may include direct thermal damage, smoke inhalation or systemic CO or CN toxicity. Thermal damage is supraglottic as the upper airway is designed for heating inspired air and dissipates the heat efficiently. The exception is pressurized steam as this has the thermal capacity to transmit heat distal to the cords. The first clinical examination, chest X-ray and arterial blood gases may be normal. Clinical demise may occur more than 24 hours later when airway oedema becomes maximal. If there is CO or CN poisoning tachypnoea may not occur as the carotid bodies respond more to the PaO_2 than the arterial oxygen content. If any of these signs are initially abnormal it suggests significant inhalational injury. There should be a high index of suspicion if there:

- is a history of impaired consciousness or the fire was in an enclosed space;
- are oropharyngeal inflammation or deposits of soot or carbonaceous sputum;
- is burnt nasal hair and eyebrows;
- are facial burns especially lips and nose;
- is stridor or clinical signs of respiratory distress.

Initial management is chiefly supportive and should be proactive and comprehensive. The need to intubate is a clinical decision based on the initial assessment of the respiratory status, the damage to the airway and the likelihood of further deterioration. Some patients will die at the scene. 50% of those reaching hospital with inhalation injury will require intubation and the rest careful monitoring for 48 hours.

3. Endotracheal intubation ensures a safe airway. If delayed, it may be more difficult due to increasing airway oedema. It facilitates the basic treatment of inhalational injury by:

- warmed, humidified, 100% oxygen with IPPV and PEEP to minimize atelectasis;
- physiotherapy with tracheobronchial toilet;
- desloughing of dead bronchial mucosa.

Other injuries, burns and sepsis predispose to ARDS and should be treated aggressively. CO and CN poisoning should be treated. Routine antibiotics and steroids are not indicated.

4. Beneficial uses of the fibreoptic bronchoscope in inhalational injury include the assessment of the extent and severity of the airway and lung injury, the therapeutic desloughing of dead bronchial mucosa and the facilitation of a difficult intubation.

5. Cyanide causes non-specific symptoms and signs due to tissue hypoxia. Serum analysis of cyanide levels is slow. The following should make one suspicious of cyanide poisoning:

- normal PaO_2, metabolic acidosis, high blood lactate and mixed venous oxygen saturation >75%;
- decrease in the pulse oximeter saturation reading due to cyanohaemoglobin;
- anion gap >12 μmol/L.

Drug treatment of cyanide poisoning includes amyl nitrite, sodium nitrite and sodium thiosulphate. Dicobalt edetate is toxic and only recommended in severe poisoning.

Key reference:

Langford RM, Armstrong RF. Algorithm for managing injury from smoke inhalation. *British Medical Journal* 1990; **299**:902–905.

Answers to 4.5

1. Trainees should practise difficult intubation by intentionally malpositioning the patient, the laryngoscope or cricoid pressure to produce a grade 3 or 4 laryngoscopy. The gum elastic bougie (GEB) should be available for every anaesthetic. On insertion into the trachea one can often detect a bumping sensation as the tip of the GEB catches on the tracheal rings. It should lodge in a tertiary bronchus. If it continues to pass caudally it is assumed to be in the oesophagus and should be removed. Successful intubation is more likely if the laryngoscope is kept in position and the tracheal tube is rotated anticlockwise through 90°, i.e. with the tip lying anteriorly.

2. The Combitube airway is a double lumen tube with two cuffs. One cuff inflates in the oropharynx to secure the tube. The other cuff, which is distal, inflates in and seals the oesophagus or the trachea. The shorter (tracheal) channel is open at the distal tip. The longer (oesophageal) channel is closed at the distal tip but has side holes in its middle 'pharyngeal' portion. The tube may be introduced blindly and then the cuffs inflated ($\approx$100 mL in the proximal and $\approx$15 mL in the distal). If ventilation through the shorter tracheal channel shows this to be sited in the trachea then ventilation can continue as with a standard tube. If there is gastric bubbling and axillary breath sounds are absent the distal tip is sited in the oesophagus. The patient should then be ventilated through the longer oesophageal channel (via its pharyngeal holes) and the tracheal channel should be used to aspirate gastric content.

3. Various light wands have been developed and may be successful in 98% of cases. They consist of a malleable intubating stylet with a handle and a distal end that illuminates. The tracheal tube is mounted over the stylet which is angulated anteriorly through 90° at its distal end. It is inserted orally and the room lights are dimmed. When the light is seen in the larynx the tracheal tube is released and slipped over the stylet into the trachea. False positives occur in children and adults with thin necks as the light can shine through the oesophagus and trachea. False negatives may occur in patients with thick necks, scarring or tumours.

4. If cricoid pressure is not used, there is a 90% success rate of blind intubation when a 6 mm cuffed tube is passed through a size 3 or 4 laryngeal mask airway (56% with cricoid pressure). A GEB can also be inserted through a laryngeal mask airway (LMA) which is then removed and a larger tracheal tube sited. A longitudinally split LMA has been described. This can guide a fibreoptic bronchoscope (loaded with a tracheal tube) and then be removed, allowing intubation.

5. Tests which help confirm correct siting of a tracheal tube include:

- observing the tube pass between the glottis or anterior to the arytenoid cartilages, seeing bilateral chest expansion (may be absent in ankylosing spondylitis) or exhaled water condensing in the tube;
- auscultation of breath sounds in both axillae and the absence of gastric bubbling;
- continual presence of CO_2 in the exhaled gas detected by capnography or devices which show a change in colour;
- fibreoptic endoscopy;
- marked improvement in oxygen saturation following ventilation;
- Wee oesophageal detector device (1988);
- adequate movement of the reservoir bag with spontaneous ventilation.

Key reference:

Benumof JL. Management of the difficult adult airway. *Anesthesiology* 1991; **75**:1087–1110.

Answers to 4.6

1. (a) Train of four stimulation (TOF).
   (b) Post-tetanic count (PTC).
   (c) Double burst stimulation (DBS$_{3,3}$).

2. TOF does not require a control value or a measuring device. In order to assess the depression of first twitch (T1%) compared to the pre-relaxant control anaesthetists would have to remember their manual or visual assessment of this control. Therefore to assess T1% a measuring device, e.g. a mechanomyograph or electromyograph, is necessary. The TOF stimulus allows assessment of neuromuscular blockade (NMB) by counting the number of twitches detectable either visually or manually (TOF count) and by the value of the fourth response divided by that of the first response (TOF ratio). There is a correlation between the TOF count and TOF ratio and T1% (*see* Table 4.6) although there may be some variation between muscle relaxants.

3. Each stimulus is:

- 0.2 ms duration and of square waveform to prevent repetitive firing of the nerve
- of supramaximal intensity, i.e. of a current greater than that necessary to achieve the maximum muscle effect. This ensures all muscle fibres are always recruited.

The TOF stimuli have intervals of 500 ms (2 Hz) to ensure that the muscle will have recovered its pre-contracted physical state and the responses are detectable as separate twitches. This is slow enough to prevent transmitter facilitation and fast enough to produce significant depletion of the immediately available acetylcholine store. Four stimuli are used because during NMB, stimulation at 2 Hz causes maximum fade at the fourth response, further responses being equal or greater than the fourth. Fade is present if the TOF ratio is less than one.

Table 4.6 Correlation of clinical signs and degree of NMB as assessed by ulnar *n*. stimulation.

T1 %	TOF %	No. of twitches	Clinical correlation
100	100	4	Normal
100	95	4	Normal
95	75	4	Head lifting sustained for 5 s Adequate ventilation, cough and maintenance of airway
35	low	4	Inadequate tidal volume and maintenance of airway
25	0	3	Poor surgical abdominal relaxation
20	0	2	Abdominal relaxation with volatiles
10	0	1	Abdominal relaxation without volatiles
5	0	0	Jaw/larynx paralysed, ideal for intubation
0	0	0	Diaphragmatic movement possible

4. PTC is used when the degree of NMB is so deep that there is no response to the TOF stimulation. The interval following the 5 s 50 Hz tetanus is three seconds as this maximizes the post-tetanic facilitation. The number of twitches detected during the following 1 Hz stimulation is inversely related to the interval until the first response of TOF stimulation becomes detectable. This interval varies between muscle relaxants. The duration and intensity of NMB shows great variation between patients and with temperature, pH, PaCO$_2$, renal and hepatic function and electrolyte status. The aims of NMB monitoring include optimal surgical relaxation and safe recovery after the anaesthetic. During surgery the TOF count is adequate to assess if more relaxant is necessary and if neuromuscular recovery is sufficient to give reversal agents. The ability to adequately reverse NMB depends on the degree of NMB when the reversal agents are given.

Key reference

Beemer GH. *Baillière's Clinical Anaesthesiology* 1994; **8** (2):395–416.

Answers to 4.7

1. The illustration shows a 'Ciaglia' percutaneous dilational tracheostomy (PDT) kit (Cook Critical Care) with a standard Portex tracheostomy tube (TT). This may be performed under local or general anaesthesia. A separate anaesthetist should be responsible for monitoring, analgesia and the upper airway. The indications for PDT are the same as for standard surgical tracheostomy and include:

- long term airway control for respiratory failure patients who are difficult to wean and those with a reduced ability to protect their airway, e.g. post head injury;
- post upper airway surgery;
- acute upper airway obstruction; PDT is not ideal as cricothyroid puncture and cricothyrotomy are quicker, easier and have less complications.

Relative contraindications of DPT include large goitre, obesity, malignant infiltration, coagulopathy and age below 16 years.

2. The trachea has 16 to 20 C-shaped rings. It starts at the cricoid cartilage (C6) and passes posteriorly to end at the carina at the level of the angle of Louis (T4 in the cadaver but T5 to T6 in a live adult). About one third lies above the sternal notch. The thyroid isthmus lies over the 2nd to 4th tracheal rings.

3. 100% oxygen is given and the tracheal tube retracted into the larynx. Skin infiltration with local anaesthetic and adrenaline reduces oozing during the procedure. A transverse 2 cm skin incision is made half-way between the cricoid ring and the sternal notch. The pretracheal fascia, which invests the strap muscles, is bluntly dissected. A needle and cannula is then inserted between the first and second tracheal rings. It is directed at 90° to the axis of the trachea to prevent it entering below this level and damaging the thyroid isthmus. If the space above is used the cricoid may be damaged and lead to subglottic stenosis. Aspiration of air confirms airway entry and tracheal tube movement checks the needle hasn't transfixed it. A guide wire is inserted and successive dilators up to 36FG are passed over a guiding catheter. Finally, the TT is mounted on one of the smaller dilators and inserted. The cuff is inflated to 20 mmHg.

4. Early complications include:

- bleeding from thyroid veins and the communicating veins between the anterior jugular veins;
- misplacement or obstruction of the TT;
- extubation;
- oesophageal ulceration and perforation;
- pneumothorax;
- infection of the stoma (15%);
- cardiovascular collapse if the patient has hypercarbia that is rapidly reversed.

5. The advantages of this technique over the standard surgical technique include the following: it is quicker; a surgeon is not required; there is less bleeding as the tube has a tamponade effect on the relatively small tissue opening; it can be done at the bedside so the risks and expense of going to theatre are reduced.

6. The track is usually formed by 5 days. Prior to this there may be some difficulty replacing the TT if it falls out. The standard TT can be replaced by others including:

- plastic TT with port for suctioning above its cuff; this can also be used for speaking by instilling oxygen down the suction tube;
- uncuffed silver tube (sizes 28–34) which can have a valved inner tube for speaking;
- fenestrated uncuffed speaking tube.

Key reference:

Manara AR. Percutaneous tracheostomy. *Current Anaesthesia and Intensive Care* 1994; 4:41–46.

Answers to 4.8

1. (a) Infantile pyloric stenosis.
1. (b) Ramstedt's operation (pyloromyotomy).

2. Waves of peristalsis can be observed moving across the upper abdomen when the infant sucks and an olive-shaped mass is palpable in the epigastrium. There usually is weight loss, and dehydration as evidenced by reduced skin turgor, sunken eyeballs, depressed fontanelles, dry mucous membranes and a decrease in the urine output. The blood pressure may be low and the pulse fast and thready. Jaundice is seen in 2% of the cases.

3. (a) The metabolic consequences include dehydration, hypokalemia, hypochloraemia, metabolic alkalaemia and a paradoxical aciduria. The haemoconcentration reflects dehydration.
3. (b) Emergency resuscitation of the infant is a priority. Surgical treatment is not an emergency.

4. The volume deficit, metabolic derangements and acid–base imbalance should be corrected prior to surgery. A bolus of 20 mL/kg of 0.9% saline can be administered initially whilst further fluid administration is titrated against the level of hydration, haemodynamic parameters and urine output. Potassium supplementation (daily requirement = 3 mmol/kg/day) is usually necessary once urine output is established. Surgery can be safely undertaken after haemodynamic stability has been restored and pH = 7.3 – 7.5, Na^+ >135 mmol/L, Cl^- >90 mmol/L and HCO_3^- <30 mmol/L.

5. Ensure that resuscitation is adequate before administering anaesthesia. Monitoring should include non-invasive blood pressure, electrocardiograph, pulse oximeter, precordial stethoscope and a peripheral temperature probe. A nasogastric tube is usually in place and this should be aspirated. Pre-oxygenation is achieved via a facemask. Atropine in a dose of 20 μg/kg may be given prior to induction of anaesthesia. The choices for tracheal intubation in this case are controlled rapid sequence induction with cricoid pressure, gaseous induction (e.g. oxygen and halothane) or awake intubation.

Additional notes

1. Pyloric stenosis results from a combination of hypertrophy of the pyloric smooth muscle and mucosal oedema. It is seven times commoner in boys, and presentation is usually between 2 and 6 weeks with regurgitation and nonbilious projectile vomiting, resulting from gastric dilatation and delayed gastric emptying. Pyloromyotomy involves dividing the pyloric muscle along its entire length until the mucosa protrudes into the incision.

3. H^+, Cl^-, Na^+ and K^+ are lost in considerable amounts during vomiting. Initially serum pH is defended by excretion of alkaline urine that contains Na^+ and K^+. When Na^+ and Cl^- are depleted, ECF volume is defended over pH. Thus Na^+ and Cl^- are retained by the kidney and H^+ is lost resulting in paradoxical aciduria. This worsens the existing alkalaemia.

5. In addition to the special considerations necessary for neonatal anaesthesia it must be remembered that there is a potential danger of vomiting and aspiration during induction of anaesthesia and tracheal intubation.

Key references:

Steward DJ. *Manual of Pediatric Anesthesia* 3rd ed. Churchill Livingstone, New York 1990; 229–231.

Stehling L (ed). *Common Problems in Pediatric Anesthesia* 2nd ed. Mosby-Year Book Inc., St. Louis, Missouri 1992; 73–77.

Answers to 4.9

1. Ventricular tachycardia (VT).

2. Pre-existing cardiac disease (ischaemic heart disease, valvular heart disease, congestive and hypertrophic cardiomyopathy, primary electrical disease), electrolyte disorders (poor renal function, hyperkalaemia), intra-operative hypoxia, hypotension, hypercarbia and acidaemia, injection of adrenaline-containing local anaesthetic as part of surgical technique, effect of isoflurane on catecholamine sensitized myocardium, undetected hypermetabolic states (hyperthyroidism, phaeochromocytoma, malignant hyperpyrexia).

3. Rapidly assess airway, breathing and circulation.
If laryngeal mask airway position is unsatisfactory, secure airway by other means.
Administer 100% O_2 with intermittent positive pressure ventilation.
Ask surgeon to stop operating, discontinue anaesthesia.
If carotid pulse is absent, deliver precordial thump – this is a monitored cardiac arrest.

4. Pulseless VT is treated as ventricular fibrillation. The ERC 1992 guidelines recommend three consecutive d.c. shocks at 200 J, 200 J and 360 J. Having secured the airway and vascular access, adrenaline 1 mg i.v. is given. Basic life support must be continued (5:1= compressions:ventilation, two operators) for 10 sequences followed by a further series of three shocks, each at 360 J. Adrenaline 1 mg i.v. is given every 2–3 minutes to increase the efficacy of basic life support which should not be interrupted for more than 10 s except for defibrillation. After three cycles of three shocks each, other drugs may be considered. $NaHCO_3$ (50 mmol or calculated from base deficit of arterial blood) to correct acidosis, and lignocaine, amiodarone or bretylium may be tried in this dire situation. Calcium, magnesium or potassium salts may be useful in specific circumstances.

Notes

1. Wide complex tachycardias (WCT) may also result from supraventricular tachycardias (SVT) with aberrant intraventricular conduction or pre-existing bundle branch block. Making the distinction can be difficult and if the patient is symptomatic it is more important to treat than to make an ECG diagnosis. The commonest cause of WCT, particularly in patients with underlying heart disease, is VT, which is potentially life threatening.

In VT, the rate is usually between 100 and 200/min and the rhythm regular unless it is paroxysmal: P waves are absent or there is complete a–v dissociation. The QRS complex is wider than 0.12 s. Diagnostic criteria include fusion beats (ventricular depolarization from two different foci, usually an atrial impulse depolarizing the ventricle that is already partially depolarized by a ventricular ectopic), capture beats (resumption of atrial control of ventricular depolarization producing a normal QRS complex in the midst of a–v dissociation), changes in axis (*torsades de pointes*) and concordance (all the V leads have similar vectors), all of which are absent in SVT with aberrant conduction. Other causes of WCT include pre-excitation syndromes, hyperkalaemia, drugs (e.g. procainamide) and ventricular pacing.

3. If a pulse is present, d.c. cardioversion with a stepwise increase in energy (50 J, 100 J, 200 J, 360 J) should be tried. Further cardioversion after antiarrhythmic drug therapy may be required. Adenosine i.v. is a useful diagnostic tool that may help distinguish this rhythm from a SVT.

Key reference:

Advanced Life Support Working Party of the European Resuscitation Council. Guidelines for advanced life support. *Resuscitation* 1992; **24**:111–121.

Answers to 4.10

Two thirds of normal healthy parturients suffer severe or intolerable pain during labour. There have been many recent advances in the techniques available for pain relief during labour. It is important that pregnant women are educated about the different options available to them to enable them to make an informed choice regarding technique of analgesia. Advice should be honest and unbiased and take into consideration special maternal or foetal needs (e.g. maternal disease with implications for anaesthesia/foetal malpresentation).

Analgesic techniques available include:

- Nonpharmacological techniques: hypnosis; psychoprophylaxis; relaxation and breathing techniques; transcutaneous electric nerve stimulation (TENS).
- Inhalational analgesia: Entonox
- Parenteral opioids: intramuscular (mainly pethidine), intrathecal and patient controlled i.v. analgesia.

Epidural analgesia: Explain the technique in lay language and ensure that the parturient understands that co-operation from her is important during the siting of the epidural. Cover the technical details briefly: insertion of intravenous drip, positioning, the need for asepsis, the need for the parturient to remain still during the procedure. Reassure her that the procedure will in most instances be carried out in the interval between contractions and that local anaesthetic infiltration will precede insertion of the epidural needle. Inform the parturient that a catheter will be sited in the epidural space to allow the administration of analgesia throughout the period of labour.

Advantages of epidural anaesthesia:
Epidural analgesia produces labour during which the mother is able to feel the uterine contractions and the delivery of her baby without pain. Refinements include epidural infusions with low concentrations of LA ± opioids and patient controlled epidural analgesia (PCEA). Epidural analgesia improves the conditions for assessing the progress of labour by vaginal examination and foetal blood sampling.

Obstetric manipulations and assisted delivery (e.g. forceps, ventouse) can be carried out with the full co-operation of the mother. If necessary, a Caesarean section can be performed under an extended epidural block.

Elimination of pain will reduce the hyper-hypoventilation cycle and restore maternal PaO_2 and $PaCO_2$ to normal. It decreases catecholamine release and minimizes maternal and foetal acidosis resulting in an increase in uterine blood flow and foetal oxygenation. It avoids the side effects of systemic opioid analgesia, particularly neonatal respiratory depression and delayed gastric emptying and reduced barrier pressure in the mother.

Value in special circumstances: Foetal Apgar scores are improved and perinatal mortality reduced by the use of epidural analgesia for breech delivery. In PET, complete pain relief is provided, preventing further rises in blood pressure and improving renal blood flow. With maternal cardiac and respiratory disease, pregnancy increases demands, and an epidural facilitates a controlled instrumental delivery.

Potential disadvantages:

- Incomplete analgesia due to anatomical or technical difficulties.
- Post-dural puncture headache.
- Hypotension and consequences for the foetus.
- Motor block, urinary retention, shivering.
- Prolonged second stage of labour.
- Higher rate of instrumental delivery.
- Backache (partly due to abnormal postures).

Key references:
Crowhurst JA. Analgesia for labour. *Current Opinion in Anaesthesiology* 1994; 7:224–230.

Reynolds F. Epidural analgesia in obstetrics. *British Medical Journal* 1989; **299**:751–752.

Answers to 4.11

1. Reflex sympathetic dystrophy (RSD) is a spectrum of painful limb disorders in which a combination of sympathetic, sensory and motor dysfunction occurs following tissue damage. The distribution of pain in RSD is usually diffuse and not localized to the area of damage, or to a specific dermatome if nerve damage is involved. Sympathetic function can be hyper- or hypoactive and this may vary over time. RSD may start within a week of injury and progress to osteoporosis and muscle atrophy (Sudek's atrophy). The affected limb should be compared with the contralateral side. Symptoms and signs of RSD include:

- skin pallor, sweating, goose-flesh and altered temperature in the affected part;
- *limb tremor, swelling and stiffness:* this may be exacerbated by immobilization used to try to reduce the pain;
- *allodynia:* stimuli that are normally non-painful cause pain;
- *hyperalgesia:* stimuli that are normally painful cause severe pain;
- *hyperpathia:* minor repetitive cutaneous stimuli are perceived initially as an abnormal dull sensation but after a delay an excruciating pain develops;
- *hyperaesthesia:* extreme hypersensitivity to cutaneous stimulation.

2. The rôle of the sympathetic nervous system in pain is complex. For example, sympathetic efferents modulate transmission in afferent pain neurones. Therapeutic sympathetic blockade by drugs or surgery works in more ways than just vasodilatation. The effects of guanethidine are similarly complex. It appears to be a false transmitter with a biphasic effect. Initially it displaces noradrenaline (NA) from its storage sites in sympathetic nerve endings and then it stops NA re-uptake into those sites. However, in dentistry the analgesic effect of guanethidine on dentinal pain does not involve NA pathways or local anaesthesia. When used in high doses in intravenous regional (IVR) blocks it may inhibit the axonal movement of nerve growth factor, causing axonal regression. The initial release of NA may cause vasoconstriction or an increase in pain. This may compromise the viability of an ischaemic limb or be excruciating if a patient is already in extreme pain. The initial dose of guanethidine should therefore be small and these effects may be offset by combining the guanethidine with:

- a local anaesthetic;
      or
- an α-adrenergic blocker, e.g. phentolamine.

As guanethidine replaces the NA and stops its re-uptake, further doses of guanethidine do not cause further release of NA or more pain.

3. Initially, systemic release of NA may cause hypertension followed by postural hypotension due to dilatation of venous capacitance vessels and myocardial depression. This should initially be treated by ensuring that the patient is supine, raising the legs and giving i.v. fluids. Postsynaptic NA receptors will be hypersensitive to exogenous catecholamine vasoconstrictors so if these are necessary the dose should be reduced. Guanethidine is a quaternary amine so it does not cross the blood brain barrier. Reserpine, a similar drug, can be used for IVR sympathetic block but is a tertiary amine and so can cause mental depression with repeated doses.

4. Even if the first block is not beneficial it should be repeated as the effect is cumulative. Treatment of RSD in this scenario includes active physiotherapy and not immobilization.

Key reference:

Wall PD, Melzack R (eds). *Textbook of Pain* 3rd ed. Churchill Livingstone, New York, 1994; 1035–1052.

Answers to 4.12

1. Fibreoptic bronchoscope (FOB). The specifications of FOBs vary. The one shown is an intubating FOB. These tend to be thinner and longer than diagnostic bronchoscopes. Intubating FOBs have external diameters from 6 mm down to 2.7 mm which allows intubation with a 3 mm ID tracheal tube. They are about 60 cm long and have a depth of focus of about 3 – 50 mm. The shaft contains:

- two fibreoptic channels: one transmits the image and the other a strong light source. The fibres are arranged in bundles called guides. Each fibre has a diameter of about 10 – 20 µm;
- anterior and posterior longitudinal wires to control movement of the distal tip;
- suction channel of about 1 – 2 mm.

2. The lever on the handle is attached to the longitudinal wires that control movement of the distal 2 cm of the scope. This tip can only move in one plane. The lever is labelled for this up or down movement of the tip which is usually limited to 90°–120° each way. The image has a black peripheral notch which indicates the anterior or 'up' direction. The scope is manoeuvred using this control lever, axial rotation of the whole scope and protrusion and retraction of the whole scope. The scope should be flexible enough to go around corners but rigid enough to allow control of movement.

3. Before using the FOB one should check:

- the aspiration channel is patent: inject with a syringe or aspirate with suction tubing;
- the light source and its channel: connect to source and shine the tip at a surface;
- the lens and viewing channel: direct it at some printed letter and examine the image's focus, brightness and whether it is fogged;
- the tip responds to the lever control on the handle.

4. Delivering oxygen down the FOB reduces hypoxic episodes and can help to disperse secretions and prevent fogging of the lens. However, inflation of the stomach occurs if the scope enters the oesophagus. Barotrauma may occur if, when the trachea is intubated, the FOB occludes the tracheal tube. Other uses of this channel include the following:

- aspiration of secretions, blood;
- instilling saline to disperse secretions;
- passage of flexible biopsy forceps;
- spraying local anaesthetic in the 'spray as you go' technique;
- a guide wire can be inserted retrogradely from the larynx out of the mouth or nose and then up this channel. If the FOB is loaded with a tracheal tube this can then be inserted in the trachea.

5. The image may be unrecognizable due to fogging, secretions or the tip abutting onto mucosa in the oesophagus or one of the piriform fossae. Blowing oxygen or sucking via the suction channel or manipulating the tip may help. Reducing the room lighting may show the tip's position. If no better, the FOB should be withdrawn until the anatomy is recognized. The distal lens surface can be cleaned and defogged by wiping with a dry cloth, using a hydrophobic agent, e.g. silicone spray, or warming the tip in warm soapy water.

6. Between patients the FOB should be decontaminated, immersed in water to check for leaks and then immersed in 2% glutaraldehyde for 15–20 minutes. Oxygen is then blown through it and it is suspended to dry. A leak will allow glutaraldehyde to infiltrate the outer casing and damage the fibres.

Key reference:

Morris IR. Fibreoptic intubation. *Canadian Journal of Anaesthesia* 1994; **41**:996–1008.

OSCE cycle 5 – answers

Answers to 5.1

1. A = inspiratory phase.
   B = expiratory phase.
   C = upstroke reflecting mixture of anatomical deadspace and alveolar gas.
   D = alveolar plateau representing mainly alveolar gas with some alveolar dead-space gas from underperfused alveoli
   E = end-tidal PCO_2.

2. Sidestream analysers are affected by measuring delays and loss of gas, and the tiny sampling tubes are prone to occlusion. Mainstream analysers have a faster response time but are cumbersome to use, and susceptible to damage and contamination with secretions.

3. A sudden and sustained decrease in the end-tidal CO_2 concentration is a highly sensitive and specific indicator of pulmonary gas embolism. Low output circulatory failure, hypothermia and excessive mechanical ventilation could also result in a sustained decrease in end-expired CO_2. An abrupt loss of CO_2 might indicate airway obstruction, cardiac arrest or disconnection of the breathing system.

4. A Doppler ultrasound probe placed over the right side of the heart is very sensitive and can detect quantities of gas as small as 0.5 ml. Transoesophageal echocardiography is even more sensitive than Doppler ultrasonography but lacks specificity. Both techniques can detect intracardiac gas before haemodynamic changes become apparent.

Decreased pulmonary perfusion following gas embolism leads to an increase in alveolar deadspace and a decrease in end-tidal PCO_2 which is an early sign. This is accompanied by increases in end-tidal nitrogen. The pulmonary artery pressure rises early due to intense pulmonary vasoconstriction.

The decrease in systemic blood pressure, increase in central venous pressure and evidence of right heart strain on the ECG are late signs and are suggestive of massive pulmonary gas embolism. Approximately 30 mL of air are required for the classical mill-wheel murmur to be heard.

5. The immediate management would include:

- stop surgery;
- discontinue insufflation of gas into peritoneal cavity;
- administer 100% O_2 and discontinue N_2O;
- insertion of a CVP line which can be used both to confirm the diagnosis and to aspirate gas bubbles from the right atrium (CVP catheters with multiple orifices that are designed to facilitate bubble aspiration are available.)
- haemodynamic support with fluids and vasopressors as necessary;
- PEEP: the use of positive end-expiratory pressure in the management of gas embolism is controversial.

Notes

On inspiration the PCO_2 decreases to zero. On expiration the gas emerging first is deadspace gas (both anatomical and apparatus) and this, like the inspirate, has a PCO_2 of zero. The upstroke represents a mixture of deadspace gas (anatomical and alveolar) and alveolar gas. The nearly horizontal alveolar plateau is produced mainly by alveolar gas. The value at the end of the expiratory plateau represents the end-tidal PCO_2.

Key references:

Knill RL. Practical CO_2 monitoring in anaesthesia. *Canadian Journal of Anaesthesia* 1993; **40**:R40–R44.

Bhavani-Shankar K, Moseley H, Kumar AY, Delph Y. Capnometry and anaesthesia. *Canadian Journal of Anaesthesia* 1992; **39**:617–632.

Answers to 5.2

1. Hollow-fibre haemodialysis filter.

2. Afferent blood flow and efferent return to the patient are, by convention, described as the patient's arterial and venous lines respectively even if both are from a patient's vein. The third port is the filtrate output during haemofiltration. The fourth port is used for the input of dialysis fluid during haemodialysis or haemodia-filtration.

3. Standard (unfractionated) heparin which may cause thrombocytopenia after 6–10 days by an immune mechanism. Low molecular weight heparins can be given once daily and have less effect on platelets but cross-reactivity may occur. Danaparoid sodium is not derived from commercial heparins and shows less cross-reactivity. Prostacyclin reduces platelet aggregation but not the number of platelets. It has a half-life of three minutes and so is given as an infusion and its anticoagulant effect wears off quickly on cessation. It may cause hypotension by peripheral vasodilatation if it passes into the patient's systemic circulation.

4. Predilution, suction assist, increased filter blood flow and low blood viscosity.

Notes on basic principles of renal support

Diffusion is the movement of solutes from a region of high to one of low concentration. Dialysis is when this process occurs across a semipermeable membrane. Large molecules move more slowly than small molecules so small molecules will be dialysed more efficiently. The concentrations across the membrane will tend to equilibrate so the dialysis fluid must be continuously replaced to maintain the concentration gradient. Pure haemodialysis (HD) without haemofiltration removes solutes but not water from the blood. In practice during HD a suction pressure causes some filtration as well as dialysis. If the dialysis of osmotically active solutes out of the intravascular compartment occurs quickly, the body may not be able to compensate. Water passes by osmosis into the intracellular compartment, producing disequilibrium syndrome. The cellular oedema is most marked in neural tissue and can cause symptoms from nausea to coma. The loss of intravascular volume may cause hypotension which can be treated with replacement fluid but in the critically ill, vasoconstrictors or inotropes may also be appropriate.

Haemofiltration (HF) produces a filtrate by convection, i.e. bulk movement of water across the filter which takes solutes with it (solvent drag). Synthetic filters allow passage of molecules of 20–40 kDa size so water, urea, creatinine and electrolytes pass into the filtrate in the same composition as in the blood. The volume of filtrate depends on the trans-membrane pressure (TMP), membrane characteristics and the blood composition (protocrit and haematocrit) and flow.

$$TMP = \frac{(P_A + P_V)}{2} + P_{Vac}$$

P_A = pressure in arterial line
P_V = pressure in venous line
P_{Vac} = suction pressure in filtrate line

HF doesn't change the concentration of blood solutes until the blood is diluted by replacement fluid. Intravascular volume changes are slower so cardiovascular stability is better than with HD.

Key references:

Jacobson DW, Webb AR. Acute renal support in the ITU. *Current Anaesthesia and Critical Care* 1992; 3:150–155.

Dickson DM, Hillman KM. Continuous renal replacement in the critically ill. *Anaesthesia and Intensive Care* 1990; **18**:76–101.

Answers to 5.3

1. Patients continue to die during anaesthesia due to inability to maintain the airway or intubate the trachea. Causes of failed tracheal intubation include inexperience of the anaesthetist, inadequate anaesthesia or paralysis, inappropriately placed cricoid pressure, incorrect positioning and multiple anatomical factors. It occurs in about 0.3% of obstetric and 0.04% of general surgical patients. Difficult intubation (DI) may occur despite a good view of the larynx, e.g. if sentinel teeth are present, but generally DI is associated with a poor laryngoscopic view. Cormack and Lehane graded laryngoscopy according to the structures that were visible:

Grade 1: most of the vocal cords visible;
Grade 2: only the posterior vocal cords visible;
Grade 3: only the epiglottis visible;
Grade 4: epiglottis not visible.

Grades 3 and 4 are regarded as difficult and comprise 1 – 3% of all intubations. Recognition of DI requires a combination of screening tests to assess its multiple anatomical causes. Screening criteria in the history and physical examination may fail to detect 50% of patients who are a DI unless these tests have a high false positive rate. There is a large inter-observer variation in this pre-anaesthetic analysis. This does not reduce its importance but stresses that one must always be prepared for these unforeseen emergencies. Recognition of risk allows provision of a plan of action including the availability of equipment and anaesthetists experienced in difficult airway management.

2. Direct questioning of the patient, an information bracelet or the notes may reveal a previous DI. Indirectly, awareness during a previous intubation may have been due to the induction agent wearing off while intubation was prolonged and difficult. Numerous diseases are associated with an increased risk of DI; e.g. hypothyroidism can result in a large myxoedematous tongue and hyperthyroidism can result in tracheal compression and deviation due to goitre. Diseases progress and the previous ability to intubate a patient does not guarantee a similar outcome.

3. The Mallampati test assesses the size of the tongue relative to the oropharynx. The patients sit upright facing the examiner. They open their mouths as wide as possible and protrude their tongues as far as possible. The examiner sits at the same level and observes which anatomical structures are visible:

Class 1: soft palate, faucial pillars and uvula;
Class 2: soft palate and faucial pillars only;
Class 3: soft palate only.

Samsoon and Young added Class 4 which is when the soft palate is not visible. The faucial pillars are the pair of mucosal folds with the palatine tonsil between them. The anterior pillar contains palatoglossus and the posterior pillar, palatopharyngeus. The view improves on saying 'Ah' so the test should be done without speech. Supination gives a slightly poorer view but has little effect on the classification. If a patient cannot sit up the test can still be usefully performed while supine.

4. The Wilson Risk Sum Index is the sum of the scores given to five features: weight, head and neck movement, jaw movement, receding mandible and buck teeth. Each scores 0, 1 or 2. The greater the score, the more likely a DI.

5. The head is fully extended on the neck with the mouth closed. A thyro-mental distance ≤ 6.5 cm or a sterno-mental distance ≤ 12.5 cm predicts a DI is likely.

Key reference:

Cobley M, Vaughan RS. Recognition and management of difficult airway problems. *British Journal of Anaesthesia* 1992; **68**:90–97.

Answers to 5.4

1. Haematoma block (direct injection of local anaesthetic into the fracture site; this provides analgesia but no muscle relaxation): triple block of the radial, median and ulnar nerves at the elbow: intravenous regional anaesthesia (IVRA) (Bier's block): brachial plexus block: general anaesthesia.

2. It is an easy technique to learn, simple to perform, demands no technical expertise, provides good analgesia and motor paralysis and has a high success rate. It can be used for both open and closed surgical procedures of up to 90 min duration. Continuous IVRA techniques have been described for longer procedures. The block can be established quickly, supplementary medication is not necessary and patients spend less time in hospital than when general anaesthesia is used.

3. IVRA should never be performed by a single operator-anaesthetist. The person performing the block must be capable of instituting CPR, possess airway management skills and be able to deal with complications of the procedure (e.g. seizures). Guidelines for pre-operative fasting must apply as for general anaesthesia. Resuscitation drugs and equipment, monitoring equipment and other drugs (thiopentone, suxamethonium, diazepam) must be available. The anaesthetic machine and double cuff tourniquet must be checked. Each cuff must be tested independently for leaks and ability to maintain pressures that are 100 mmHg higher than arterial occlusion pressure. With some machines the pressure gauge indicates the pressure within the machine and not the pressure in the cuff. Luer-lock connections will prevent disconnections at high pressure.

4. The general contraindications to regional anaesthesia (non-cooperation, coagulopathy, local or generalized sepsis, progressive neurological disease, known allergy to local anaesthetic) apply. Other contraindications are

hypertension, sickle cell disease, scleroderma, and peripheral vascular disease. Relative contraindications include pregnancy, epilepsy, liver dysfunction, serious cardiac disability and children under 10 years of age.

5. *Local anaesthetic toxicity.* This may occur with inadvertent absolute overdoses or when the tourniquet fails or is accidentally released during the procedure. Potentially fatal adverse effects include convulsions, coma and cardiovascular collapse. With meticulous attention to detail, only minor neurological sequelae (dizziness, tinnitus, nystagmus, diplopia and drowsiness) were reported by a Canadian group reviewing 20 years' experience with Bier's blocks.

Tourniquet pain. Discomfort due to direct compression of tissue is usually felt after about 30 min: after 60 min the pain may cause considerable distress. This can be minimized by inflating the proximal cuff first and inflating the distal cuff 10 min after injection. The distal cuff will overlie anaesthetized skin and the proximal cuff may then be deflated.

Methaemoglobinaemia. Prilocaine is metabolized to O-toluidine which oxidizes haemoglobin to methaemoglobin. Provided the dose does not exceed 600 mg, clinically significant levels of methaemoglobin do not develop and there is no interference with oxygen transport. It is usually self limiting, and can be treated with i.v. methylene blue.

Others. The overall incidence of adverse effects in the Canadian retrospective study was 1.6%. Prilocaine may cause pain on injection. The cuff may cause pressure injury to nerves (e.g. peroneal nerve damage after lower limb IVRA), and may cause soft tissue necrosis if applied closely to the humeral epicondyles.

Key references:

Brown EM, McGriff JT, Malinowski RW. Intravenous regional anaesthesia (Bier block): review of 20 years' experience. *Canadian Journal of Anaesthesia* 1989; 36:307–310.
Benumof JL (ed). *Clinical Procedures in Anesthesia and Intensive Care* 1st ed. JB Lippincott Company, Philadelphia 1992; 807–819.

Answers to 5.5

1. Give 100% oxygen.

2. Differential diagnosis of shivering:

- seizures caused by hypoxia, drugs, eclampsia of pregnancy and metabolic derangement, e.g. hypoglycaemia;
- tetany;
- parkinsonian tremor;
- oculogyric crisis secondary to anti-dopaminergic antiemetic drugs.

3. Causes of peri-operative hypothermia are:

Method	Cause	Prevention
Convection	Draughts	Insulating cover Reduce air replacement rate
	Cold i.v. fluids, including blood	Blood warmer
Conduction	Directly to table	Warming blankets and mattresses
	Cold irrigating fluid	Warm irrigants
	Cold i.v. fluids, including blood	Blood warmer
Radiation	Between the patient and any object of lower temperature	Insulating cover reduces radiant heat loss and overhead lights heat patient
Evaporation	Anaesthetic: cold dry gas and high gas flows	Heater, humidifier, and low gas flows and circles
	Surgical: cold skin cleaning fluid	Warm the theatre and the cleaning fluid
	Large wound	Drape
	Insensible loss	Warm theatre

All anaesthetics affect thermoregulation via the hypothalamus except ketamine. There is no behavioural response; effector responses and hypothalamic function are impaired; and basal metabolic heat production is decreased. The transfer of heat between two objects by any method depends on their temperature difference. The most important factor causing peri-operative hypothermia is a low theatre temperature. The most rapid rate of heat loss during anaesthesia occurs at induction, due to vasodilatation and central redistribution of peripheral cold blood. The core temperature falls by 0.5–1.5 °C. *The critical ambient temperature* is that which maintains the patient normothermic and it varies with the type of surgery and anaesthetic. For surgery not involving body cavities and anaesthesia that is light enough to allow some degree of thermo-regulation, it is 21 °C.

4. Post-operative risks of hypothermia include:

- hypoxia, myocardial ischaemia, arrhythmias and cerebral ischaemia;
- coagulopathy, because the clotting cascade is enzymatic and platelet function is temperature dependent;
- prolongation of action of drugs;
- subjective unpleasant sensation of cold.

The normal thermoregulatory responses to hypothermia may cause cardiorespiratory distress. A 500% increase in carbon dioxide production, metabolic rate, and consumption of oxygen can occur without obvious shivering. If the patient is breathing air this may not provide an adequate oxygen delivery and even if given oxygen the patient may still have to increase cardiac output to meet the demand. Peripheral vasoconstriction increases afterload and myocardial work.

Key reference:
Barash PG (ed). *ASA Refresher Courses in Anesthesiology*. JB Lippincott Company, Philadelphia 1993; **21:** Ch. 7.

Answers to 5.6

General anaesthesia

Advantages:

- more rapid induction of anaesthesia;
- less associated hypotension and cardio-vascular instability;
- better control of the airway and ventilation;
- preferred mode of anaesthesia in patients with pre-existing neurological disease or coagulopathies;
- alleviates patients' fear of needle insertion in the back or of being awake during surgery.
- reliable, reproducible, controllable method.

Disadvantages:

- pulmonary aspiration of gastric contents;
- risk of failed tracheal intubation;
- lower Apgar scores due to placental transfer of anaesthetic agents;
- inadvertent maternal awareness;
- reduced uterine muscle tone due to high concentrations of inhaled anaesthetics which may increase postpartum blood loss;
- excessive IPPV, resulting in foetal acidosis and hypoxia due to reduced uterine and umbilical blood flow and the increased affinity of maternal haemoglobin for oxygen (Bohr effect);

Regional anaesthesia

Maternal advantages

- pulmonary inhalation of gastric contents is avoided;
- careful controlled regional anaesthesia avoids the hazards of tracheal intubation;
- encourages active participation of the parturient, baby's father and other staff at delivery;
- avoids unintended awareness;

- significantly reduces blood loss;
- more rapid mobilization and reduced incidence of post-operative morbidity (e.g. pyrexia, cough);
- epidural opiates given post-operatively significantly improve quality of analgesia.

Foetal advantages:

- better Apgar scores demonstrated with regional techniques;
- time to onset of sustained respiration is shorter in this group;
- babies are more alert.

Disadvantages:

- hypotension due to extensive sympathetic blockade can cause reduced placental perfusion;
- large doses of local anaesthetic required to produce adequate epidural block – risk of toxicity from accidental intravascular injection: convulsions, cardiovascular collapse;
- vomiting may occur due to hypotension, eventration of the uterus, or intravenous ergometrine;
- technical difficulties – inadequate anaesthesia due to missed segments/unilateral blocks;
- time required to establish adequate epidural block;
- risk of post-dural puncture headaches;
- accidental subarachnoid injection of epidural dose of local anaesthetic can lead to total spinal anaesthesia.

Key references:

Datta S. *The Obstetric Anesthesia Handbook*. Mosby Year Book, Missouri 1992; 149–181.

Reynolds F (ed). *Epidural and Spinal Blockade in Obstetrics*. Bailliere Tindall, London 1990; 127–138.

Answers to 5.7

1. The picture shows a minitracheotomy (MT) kit. The one shown is a Portex Mini-Trach II kit. It comprises in the order of use:

- scalpel;
- 16 standard wire gauge (s.w.g.) 2 cm long Tuohy needle and syringe;
- 50 cm Seldinger guidewire;
- 7 cm long curved tissue dilator;
- 4 mm ID tracheal cannula and introducer;
- 15 mm taper mount and neck tapes.

The patient is placed supine with maximum extension of the lower and upper cervical spine. This may require a pillow sited under the shoulders. The skin is cleaned and local anaesthetic infiltrated. A 1 cm long vertical midline cut is made superficially with the scalpel between the thyroid and cricoid cartilages. The Tuohy needle is inserted until air is aspirated, confirming entry to the airway. The Seldinger guidewire is passed and the Tuohy needle removed. The curved dilator enlarges the channel and then the MT tube is inserted over its introducer. The tube is flanged to stop aspiration. A 10 FG suction catheter passes through the MT tube. The original standard kit does not use a Seldinger wire and the scalpel is inserted up to the hilt. It has a 1.4 cm long blade with plastic guard to prevent it piercing the posterior tracheal wall. The introducer is then passed into the trachea and the MT tube rail-roaded over this.

2. The main indication for MT is treatment of sputum retention. Sputum that is produced at the periphery moves into the larger airways by coughing, postural drainage and the mucociliary action of respiratory epithelium. Sputum retention occurs if the amount of sputum produced exceeds the ability of the patient to remove it. If respiratory failure occurs this exacerbates the retention so MT may be used prophylactically in patients at high risk of post-operative sputum retention. Treatment of sputum retention also includes:

- good analgesia and physiotherapy;
- direct pharyngeal and intratracheal suction;
- intermittent bronchoscopic aspiration;
- tracheal intubation or tracheostomy.

3. Invasive treatment of sputum retention aims at removing sputum from the large airways but is not ideal as it prevents glottic function. The advantages of MT include:

- it is relatively non-invasive;
- glottis unaffected: can cough, talk and eat;
- allows frequent tracheal toilet;
- no sedation required;
- can give humidified oxygen, drugs and take sputum samples for culture.

4. Immediate complications of MT are less likely with the Seldinger technique but include:

- misplacement in the subcutaneous tissues, mediastinum or the oesophagus;
- haemorrhage: this procedure should not be performed if coagulopathy is present.

5. In contrast to previous 'high' tracheotomies, serious long term problems are minimal, probably due to the smaller tube used, its bio-compatibility and the short duration of use. Generally, the site is healed within six days of decannulation and there is no increase in hoarse voice or laryngeal damage. Other indications for MT include:

- securing the airway in acute upper airway obstruction or prior to laryngeal surgery;
- treatment of respiratory failure with high-frequency jet ventilation.

Key reference:

Ryan DW. Minitracheotomy. *BMJ* 1990; **300**:958–959.

Answers to 5.8

The aims of pre-operative anaesthetic assessment for lung resection are twofold: exclusion of those patients who will not survive the post-operative period and optimizing the cardio-respiratory function of those submitted to surgery. Post-operative survival depends on many factors. 90% of these patients smoke. Chronic obstructive airways disease (COAD) and ischaemic heart disease are common. No single test is both a sensitive and specific predictor of post-operative survival. In the majority of cases the decision to proceed with surgery is made on the history and basic tests, i.e. arterial blood gases and spirometry. If these suggest non-survival a series of progressively more invasive tests may be done. These culminate in occlusion of the appropriate pulmonary artery or bronchus, so simulating the post-operative state. The history includes exercise tolerance. The ability to walk up five flights of stairs (or two easily) suggests the patient will tolerate a pneumonectomy.

1. (b) Hypercapnia ($PaCO_2$ >45 mmHg) correlates with post-thoracotomy respiratory morbidity. It signifies that the lungs' ability to compensate is exceeded. Hypoxia can be due to many causes. If the part of the lung to be resected is responsible for a large shunt, surgery may improve overall oxygenation.

2. Minimal pre-operative spirometric values that suggest a patient will tolerate a pneumonectomy include:

- FEV_1 (forced expiratory volume in 1 second) >2 L
- FEV_1 >50% of FVC (forced vital capacity)
- FVC >2 L
- MBC (maximum breathing capacity also known as maximum ventilatory volume, MVV) >50% predicted.

MBC is the product of tidal volume and respiratory rate measured over 12 or 15 seconds during maximal breathing effort. It is expressed in litres/minute. It approximates to 35 x FEV_1. Normal MBC is > 100 L/minute.

3. As a rule of thumb 20% of cardiac output and ventilation goes to each of the lobes. The right has upper, middle and lower lobes and the left upper and lower lobes, i.e. 60% for the right and 40% for the left lung. Radioisotope scanning is more accurate. ^{133}Xenon radio-spirometry assesses ventilation and albumin-labelled ^{99}technetium assesses perfusion.

4. COAD patients need a FEV_1 ≥1 L to cough effectively. Predicted post-operative FEV_1 is:

pre-operative FEV_1 x % perfusion of lung remaining

Post-pneumonectomy survival is unlikely if the predicted post-operative FEV_1 is <0.8 L or is <40% predicted pre-operative FEV_1.

5. Eaton-Lambert or myasthenic syndrome occurs in 1% of patients with bronchial carcinoma, usually small cell. Table 5.8 gives some comparisons with myasthenia gravis.

Table 5.8 Myasthenic conditions

	Myasthenia gravis	Myasthenia syndrome
Sex	Female	Male
Auto-immune site destroyed	Postsynaptic ACh receptors	Presynaptic ACh release sites
Response to exercise	Fatigue	Increased power then fatigue
Response to:		
Suxamethonium	Resistant	Sensitive
Non-depolarizers	Sensitive	Sensitive
Anticholinesterases	Good effect	Minimal effect

Key references:

Kaufman L, Ginsburg R (eds). *Anaesthesia Review 11*. Churchill Livingstone, Edinburgh 1994; 87–107.

Kaplan JA (ed). *Thoracic Anesthesia* 2nd ed. Churchill Livingstone, New York 1991; 1–18.

Answers to 5.9

1. Rheumatoid arthritis (RA).

Hand signs include:

- symmetrical deforming arthropathy;
- spindle fingers: swelling of the proximal interphalangeal joints (PIP) and the metacarpophalangeal joints (MCP) with sparing of the terminal interphalangeal joints (TIP);
- swan-neck deformity (PIP hyperextension and fixed flexion of MCP and TIP);
- ulnar deviation of the fingers;
- wasting of the small muscles of the hand;
- Z-deformity of the thumb;
- boutonnière deformity: flexion deformity of PIP with extension contractures of MCP and TIP;
- palmar erythema and nodules;
- nail-fold infarcts and vasculitis;
- steroid stigmata: thin atrophic skin and purpura (look for Cushingoid face).

2. Causes of anaemia in RA:

- gastrointestinal (GIT) bleeding due to non-steroidal anti-inflammatory drugs (NSAIDs) and steroids (hypochromic microcytic);
- anaemia of chronic disease (normochromic normocytic);
- megaloblastic anaemia due to associated pernicious anaemia or folate deficiency;
- bone marrow suppression (indomethacin, gold, penicillamine);
- Felty's syndrome (rheumatoid arthritis, neutropenia and splenomegaly) .

Thrombocytopenia may also occur with NSAIDs, penicillamine, gold, steroids, the immunosuppressants (azathioprine, methotrexate, chlorambucil, cyclophosphamide) and sulphasalazine.

Neutropenia and leucopenia may be caused by NSAIDs, sulphasalazine, immunosuppressants and gold.

3. Lung pathology in RA:

- minor pleural effusions (the commonest) occurring mainly in middle aged men;
- obliterative bronchiolitis (penicillamine);
- fibrosing alveolitis;
- rheumatoid nodules in the lung (if in coal miners with pulmonary fibrosis, this is called Caplan's syndrome);
- costovertebral joint fixation may cause a restrictive pattern of lung disease.

4. Cardiovascular complications of RA:

- coronary arteritis causing ischaemic heart disease and conduction defects;
- pericardial effusion and fibrosis;
- myocardial fibrosis.

In practice, the siting of radial arterial lines may be difficult due to wrist deformity and calcification of the artery. Central venous lines may prove technically difficult due to cervical immobility and flexion deformities.

5. The normal albumin loss is 20 mg/L. Stix-testing only detects levels above 150 mg/L. Between these two values micro-albuminaemia is diagnosed and is an early marker for diabetic renal disease. If stix-testing is positive a 24-hour sample should be taken. Proteinuria up to 300 mg/day may be normal but requires further investigation. Nephrotic syndrome is diagnosed by a high urinary protein loss (>3 g/day in adults), hypoalbuminaemia (<30 g/L) and peripheral oedema. Causes include penicillamine, gold and renal amyloidosis.

Key reference:

Khanam T. Anaesthetic risks in rheumatoid arthritis. *British Journal of Hospital Medicine* 1994; **52:**320–325.

Answers to 5.10

1. The high speed, his ejection from the car and the death of another occupant are all criteria which classify this patient as high risk. If on examination in the casualty department he appears to have only minor injuries he should still undergo a period of observation. The car demolishing a brick wall is important as it predicts that there was a transfer of a large amount of energy which was reflected in the change of shape of the car and wall. Human bodies are more elastic and hide internal damage.

2. 30–40% of the blood volume, i.e. 2 litres in a 70 kg man. This corresponds to a Class 3 haemorrhage.

3. Chest, cervical spine and pelvic X-ray.

4. No: it is a poor predictor of pelvic injury and may miss 50% of major pelvic fractures.

5. Rectal digital examination to exclude urethral injury which may be exacerbated by urethral catheterization.

Notes on haemorrhagic shock

As with all resuscitation the basis is airway, breathing and circulation. With respect to trauma the airway must be managed concomitantly with control of the cervical spine until cervical injury has been excluded both clinically and radiologically. 100% oxygen should be given even if the pulse oximeter reading is 100% and only reduced when the patient is stable and arterial blood gases confirm adequate oxygenation.

Haemorrhagic shock can be divided into four classes depending on the patient's mental state, pulse, blood pressure, peripheral perfusion and respiratory rate. This classification guides therapy but one should continually reassess the patient and monitor the response to therapy.

In Class 1 (<15% of blood volume lost), a fit young adult can compensate with no signs or symptoms and without requiring transfusion. However, with increasing age or ischaemic heart disease, symptoms and signs may occur with less blood loss. Conversely a pregnant woman may lose more than 20% of her blood volume with no signs or symptoms although uterine perfusion is decreased and there may be foetal distress. Patients on ß-blockers may not be able to respond with a reflex tachycardia.

In Class 2 (15–30% blood loss) compensatory mechanisms become apparent. The pulse increases to above 100/minute. Systemic vascular resistance rises, increasing diastolic pressure, maintaining systolic pressure and delaying capillary refill. (Normally, pressing on the thumb nail blanches it and releasing it causes a reperfusion flush within 2 seconds. It is absent if the patient is hypothermic.)

In Class 3 (30–40% blood loss) both systolic and diastolic pressures fall, the systolic falling below 100 mmHg, and the pulse increases to 120/minute or greater.

In Class 4 (>40% blood loss) the blood pressure becomes low or unrecordable and there may be either a tachycardia or preterminal bradycardia.

From Class 2 to Class 4 there is a deterioration in mental state which may manifest as agitation, aggression and drowsiness. If the blood loss exceeds 50% of blood volume the patient will be unconscious and have no pulse and should be intubated and ventilated with 100% oxygen and treated as in the electromechanical dissociation algorithm of the European Resuscitation Guidelines (*see* OSCE 2.10).

Key references:

Skinner D, Driscoll P, Earlam R (eds). *ABC of Major Trauma.* BMJ Books, London 1991; 20–24.

Robertson C, Redmond A. *The Management of Major Trauma.* Oxford University Press 1992; 31–43.

Answers to 5.11

1. Sinus bradycardia. (Always check paper speed before making diagnosis.)
Sinus bradycardia occurs when the sino-atrial node fires at a rate less than 60 beats/minute. In an infant, sinus bradycardia is defined as a rate less than 100 beats/minute.
The morphology of the ECG is normal with a constant P-R interval >0.12 s, unless AV block is present at the same time.

2. The rate of sinus node discharge reflects the balance between parasympathetic and sympathetic influences on the heart. Heart rates below 40 beats/minute are poorly tolerated even by healthy individuals and may adversely affect cardiac output. Sinus bradycardia accounts for 11% of intra-operative arrhythmias. Sinus bradycardia may be found in or caused by:

Normal physiological states:
• well trained athletes;
• sleep (REM sleep has been associated with sinus arrest);
• pronounced sinus arrhythmia.

Increased vagal tone:
• oculocardiac reflex during eye surgery;
• traction on peritoneum;
• distension of hollow viscus;
• vasovagal syncope;
• carotid sinus massage.

Drugs:
Cholinergic agents, suxamethonium, neostigmine, opioids, beta blockers, calcium channel blockers, clonidine, encainide.

Intracranial pathology:
• meningitis;
• raised intracranial pressure (Cushing's reflex).

Disease states:
• myocardial infarction;
• cervical and mediastinal tumours;
• hypothyroidism;
• hypothermia, hypoxia;
• gram negative sepsis.

3. A bradycardia (ventricular rate <60/min) need not always arise form the sino-atrial node.
The two questions that have to be addressed are:
(a) Does the patient show significant symptoms and signs? These are:

• chest pain;
• dyspnoea;
• congestive cardiac failure;
• systolic blood pressure <90 mmHg;
• altered mental status.

(b) Does the bradycardic rhythm have the potential to cause cardiac standstill?
Two bradycardic rhythms that could potentially lead to cardiac standstill, particularly after myocardial infarction, are Mobitz Type II second degree heart block and complete AV dissociation. If these are present, a pacemaker is indicated.

4. The initial treatment is atropine 0.5–1 mg. If symptoms persist, this dose can be repeated. Lower doses of atropine may cause an initial parasympathomimetic effect, probably via a central mechanism. Ephedrine, aminophylline and hydralazine may be useful in some patients with sinus bradycardia. A continuous infusion of isoprenaline (2–10 μg/kg/min) may be used to accelerate the heart rate but if the bradycardia proves refractory, external or transvenous electrical pacing may be necessary.

Key references:

Braunwald E (ed). *Heart Disease* 4th ed. WB Saunders Company, Philadelphia 1992; 674.

The Advanced Life Support Group. *Advanced Cardiac Life Support* 1st ed. Chapman & Hall, London 1993; 103–104.

Answers to 5.12

1. Inadvertent subarachnoid injection of local anaesthetic, inadvertent intravascular injection of local anaesthetic, haemorrhage – concealed/ overt, amniotic fluid embolism, pulmonary embolism, eclampsia, previously undetected cardiac disease (e.g. myocarditis).

2. Summon cardiac arrest and obstetric teams. Assess airway, breathing and circulation to establish diagnosis. Institute basic life support with minimal delay. Use a wedge or frame to tilt the pelvis by 30° or pull the uterus to the left and upwards to lift it off the inferior vena cava to improve venous return. Monitor ECG rhythm and follow appropriate European Resuscitation Council (1992) algorithm for advanced life support. Tracheal intubation may be difficult but would be advantageous if performed early. Any obvious primary cause of cardiac arrest (e.g. haemorrhage) must be corrected rapidly. If basic and advanced life support measures are not successful within 5 minutes, immediate Caesarean section must be performed as part of maternal resuscitation. Urgent surgical delivery will completely relieve aortocaval compression and also improve foetal outcome. Cardio-pulmonary resuscitation must be continued throughout the procedure and if external cardiac compression is ineffective, open chest cardiac massage must be considered. If resuscitation is successful, appropriate intensive care follow up must be arranged.

3. *Airway:* tracheal intubation may be hindered by a full set of teeth, obesity of the neck, engorged breasts interfering with direct laryngoscopy, and glottic and supraglottic oedema. Maintain cricoid pressure during bag and mask ventilation to minimize risk of regurgitation and aspiration (intragastric pressure is higher and gastric emptying may be delayed).
Breathing: the metabolic rate and O_2 consumption are increased at term. This, combined with a splinted diaphragm, decreased functional residual capacity (FRC), and poor chest compliance may render ventilation difficult.
Circulation: aortocaval compression in the supine position decreases venous return and cardiac filling. Massage of an empty heart is ineffective. External cardiac compression is rendered difficult by the angle of application, the flared ribcage and the raised diaphragm. Recently, a 'human wedge' has been described where a person kneels on the floor sitting on his heels. The patient is positioned so that her back lies on the thighs of the 'human wedge'. The 'human wedge' stabilizes the patient's shoulders with one arm and the pelvis with the other. Basic life support is effective in this position.

4. Hypertensive disease – 18.4%, pulmonary embolism – 16.9%, haemorrhage–15.4%, ectopic pregnancy – 11%, amniotic fluid embolism – 7.4%, abortion – 5.1%, sepsis – 4.4% (excluding abortion), anaesthesia – 2.2%, ruptured uterus – 1.5%, other direct causes – 17.6%.

Notes

The estimated incidence of maternal cardiac arrest is 1:30 000 pregnancies. Survival is exceptional and depends upon rapid and appropriate action as the pregnant female withstands hypoxia poorly.
Bupivacaine toxicity is marked by seizures and profound hypoxia, hypercarbia and acidaemia. Early administration of 100% O_2 and $NaHCO_3$ is necessary for resuscitation to be successful. Bretylium tosylate 5 mg/kg i.v. is the preferred treatment for refractory ventricluar fibrillation (VF) in bupivacaine toxicity. It may take up to 30 min to become effective and advanced life support must be continued throughout. If effective, the bolus dose is followed by infusion of 1–2 mg/kg/h.

Key references:

Evans TR (ed). *ABC of Resuscitation* 2nd ed. British Medical Journal, London 1990; 50–53.
Report on confidential enquiries into maternal deaths in the United Kingdom 1988–1990. HMSO, London 1994.

OSCE cycle 6 – answers

Answers to 6.1

1. There is a macrocytosis (normal mean corpuscular volume is 80 – 96 fL), leucopenia and thrombocytopenia. General causes of a macrocytosis include:

- megaloblastic anaemia due to Vitamin B_{12} or folate deficiency;
- haemorrhage or haemolysis, which also cause a reticulocytosis;
- alcoholism and cirrhosis;
- marrow aplasia or leukaemia;
- myxoedema.

Macrocytosis occurs in 60% of those with a current alcohol problem but usually resolves with 2 to 3 months abstinence. The legal blood alcohol limit for driving a car in the United Kingdom is 80 mg/dL. This patient has therefore been drinking heavily in the previous few hours. Alcohol is directly toxic to the bone marrow and alcoholism results in malnutrition and vitamin deficiencies. Hence megaloblastic anaemia, macrocytosis, leucopenia and thrombocytopenia can all occur.

2. The following strongly suggest a chronic alcohol problem:

- urinary alcohol >120 mg/dL (>200 mg/dL is diagnostic);
- raised gamma glutamyl transferase with a normal alkaline phosphatase;
- macrocytosis.

3. A blood alcohol >250 mg/dL is associated with an increased surgical risk. This must be balanced against the urgency of surgery. Problems of acute alcoholic intake include:

- reduced sensitivity to anaesthetic agents;
- full stomach, as alcohol delays emptying;
- hypoglycaemia and hypokalaemia;
- hypothermia;
- dehydration: alcohol inhibits ADH release.

Complications of chronic alcohol intake include psychosocial problems and:

- CVS: cardiomyopathy, cardiac beri-beri and recurrent arrhythmias;
- RS: 20% have chronic bronchitis;
- liver dysfunction: cirrhosis, coagulopathy, low albumin and oesophageal varices;
- GIT: gastritis; pancreatitis causes further malnutrition and steatorrhoea;
- haematological disorders;
- CNS: seizures, Korsakoff's psychosis and Wernicke's encephalopathy. The history from the patient may not be accurate due to memory loss or confabulation;
- skeletal: osteoporosis and myopathy;
- autonomic and peripheral neuropathy due to B_{12}, folate, B_6, and B_1 deficiencies.

4. Delirium tremens (DTs) due to acute alcohol withdrawal usually occurs within 48 hours of stopping alcohol. It may be preceded by coarse generalized tremor, disorientation, agitation, auditory and visual hallucinations or seizures. It presents signs of an overactive sympathetic system with hyperthermia, hypertension, tachycardia, sweating and dilated pupils. The differential diagnosis includes malignant hyperthermia, sepsis and other causes of delirium e.g. withdrawal from benzodiazepines. Management is supportive and sedative. Assessment should include a septic screen as DTs may be precipitated by sepsis. Treatment is supportive and includes the following:

- correction of hypoglycaemia, dehydration, and malnutrition with i.v. dextrose, trace elements and multivitamins;
- alcohol, chlormethiazole or benzodiazepines may be used for sedation but all cause both hypotension and respiratory depression and so should be closely monitored.

Key reference:

Kumar P, Clark M. *Clinical Medicine* 3rd ed. Baillière Tindall, London 1994; 172–173, 982–985.

Answers to 6.2

1. ECT may be used in the treatment of major depressive illness in patients who are refractory to medical treatment, in patients who are unable to tolerate the side effects of anti-psychotic medication and in patients with acute deterioration in their symptoms. A brief pulse of electrical current is delivered across two electrodes applied to the anterior temporal areas of the scalp. The stimulus is in a square wave form and usually, 80 V is applied for a duration of 0.1–0.3 s to produce a modified grand mal seizure with a tonic phase of 10–15 s followed by a clonic phase of 30–50 s. A series of treatments is usually given over a 2–3 week period. General anaesthesia is provided during ECT:

• to render the patient unaware of the treatment, which is unpleasant;
• to modify the motor component of the seizures induced by ECT, so that injury to the patient is prevented (e.g. fractures of bones, biting of tongue).

2. Physiological effects:

• *Cardiovascular system:* ECT causes an initial vagal discharge with bradycardia and hypotension. Intense parasympathetic stimulation upon application of the current may result in asystole. There follows activation of the sympathetic nervous system with consequent hypertension and tachycardia which lasts 5–10 minutes. Both cardiac output and myocardial O_2 consumption are increased. Atrial or ventricular arrhythmias may be precipitated. ECG changes often occur and include prolongation of the PR and QT intervals and inversion of T waves.
• *Central nervous system:* ECT causes increases in cerebral blood flow, cerebral metabolic rate and intracranial pressure. The intraocular pressure is also raised.

• *Other:* Intragastric pressure is raised. There is an increase in plasma levels of ACTH, cortisol and catecholamines.

3. The absolute contraindications to ECT are:

• myocardial infarction within 3 months;
• cerebrovascular accident within 3 months;
• intracranial surgery within 3 months;
• intracranial mass lesion;
• phaeochromocytoma.

4. *Tricyclic antidepressants:* these drugs (e.g. amitriptyline, imipramine and doxepin) prevent re-uptake of noradrenaline and serotonin. The use of directly-acting sympathomimetic drugs must be avoided as the interaction may cause intra-operative hypertensive crises. Anticholinergic drugs have additive antimuscarinic side effects with the tricyclics and can cause post-operative confusion and delirium.
Monoamine oxidase inhibitors: these inhibit the enzymatic breakdown of noradrenaline, serotonin and dopamine. Interaction with sympathomimetic amines may cause hypertensive crises. They interact with opioid analgesics and produce either excitation or depression of the CNS. Phenelzine has been reported to reduce plasma cholinesterase in 40% of patients taking it. Both the MAOIs and the tricyclics augment the effects of barbiturates.
Other drugs: lithium prolongs the action of pancuronium and suxamethonium. The newer serotonin uptake inhibitors (e.g. fluvoxamine, fluoxetine, paroxetine and sertraline) are less sedative, less cardiotoxic and cause fewer anticholinergic side effects.

Key references:

Miller RD (ed). *Anesthesia* 4th ed. Churchill Livingstone, New York 1994; 2269–2273.

Davison JK, Eckhardt III WF, Perese DA. *Clinical Anesthesia Procedures of the Massachusetts General Hospital* 4th ed. Little Brown, Boston 1993; 486–490.

Answers to 6.3

1. Malignant hyperthermia (MH). Other causes of intra-operative tachycardia include:

- light anaesthesia: absence of sweating and dilated pupils are inconclusive but check presence of volatile in vaporizer and doses of drugs given. Give test dose of opiate;
- hypovolaemia: look for hypotension and poor perfusion and give a fluid challenge.
- hypercarbia: check the capnograph. Causes include excess CO_2 production in sepsis and thyrotoxicosis or rebreathing, e.g. due to exhaustion of soda lime or disconnection of the inner tube of a Bain circuit;
- thyrotoxicosis.
- phaeochromocytoma.

2. No sign is pathognomonic of MH. The clinical presentation varies from normal to a fulminant crisis. The clinical and biochemical features can be explained by the pathophysiology. Following a trigger agent (the disease can be triggered by any volatile agent or depolarizing muscle relaxant) the skeletal muscle becomes hypermetabolic. There is a massive increase in O_2 consumption, CO_2 and heat production. When the local energy demand exceeds supply anaerobic metabolism produces a metabolic acidosis. The actin–myosin coupling requires energy to uncouple so the muscle becomes rigid. Signs of MH include:

- difficult intubation due to masseter spasm that is not relieved by muscle relaxant;
- flushed skin due to hypercarbia;
- tachycardia;
- cyanosis due to increased oxygen consumption despite an increased inspired oxygen concentration;
- hypercarbia despite increased ventilation: this may present on capnography or as a hot soda lime canister;
- arrhythmias due to the acidosis and hyperkalaemia;
- rise of core temperature of >2°C/h.

3. The following investigations are indicated:

- arterial blood gases are the most important: hypercarbia, hypoxaemia, respiratory acidosis and metabolic acidosis;
- full blood count may show a high white cell count (infection), a low haemoglobin (hypovolaemia) or low platelet count (disseminated intravascular coagulation);
- electrolytes: hyperkalaemia suggests MH;
- coagulation: to assess disseminated intravascular coagulation;
- creatine kinase: raised, but not diagnostic due to wide overlap with normal values.

4. Dantrolene: is available as vials of 20 g dantrolene sodium, 3 g mannitol (to maintain isotonicity), and enough NaOH to produce a solution of pH 9.5 (so that it dissolves) when reconstituted with 60 mL of sterile water. Extra mannitol for renal protection is probably unnecessary. Dantrolene has no side effects in the short term but should be given by CVP as it is irritant.

5. These do not affect your management. Exposure to known triggering agents does not always provoke a response so a previous uneventful anaesthetic does not exclude the diagnosis. MH can be triggered by residual volatile agent in the breathing circuit. The initial management of the patient is clinical: the diagnosis is only confirmed by *in vitro* contracture testing of muscle biopsies at a later date. In the future, diagnosis may be aided by genetic testing or MRI techniques.

Key reference:

Fisher MMcD (ed). *Clinical Anaesthesiology* 1993; **7**: 343–356.

Answers to 6.4

1. (a) Body Mass Index = Weight [kg] divided by Height^2 [m^2].
   (b) This patient's BMI = 44.98
   (c) Obesity can be classified on the basis of Body Mass Index as follows:

Underweight	<20
Normal	20–25
Overweight	25–30
Obese	30–40
Severely obese	>40

2. Medical complications include:

- sudden death;
- Pickwickian syndrome comprising hypersomnolence, daytime hypoventilation, hypercapnia, hypoxia, polycythaemia and cor pulmonale;
- congestive cardiac failure;
- association with hypertension/diabetes mellitus/hyperlipidaemia;
- nephrotic syndrome/renal vein thrombosis;
- obstructive sleep apnoea;
- immobility which restricts normal daily activities/psychosocial problems.

3. Functional residual capacity (FRC) is decreased due to the decrease in chest wall compliance caused by truncal obesity. The reduced FRC may fall within the closing capacity range in the upright position resulting in ventilation–perfusion mismatching or right-to-left shunting, both of which will result in arterial hypoxaemia. The decreased chest wall compliance, in conjunction with the need to increase minute ventilation in order to maintain normocapnia, increases the work and oxygen cost of breathing. The increase in BMI also increases oxygen consumption.

Despite a low PaO$_2$ many obese patients can sustain an adequate minute ventilation which maintains normocapnia. With increasing obesity and age, some patients become unable to maintain normocapnia. As the PCO$_2$ rises, they become reliant on the hypoxic ventilatory drive.

4. *Transporting and positioning of patient on operating table:* For elective procedures it is probably easier for the patient to walk to theatre than be transported on a trolley; it may be necessary to use two tables. Asking the patient to position himself on the table minimizes the need for lifting. Appropriate padding and protection of pressure points is important; both tables must be adjusted simultaneously when changing table position.

Induction: Venous access may be difficult. Gastro-oesophageal reflux is common, so premedication with H$_2$-blockers is prudent. Awake intubation or a controlled rapid sequence induction may be necessary. Airway control and tracheal intubation may be difficult.

Maintenance: Direct blood pressure measurement may be preferred (a cuff of appropriate size is needed for NIBP measurement). Serial arterial blood gases, airway pressure and end-tidal CO$_2$ measurement will yield useful information intra-operatively. Intra-operative hypoxia is not uncommon and a minimum FIO$_2$ of 0.5 must be used. Haemodynamic swings are poorly tolerated and PCWP monitoring may be necessary, particularly in patients with the Pickwickian syndrome. Pneumatic compression leggings will minimize the risk of DVT.

Recovery: May be prolonged due to altered drug handling, increased sequestering of lipid soluble agents and residual neuromuscular blockade. Post-operative respiratory depression and hypoxia are common and severely obese patients are best managed in an ITU/HDU after surgery.

Key references:

Andreoli TE, Bennett JC, Carpenter CCJ, Plum F, Smith Jr LH (eds). *Cecil Essentials of Medicine* 3rd ed. WB Saunders, Philadelphia 1993; 434–436.

Miller RD (ed). *Anesthesia* 4th ed. Churchill Livingstone, New York 1994; 912–915.

Answers to 6.5

1. Magnetic Resonance Imaging (MRI) scan of the head and neck. MRI is a non-invasive diagnostic procedure that does not involve ionizing radiation. It is different from, rather than superior to, computerized tomography (CT) and has different indications and strengths. It is still developing but is now common in the United Kingdom. This scan shows distortion due to a nearby metallic object that need not be ferromagnetic (i.e. able to be attracted to magnets). This example was due to the wire spiral of an armoured orotracheal tube. Other causes include tattoos, cosmetics and monitoring equipment. The image can also be distorted by radiofrequency signals, e.g. FM radio waves. A Faraday cage may surround the scanner to reduce this interference. Care should be taken as monitoring leads may act as antennae and transmit these signals across the cage. Problems of anaesthetizing for MRI include:

• poor access and visibility of the patient;
• malfunction of monitors;
• ferromagnetic nature of anaesthetic equipment (including monitoring equipment);
• distortion of MRI picture by currents produced by monitors.

2. Indications for anaesthesia for MRI:

• Protection of the airway in an unconscious patient and hyperventilation in head injured patients.
• Patients who cannot keep still, e.g. children, claustrophobia, low IQ and sensitivity to noise. Some patients may be helped by ear plugs, counselling or turning prone. Sedation may be more appropriate but monitoring is still mandatory.

3. A 'quench', i.e. a leak of liquid helium (4K) or nitrogen (77K) can result in sudden asphyxia with no warning to staff. An oxygen analyser should monitor the ambient oxygen concentration and be set to alarm at 19–20%.

4. Risks of MRI scanning to patients include:

• Missile effects: ferromagnetic objects (FMO) are attracted to the centre of the magnet and may hit the patient or the staff. Even small objects are dangerous as the kinetic energy delivered depends on the square of the velocity. Objects within the 50 Gauss line should be fixed or nonferromagnetic. Any object entering the scanning room should be checked to ensure that it is nonmagnetic.
• Movement of FMOs in the patient: the risk of alignment in the field or attraction to the magnetic centre depends on the site and nature of the FMO; e.g. intraorbital foreign bodies may be dangerous but modern heart valves and sternal wires that are relatively fixed are not.
• Malfunction of implanted devices: pacemaker reed switches may be turned off by magnetic fields as low as 5 Gauss; automatic defibrillators and spinal cord stimulators may be affected. These patients should be excluded from the MRI suite by the preoperative history.
• Burns: RF pulses heat the outer body more than internal organs. Children and heat sensitive organs, i.e. testes and eyes, may be affected more but there are United Kingdom Standards which protect against this risk. In practice, current induced in monitoring wires next to the patient is the commonest cause of burns. The patient should be insulated from leads which should be kept as far as possible from the field and not coiled. A quench may result in cold injury.
• Biological hazards: magnetic fields can cause physiological changes, e.g. in blood pressure, but no pathological changes have occurred with MRI scanning.
• Hearing loss (coil movement is very loud).

Key reference:

Menon DK, Peden CJ, Hall AS, Sargentoni J, Whitwam JG. Magnetic resonance for the anaesthetist. *Anaesthesia* 1992; **47**:240–255, 508–517.

Answers to 6.6

1. Mechanical support devices include:

- *Intra-aortic balloon pump:* This is usually passed via the femoral artery into the descending thoracic aorta. It is alternately inflated and deflated. Inflation of the balloon is with helium and is timed to occur on the dicrotic notch of the arterial pulse wave with deflation just before the upstroke of the next wave. It can augment intrinsic cardiac output by 10–20%.
- *Haemopump:* This consists of a spinning turbine which is located in the left ventricle and ejects blood into the aorta. It is a difficult device to position and there have been mechanical failures. It is used mainly in the management of acute heart failure following myocardial infarction or cardiac surgery.
- *Centrifugal pumps:* These are extra-corporeal pumps that may be used to support the left or right ventricles. The flow is nonpulsatile and the flow rates depend on the venous return. They are relatively cheap and not technically demanding.
- *Ventricular assist devices:* These artificial ventricles work in conjunction with the failing native ventricle. The assistance provided is up to 100% of the desired output. These devices consist of a blood sac (reservoir) made of biocompatible material, valves for unidirectional flow, and a power source (pneumatic or electrical) to drive the system.
- *Total artificial heart:* These are designed to replace the native heart altogether. The implantation procedure is similar to heart transplantation. The design resembles a combination of two ventricular assist devices. They may be used as a bridge to heart transplantation.

2. Intra-aortic balloon counterpulsation supports the ischaemic failing heart by augmenting myocardial oxygen delivery and decreasing oxygen consumption. Counterpulsation involves phasic displacement of blood within a fixed intravascular space, synchronized with the cardiac cycle, to reduce blood volume in the ascending aorta during systole and augment aortic root blood volume during ventricular diastole. This modifies the normal aortic root pressure pattern and results in a decrease in systolic pressure and an increase in diastolic pressure in the aortic root. The improved left ventricular ejection results in decreased end-diastolic ventricular volume and pressure. There is an increase in diastolic pressure–time index which increases oxygen supply and a decrease in tension–time index which reduces myocardial oxygen demand.

3. Indications include:

- *Ischaemic heart disease:* Unstable angina pectoris, cardiogenic shock or ventricular rupture following acute myocardial infarction.
- *Pre-operative support:* Improvement of myocardial function in post-infarction ventricular septal defect, prior to transplantation or surgery for failed angioplasty.
- *Post-operative support:* Intra-operative myocardial infarction, left ventricular failure following cardiopulmonary bypass.
- *Other:* Myocardial support in critically ill patients, intra-operative support for non-cardiac surgery in cardiac patients.

4. Complications include limb ischaemia distal to the insertion site due to thrombosis or embolism, bleeding, infection, arterial and aortic trauma, balloon rupture, gas embolism and renal and mesenteric ischaemia.

Key references:

Underwood MJ, Firmin RK, Graham TR. Current concepts in the use of intra-aortic balloon counterpulsation. *British Journal of Hospital Medicine* 1993; **50**:391–397.

Glenville B. Mechanical support for the failing heart. *Hospital Update* Feb. 1991; 89–95.

Answers to 6.7

1. CT brain scan showing extensive acute subdural haematoma (SDH).

Subdural haematomas are usually caused by rupture of bridging cortical veins. An SDH appears on CT scan as a crescentic, high density collection between the dura and the arachnoid. The SDH becomes isodense after a few days and progresses to become hypodense by three weeks. SDH is the most common focal intracranial lesion following severe closed head injury.

2. The aims of immediate management are to institute resuscitation and to minimize secondary injury, particularly from hypoxia, hypercarbia and hypotension.

- The relevant history must be obtained. A rapid but complete clinical examination must be undertaken. Injuries to chest, abdomen, pelvis, spine and extremities must be sought and managed appropriately. Neurological examination must include Glasgow coma score, pupillary size and reactivity, corneal reflex and assessment of the gag and cough reflexes.
- Tracheal intubation and controlled ventilation are indicated if the patient is unable to protect his own airway or if ventilation/oxygenation are inadequate. The cervical spine should be treated as 'at risk'.
- Hypovolaemia should be treated aggressively. Crystalloids should not include glucose, to minimize risk of hyperglycaemia. If there are signs of neurological deterioration, the ICP can be assumed to be elevated and 1 g/kg of mannitol given.
- The radiological investigation of choice at present in acute head injuries is the unenhanced CT scan.

3. The aims of surgical management are to:

- relieve compression of the brainstem by removal of subdural clot and contused brain;

- prevent the adverse effects of blood products on brain function.

The rapidity of surgical drainage of the SDH and the degree of associated brain damage are the major determinants of outcome.

4. The following physiological variables should be optimized:

- Systolic blood pressure should be kept at 100–160 mmHg. There are varying degrees of loss of autoregulation after head injury.
- The arterial $PaCO_2$ must be maintained around 30 mmHg and PaO_2 kept ≥100 mmHg to minimize surges in cerebral blood flow.
- Seizures increase $CMRO_2$. Phenytoin i.v. may be used to control seizures.
- After initial resuscitation, strict control of fluid balance will help reduce cerebral oedema. It is important to prevent hyponatraemia and water overload.
- ICP may be lowered with a combination of controlled hyperventilation, 30° head-up tilt, mannitol and frusemide.

5. The indications for ICP monitoring include:

- Inability to monitor serial neurological observations due to anaesthesia, or neuromuscular block to aid mechanical ventilation.
- Need for therapeutic interventions that might increase ICP (e.g. PEEP to improve oxygenation).
- Greater than 50% chance of having raised ICP: GCS ≥8 with abnormal CT scan or GCS ≥8 with normal CT scan but two other adverse prognostic features (age >40 years, hypotension, decerebrate posture).

Key references:

Cottrell JE, Smith DS (eds). *Anesthesia and Neurosurgery* 3rd ed. Mosby-Year Book Inc., St. Louis 1994; 661–684.

Oh TE (ed). *Intensive Care Manual* 3rd ed. Butterworths, Sydney 1990; 427–431.

Answers to 6.8

1. Drowning is death from asphyxia due to submersion in a fluid. It kills about two people a day in the UK. Near-drowning is survival after submersion. The submersion may be associated with trauma (especially cervical in diving incidents), alcohol, myocardial infarct, drugs, epileptic seizure, muscle diseases or suicide. Complications include hypoxaemia, hypothermia, metabolic acidosis, hypovolaemia and arrhythmias.

2. Advantages of intubation include:

- protection of the airway from gastric contents; these patients may swallow large amounts of water during submersion; a nasogastric tube will be necessary;
- airway maintenance in a comatose patient;
- facilitation of ventilation of lungs which have a decreased compliance.

Risks of intubation in these patients include:

- *Spinal cord damage:* these patients should be treated as suspected unstable cervical spinal injuries until proven otherwise.
- *Cardiac arrhythmias:* at 32 °C patients may go into spontaneous atrial fibrillation and at 28 °C into ventricular fibrillation. External cardiac massage and tracheal intubation may trigger these.

3. 10% of victims do not aspirate water and have apnoeic hypoxaemia. They may die due to vagally mediated immediate cardiac arrest (immersion syndrome). 90% of victims aspirate water. Fresh water is absorbed from the lungs quickly but dilutes surfactant, causing atelectasis. Sea water is hypertonic (3.5% salts) and causes systemic water to enter the alveoli and results in systemic hypovolaemia. The hypoxaemia is further exacerbated by pulmonary oedema due to hypoxaemia and peripheral vasoconstriction. In children basic life support started at the scene of submersion reduces mortality from 70% to 40%. Manoeuvres to remove fresh water from the lungs are unlikely to be of benefit as it is quickly absorbed. Abdominal thrusts should only be used if there is airway obstruction as they may cause gastric regurgitation. Bradycardia is common and the pulse should be carefully assessed to prevent unnecessary cardiac massage that may trigger arrhythmias. Oxygen is given until proven unnecessary. Resuscitation must continue until hospital admission when hypothermia and drugs can be excluded as a cause of coma.

4. Core temperature may be increased by:

- warming i.v. fluids and inspired gases;
- lavage of body cavities with 42°C saline: mediastinum, stomach, bladder, pleura, pericardium or peritoneum;
- extra-corporeal blood warming: haemodialysis or cardiorespiratory bypass.

5. The immediate risk is 'rewarming shock', i.e. hypotension due to peripheral vasodilatation in these hypovolaemic patients who have impaired cardiac function secondary to hypothermia, acidosis and hypoxaemia. This is exacerbated by the central movement of peripheral blood which is cold, acidic and hyperkalaemic. In severe hypothermia (core temperature <32°C) rewarming should be gradual with continuous cardiorespiratory monitoring. Hypotension is treated primarily with i.v. colloid as in the hypothermic patient vasoactive drugs and defibrillators have limited efficacy and pacemakers may trigger arrhythmias. Electrolyte abnormalities occur in the 15% that aspirate >22 mL/kg of water. Coagulopathy, renal failure and pancreatitis may occur, but are uncommon.

Key reference:

Stuart Taylor ME. Management of near-drowning. *Hospital Update* 1990; **16**:419–431.

Answers to 6.9

1. Insertion kit for a triple lumen central venous catheter (CVC). These can be sited in the internal jugular, subclavian or femoral veins. The following items are listed in an order that you may use them.

- Cleaning fluid and sterile drapes.
- Syringes, needles and local anaesthetic.
- Syringe with a plastic cannula over a needle or a large bore needle to locate and gain access to the vein.
- Seldinger guidewire to secure access.
- Scalpel or blade to facilitate catheter passage through the skin.
- Venous dilator to facilitate the triple lumen's passage through the wall of the vein as it is wider than a single lumen CVC.
- Occlusive dressing ± suture to secure the catheter.
- Saline to flush the catheter.

Advantages over a single lumen CVC are the facility for simultaneous:

- central venous pressure monitoring, blood sampling and administration of drugs, fluids and total parenteral nutrition;
- administration of drugs which need to be given separately because they do not mix, e.g. amiodarone, or because they have different actions, e.g. vasoconstrictors and inotropes.

2. The absolute contraindications to CVC insertion are inexpertness of the operator and infection at the site of insertion. Although coagulopathy should be treated prior to CV cannulation this is a relative contraindication and should be decided, as in any other clinical decision, by a risk/benefit assessment for each patient. In the presence of coagulopathy the femoral approach allows pressure to be applied over the venepuncture site.

3. The Trendelenberg position is used to ensure adequate venous filling to facilitate location of the vein and to minimize air embolism. The latter occurs if the vein is opened to air when venous pressure is less than atmospheric. The central venous pressure should be assessed clinically. If a patient has a high CVP, e.g. with congestive cardiac failure and orthopnoea, then not only is there little advantage in the Trendelenberg position but it may precipitate pulmonary oedema.

4. A chest X-ray is required to:

- exclude a pneumothorax;
- assess the position of the catheter tip: this should lie between the head of the clavicle and the arch of the azygos vein and be parallel to the walls of the superior vena cava, i.e. above the pericardial reflection.

5. Laminar flow through a cannula depends on Poiseuille's law:

$$Q = \frac{\delta P \pi r^4}{8 \eta l}$$ where

Q = flow
δP = pressure difference
r = radius of catheter
η = viscosity of the liquid
l = length of catheter

Triple lumen catheters are relatively long so even those with a 14 gauge lumen will not allow rapid transfusion. Peripheral i.v. cannulae are more appropriate as they are shorter and can be sited in the antecubital, saphenous or external jugular veins. The smallest cross-sectional area in an i.v. system is the connection of the i.v. tubing to the cannula. 'Main draining' overcomes this by plumbing the cut i.v. tubing straight into a peripheral vein. Following resuscitation a CVC may be appropriate for monitoring further fluid replacement.

Key reference:
Kaufman L (ed). *Anaesthesia Review 8*. Churchill Livingstone, Edinburgh 1991; 255–275.

Answers to 6.10

1. Soda lime is a mixture of the hydroxides of calcium, sodium and potassium with small amounts of silica and kieselguhr added to prevent disintegration of the granules. Water is present as a thin surface layer on the granules. (Composition by weight = NaOH 5%, KOH 1%, silica 0.2%, water 14–19%, $Ca(OH)_2$ to make a total of 100%.) The modern forms of soda lime do not require the addition of hardeners or KOH.

2. Soda lime is used in breathing systems to absorb expired CO_2 during anaesthesia. It can be incorporated in a single-phase (modified Mapleson C) system or into a two-phase (circle) system. CO_2 combines with the water on the granules to yield H_2CO_3 which dissociates incompletely into H^+ and HCO_3^- and further into H^+, H^+ and CO_3^{2-}. The carbonate combines with the Na^+ and Ca^{2+} ions (formed by dissociation of the hydroxides) in an exothermic reaction yielding Na_2CO_3, $CaCO_3$ and H_2O.

3. The temperature of soda lime may reach 50–60°C during the absorption of CO_2 (the newer Durasorb seldom exceeds 45°C when used in circle systems). Trichloroethylene degenerates when heated, releasing hydrochloric acid and dichloroacetylene, which breaks down further to give phosgene and carbon monoxide. Sevoflurane breaks down to a fluorinated vinyl ether known as Compound A. A safe level for Compound A in humans has not been determined. In rats, it is lethal at 340–350 ppm. Although halothane breaks down to CF_2CBrCl no adverse reactions have been reported even after extensive clinical experience with this agent in circle systems. Isoflurane and desflurane are degraded to a very small extent.

4. Exhaustion of soda lime is associated with a change in colour of the granules, a rise in temperature of the canister and increasing levels of inspired CO_2. Physical signs due to a rising CO_2 include a bounding tachycardia, increase in blood pressure, sweating, increased oozing at the surgical site and increased depth of spontaneous respiration. The time taken for exhaustion will depend upon the size of the canister, the rate of CO_2 production and the fresh gas flow used.

5. High fresh gas flows may be used both with rebreathing and nonrebreathing systems to achieve elimination of CO_2. Barium hydroxide lime can be used to absorb CO_2 in circle systems. It is a mixture of $Ca(OH)_2$ (80%) and barium hydroxide (20%). Baralyme does not absorb volatile anaesthetics, is less exothermic and requires no hardener. Activated charcoal has been used to *adsorb* CO_2 and halogenated hydrocarbons. Synthetic zeolite-containing molecular sieves, which can adsorb CO_2, hold promise and could be introduced into anaesthetic practice in the future.

Notes

Modern soda lime canisters are mounted upright to minimize channelling of gases. The granules should be of an optimal size (BP standard 3–10 Mesh in the United Kingdom). Granules that are too large decrease absorptive surface area and those that are too small increase resistance to breathing. The volume of air in the filled canister should equal the patient's tidal volume. Colour changes that signify exhaustion depend on the indicators used. Durasorb changes from pink to white when exhausted.

Key references:

Dorsch JA, Dorsch SE. *Understanding Anesthesia Equipment* 3rd ed. Williams and Wilkins, Maryland 1994; 195–196.

Holloway AM. Possible alternatives to soda lime. *Anaesthesia and Intensive Care* 1994; **22**:359–362.

Answers to 6.11

1. The Bain breathing system, described by Bain and Spoerel in 1972, is a co-axial T-piece system which conforms to the basic arrangement of a Mapleson D breathing system. It consists of an outer corrugated plastic tube, 1.8 m long with a diameter of 22 mm, within which is contained a narrower (internal diameter 7 mm) smooth plastic tube. The inner tube acts as the inspiratory limb and expiration is via the outer tube. The adjustable pressure limiting (APL) valve is located at the machine end of the system. The patient end of the Bain system has an internal diameter of 15 mm and is compatible with an angle piece, tracheal tube connector or laryngeal mask. The system incorporates a 2 L reservoir bag.

2. Examine the outer corrugated tube for cracks and leaks. Ensure that the inner co-axial tube is attached at both ends of the breathing system. Disconnection of the inner tube can lead to a dangerous increase in deadspace, particularly in children.

Connect the system to the anaesthetic machine, close the APL valve, occlude the patient end and pressurize the system. If there is no leak the pressure will be maintained. When the APL valve is opened the bag should deflate easily.

If the oxygen flow is set at a low flow rate (4 L/min), and the inner tube is occluded (finger or 2 mL syringe), the oxygen rotameter bobbin will be seen to fall provided the system is leakproof.

The integrity of the inner tube can also be assessed by activating the oxygen flush mechanism. A Venturi effect at the patient end will cause air to be drawn from the outer corrugated tubing resulting in deflation of the bag. If the inner tube is not intact, this test will cause the bag to inflate slightly.

3. It is an inefficient system for spontaneous breathing and is wasteful of fresh gas flow (FGF). There is wide variation between the recommended FGF rates for the Bain and for other T-piece systems in the published studies. The FGF rate will depend on the deadspace/tidal volume ratio, inspiratory flow pattern and the relative durations of inspiration and expiration. A FGF of 200–300 mL/kg/min is required to prevent rebreathing during spontaneous ventilation through the Bain system. The need for high flows is thought to be because the entry of fresh gas is directed at the subject's mouth resulting in turbulence within the system and leading to gas mixing in the reservoir tube. The reservoir tube cannot then store fresh gas unadulterated with expired gas. Thus, to prevent rebreathing of alveolar gas, fresh gas flow of the order of peak inspiratory flow is required. High FGFs may cause high expiratory resistance.

4. During controlled ventilation the Bain system behaves as a typical T-piece system. Controlled ventilation can be achieved by manual compression of the reservoir bag or by connecting the outlet of a ventilator (e.g. Nuffield Penlon) to the reservoir bag mount with a 1 m length of corrugated hose which prevents driving gas diluting the fresh gas flow. Fresh gas flows of 70 mL/kg/min have been recommended with ventilation of at least 150 mL/kg/min for controlled ventilation. The economy of a T-piece system is increased if there is an end-expiratory pause. Mapleson D systems make efficient use of anaesthetic gases during controlled ventilation.

Key references:

Conway CM. Anaesthetic breathing systems. *British Journal of Anaesthesia* 1985; **57**:649–657.

Bain JA, Spoerel WE. *Canadian Anaesthetists Society Journal* 1972; **19**:427–435.

Answers to 6.12

The precautions that need to be taken before IVRA is undertaken are listed in the answer to OSCE 5.4. The procedure must be explained fully to the patient and informed consent obtained. Establish non-invasive blood pressure, ECG and pulse oximetry monitoring.

Intravenous cannulae must be sited in both hands. On the affected side, the cannula must be sited distal to the injury and as distant from the tourniquet as possible. The cannula on the non-affected side is for emergency access and may be connected to an intravenous infusion. The upper arm is padded to protect the skin and a double-cuff tourniquet is applied. The arm is then exsanguinated. This can be achieved by elevation for 3 min with simultaneous digital compression of the brachial artery. Gravity drainage can be combined with the application of a Rhys-Davies exsanguinator or Esmarch bandage. The proximal cuff is then inflated to 100 mmHg greater than systolic pressure. The Esmarch bandage is removed and the time of tourniquet application noted. Absence of radial artery pulsation must be ensured prior to injection of local anaesthetic. Prilocaine (0.5%, plain, 3 mg/kg) is injected slowly at 2–3 mL/s. The distal cuff can be inflated 10 min after injection and the proximal cuff may then be deflated to minimize tourniquet-related pain. Explain to the patient that warmth and parasthesiae will be felt and the arm will appear blotchy and discoloured at this stage. Test the arm for loss of pain sensation before surgery begins. Observe and maintain verbal contact with the patient throughout the procedure so that signs and symptoms of local anaesthetic toxicity may be picked up early. A minimum tourniquet time of 25 min is recommended which allows time for the local anaesthetic to be sequestered/bound locally, thus preventing a large bolus entering the systemic circulation. At the end of the surgical procedure the tourniquet may either be deflated completely or a cycled deflation technique used (e.g. deflate for 5 s, observe, reinflate for 1 min, deflate for further 5 s, observe, reinflate for further 1 min followed by total deflation). No significant difference has been shown between the two deflation techniques in terms of post-tourniquet release blood levels of local anaesthetic. Note the time of tourniquet release and observe the patient in the recovery area for 30 min. Check circulation in the arm prior to discharge and warn the patient of possible nausea and weakness over the next 24 hours.

Notes
Escape of local anaesthetic under the tourniquet may be due to injection using excessive pressure, escape via intramedullary vascular channels or due to deep collateral circulation.

Bupivacaine is no longer used for IVRA in the UK in view of its potential cardiotoxicity. Prilocaine is considered the drug of choice because of its high pulmonary extraction and low systemic toxicity. It is as effective as lignocaine for IVRA and produces fewer neurological side effects.

Vascular engorgement of the arm due to the large volume of local anaesthetic injected and continued flow of blood through the non-compressible intra-medullary channels can cause oozing and result in an unsatisfactory surgical field. Oozing can be minimized by re-exsanguination of the arm. An Esmarch bandage is re-applied 20 min after injection, followed by complete release and immediate reinflation of the double-cuff tourniquet, prior to surgery. It has been shown that less tourniquet pain occurs with this technique.

Key references:
Benumof JL (ed). *Clinical Procedures in Anesthesia and Intensive Care* 1st ed. JB Lippincott Company, Philadelphia 1992; 807–819.

Rawal N, Hallen J, Amilon A, Hellstrand P. Improvement in i.v. regional anaesthesia by re-exsanguination before surgery. *British Journal of Anaesthesia* 1993; **70**:280–285.

OSCE cycle 7 – answers

Answers to 7.1

1. (a) Nitrous oxide cylinder showing pin-index holes on valve block.

1. (b) Although several methods have been described, the commonest process involves heating NH_4NO_3 (solid or aqueous solution) to temperatures of 245–270°C. This exothermic reaction yields N_2O and H_2O. Impurities including the higher oxides of N_2, particularly NO and NO_2, ammonia and chlorine may occur. The gas is scrubbed with permanganate, sulphuric acid and water to remove these impurities prior to medical use.

2. The pin-index system is an international standard that was introduced to prevent the interchangeability of gas cylinders on anaesthetic machines. For each gas, a unique configuration of pins projects from the yoke of the anaesthetic machine. These fit into corresponding holes in the valve block of the appropriate gas cylinder. The seven hole positions are on the circumference of a circle which has the gas port as its centre and a circumference of 9/16 inches. On the N_2O cylinder the holes are in positions 3 and 5. The pin-index renders it impossible to fit an incompatible cylinder of gas in a normal position with a single Bodok seal. The pin-index system is used for the smaller cylinders, up to size 'E'. The larger cylinders are of the bull-nose and handwheel types whose connections have specific thread patterns.

Note: No system is foolproof. There have been reports of the pin-index system being circumvented by a) using more than one Bodok seal b) fitting cylinders upside down c) filing down the pins on the yoke.

3. Filling ratio = weight of substance with which the cylinder is filled, divided by the weight of water required to fill an empty cylinder.

N_2O is stored as a liquid in cylinders (the critical temperature 36.5°C is considerably higher than room temperature 20°C). The pressure gauge indicates the SVP of the gas above the liquid at a given temperature. Rises in temperature result in rises in pressure within the cylinder, in keeping with the SVP at the new temperature. If the temperature were to rise above the critical temperature, the contents of the cylinder would become entirely gaseous, resulting in a large rise in pressure. If cylinders were filled to capacity with liquid N_2O, rises in temperature could result in large rises in pressure due to liquid expansion, with the consequent risk of cylinder rupture. Therefore in the United Kingdom, these cylinders are filled to a ratio of 0.75. In the tropics the filling ratio is further reduced to 0.67. The contents of these cylinders can be estimated by weighing the cylinder and subtracting the weight of the empty cylinder (The tare weight is given on the valve block.)

5. The gas present in body cavities is in equilibrium with atmospheric N_2. N_2O is a poorly soluble gas and diffuses into body cavities 25 times faster than N_2 diffuses out when breathing a nitrogen-free gas mixture containing N_2O through a system which allows no rebreathing. This results in a rise in pressure in noncompliant spaces and a rise in volume in compliant spaces.

Compliant: Stomach and intestines, pneumothorax, pneumoperitoneum, air embolism.

Noncompliant: Middle ear, nasal sinuses, vitreous cavity, cranium (pneumocephalus).

Tracheal tube cuffs: N_2O diffuses into these cuffs and with prolonged use may subject the tracheal mucosa to high pressures and compromise mucosal capillary blood flow. Inflation of cuffs with the inspired gas mixture or water/saline minimizes the rise in pressure.

Key references:

Atkinson RS, Adams AP (eds). *Recent Advances in Anaesthesia and Analgesia 16*. Churchill Livingstone, Edinburgh 1989; 19–42.

Dorsch JA, Dorsch SE. *Understanding Anaesthesia Equipment* 3rd ed. Williams & Wilkins, Maryland 1994; 1–23.

Answers to 7.2

1. In 1990 the previous three decades were reviewed: 30–75% of post-operative patients complained of moderate to severe pain. This had not improved during this period. Some problems were highlighted:

- the knowledge, training and attitudes of the staff including doctors and nurses;
- the patients' expectations and attitudes;
- the lack of organized acute pain teams.

There are humane, medical and economic reasons for providing good analgesia. Firstly, post-operative pain relief is a basic human right. It improves the morale and the quality of life of patients, reduces fatigue and anxiety, and promotes sleep. Medical benefits of good analgesia include:

- *Early mobilization* reducing pressure sores and deep vein thromboses and leading to faster recovery of musculoskeletal function.
- *Improved respiratory function* enabling deep breathing, coughing and co-operation with physiotherapy. This is most important for upper abdominal and thoracic surgery. Poor pain relief leads to chest infections, hypoxia and respiratory failure.
- *Less tachycardia and hypertension,* so less myocardial ischaemia and infarction.
- *Reduction of the neuroendocrine and metabolic stress effects of surgery* that may prolong the catabolic phase and reduce healing.
- *Reduction in nausea* (appropriate drugs should be given).

Economic reasons: early mobilization and less complications means a shorter hospital stay. A good acute pain service may attract patients.

2. In order for drugs to produce analgesia they must be absorbed and transported to their receptors. When a standard i.m. morphine dose is given to a group of patients their peak blood levels vary 5-fold and the time to reach these peak blood levels varies from 4 to 60 minutes. Also, the concentration of morphine in the blood that produces adequate analgesia with minimal side effects varies 4-fold. The conclusion is that one cannot predict the amount of drug a particular patient will require so the analgesic administration must be flexible. All drugs have side effects so their use must be kept within safe limits. Appropriate drugs should be prescribed in appropriate doses at appropriate intervals. Having instituted a flexible regimen, regular re-assessment is needed to maintain analgesia.

3. The one-way valve should be placed on the iv. drip tubing. If not, and the i.v. cannula becomes blocked, when the patient presses the PCA, analgesic will go up the i.v. tubing. The patient receives no analgesia and so continues to press the PCA and a reservoir of analgesic collects in the i.v. tubing. If the cannula is then unblocked the patient receives an overdose of analgesic. Syphoning may occur if the PCA is above the patient, i.e. air leaks into the syringe allowing analgesic to pass by gravity into the patient. This is prevented by siting an anti-syphoning valve in the PCA tubing.

4. A background infusion (BI) is generally no better than PCA alone unless the patient has had chronic pre-operative analgesia. The main risk of a BI is that when the patient becomes saturated with analgesic the blood level may suddenly increase. The patient may become comatose and apnoeic relatively quickly. Close monitoring is mandatory.

5. Large doses of pethidine or its use in patients with renal failure may result in norpethidine neurotoxicity.

Key reference:
Report of the Working Party on Pain after Surgery, The Royal College of Surgeons of England, The College of Anaesthetists. September 1990.

Answers to 7.3

1. Laser (**L**ight **A**mplification of the **S**timulated **E**mission of **R**adiation) surgery of the airway. Laser light is coherent, monochromatic light that is amplified and collimated. Lasers are named after their laser medium. They allow a very high power to be transferred accurately to a small area with good haemostasis. The tissue absorption of a laser depends on its wavelength. The CO_2 laser is absorbed easily by water and this limits its effects to the superficial layers of tissue. It cuts rather than coagulates. Its uses include upper airway and proximal tracheal surgery. The Nd-YAG (neodymium-yttrium-aluminium-garnet) laser requires fibreoptic transmission and produces a deeper coagulating burn whose clinical effects may be delayed by days. It may be used for debulking of tumours of the lower trachea and bronchi.

2. Hazards to staff include:

- the smoke plumes produced by burnt tissue: CO_2 lasers produce the most smoke which is of a particle size that reaches alveoli if inhaled; this may cause bronchial irritation and has the potential to be carcinogenic and infective;
- accidental irradiation of eyes and skin: CO_2 lasers may cause corneal burns and ruby lasers may coagulate retinal vessels;
- ignition of drapes, cottonoids.

Safety measures to protect staff include:

- smoke extraction at the laser field;
- theatre doors should be closed, sealed to light and have signs on them prohibiting entry to anyone not correctly protected;
- staff in theatre should wear goggles with wrap around sides; for CO_2 lasers normal glass can be used but other lasers require glass of a colour specific to that laser.

3. Hazards to the patient include airway fires, haemorrhage, pneumothorax, venous gas embolism and injury to the eyes or skin. Haemorrhage may occur from perforation of a major blood vessel as lasers can only coagulate small blood vessels. Pneumothorax can occur with pleural perforation. Nd-YAG lasers require coolant, often CO_2, which passes co-axially to the fibreoptic tip. If the laser cuts through a vein the coolant may pass intravenously to give a gas embolus.

4. Safety factors for the patient include protecting the eyes, skin and peri-operative site from aberrant lasers by shields or wet gauze. The safest anaesthetic gas mixture is the lowest inspired oxygen concentration compatible with normal oxygenation of the patient (about 30%) in helium or nitrogen as nitrous oxide supports combustion. All endotracheal tubes are flammable with some lasers. PVC tubes are quickest to ignite but even metal tubes are potentially flammable with Nd-YAG lasers. The risk is reduced by removing the radio-opaque barium strip and opaque writing. Laser proof tape may protect the tube but not the cuff which if pierced causes a leak of anaesthetic gas into the laser site which may then cause an airway fire. The Laser Flex™ tube shown has two cuffs to help prevent this. Cuffs should be filled with saline and contain dye to warn of perforation.

5. Airway fire. The source should be removed, ventilation stopped, the anaesthetic circuit disconnected and a bucket of water emptied over the operative site. Following removal of debris a new tube is inserted and the damage assessed by bronchoscopy, arterial blood gases and chest X-ray. General supportive measures are then instituted.

Key references:

Mason RA. *Anaesthesia Databook* 2nd ed. Churchill Livingstone, Edinburgh 1994; 600–604.

Miller RD. *Anesthesia,* 4th ed. Churchill Livingstone, New York 1994; 2197–2211.

Answers to 7.4

1. A good general principle is that when you are called to assess a patient who may be in a life-threatening situation your first priority is to ensure that the patient is safe. Therefore, on arrival in the recovery ward you should assess the patient's airway, breathing and circulation before progressing to the specific diagnosis and treatment.

2. Causes of post-operative apnoea include:

* prolonged effect of drugs used during the anaesthetic, including premedication, e.g. opiates, volatile agents, benzodiazepines and muscle relaxants;
* hypocapnia, acidosis;
* intra-operative cerebral insult, e.g. surgery, hypoxia, hypotension or fat emboli;
* hypoglycaemia and hyperglycaemia;
* hypothermia;
* incidental pathology, e.g. head injury, drug intoxication, dystrophia myotonica or hypothyroidism.

These factors may also interact; e.g. hypothermia and acidosis can increase the duration of action of muscle relaxants and cause cerebral depression.

3. The patient's medical history should be assessed especially for diabetes, respiratory, hepatic and renal disease, pseudocholinesterase deficiency and medications. The anaesthetic, including premedication, should be reviewed, especially the drugs used, their doses with respect to the patient's size and any periods of hypoxia or hypotension. After ensuring that the patient is being ventilated with 100% oxygen and no anaesthetic, further assessment includes:

* Clinical examination of the patient: miosis suggests narcosis but also occurs in pontine haemorrhage; an upgoing plantar reflex suggests a cerebrovascular accident but can occur in many causes of deep coma, e.g. hyperglycaemia. Spontaneous movement of limbs excludes neuromuscular blockade (NMB) as a cause of post-operative apnoea.
* A peripheral nerve stimulator: absence of fade visually or manually with a train-of-four or double burst stimulation does not guarantee a safe airway but does rule out residual NMB as a cause of post-operative apnoea. Painful stimuli should not be used to assess the patient's condition until NMB is excluded lest pain is inflicted on a paralysed and awake patient.
* Pulse oximeter and capnograph: to assess the adequacy of oxygenation and ventilation and to ensure that the $PaCO_2$ is high enough to stimulate the respiratory centre.
* A thermometer: to assess core temperature.
* Arterial blood gases: to assess blood pH and confirm the capnography and oximetry.
* BM-stix testing and blood glucose: to exclude hypo- and hyperglycaemia.
* Blood urea: uraemia can cause coma and renal failure can delay excretion of drugs.

4. The following drugs may be useful:

* Naloxone: a specific opioid antagonist which will reverse respiratory depression and sedation but also analgesia.
* Flumazenil: a specific benzodiazepine antagonist that will reverse their sedative and respiratory depressant effects.

Both these drugs act within a minute but their duration of action is much less than that of the drugs they are reversing so respiratory depression may re-occur 20 minutes later and further doses of the antagonist or a continuous infusion may be necessary.

Key reference:

Barash PG (ed). *ASA Refresher Courses, in Anesthesiolgy*. JB Lippincott, Philadelphia 1992; **20**: Ch. 5.

Answers to 7.5

1. *Cancer:* lip, mouth, pharynx, oesophagus, larynx, lung, bladder. There is a clear dose–response relationship between the number of cigarettes smoked and lung cancer mortality.
RS: chronic bronchitis, emphysema, pulmonary hypertension and right heart failure.
CVS: ischaemic heart disease and peripheral vascular disease.
Other risks: gastric and duodenal ulcers, induction of hepatic microsomal enzymes, polycythaemia and hyperviscosity, alterations in macrophage and T-lymphocyte function, abnormalities of spermatozoa, psychological effects.

2. *Decreased myocardial oxygen supply:* Carbon monoxide decreases O_2 bound to haemoglobin, causes a left shift of the O_2 dissociation curve and inactivates cytochrome oxidase in myocardium with a consequent decrease in intracellular O_2 transport. Polycythaemia, increased platelet count and aggregation, and hyperfibrinogenaemia increase blood viscosity and risk of thrombosis.
Increased myocardial O_2 demand: Nicotine increases heart rate, systolic and diastolic pressure and peripheral and coronary vascular resistance. Atherosclerosis and the reduction in the oxygen supply/demand ratio increase the risk of ischaemic heart disease.

3. Cigarette smoke is irritant to the respiratory tract, induces epithelial change and increases production of hyperviscous mucus. This, coupled with inactivation of cilia, reduces clearance of particulate matter by the muco-ciliary escalator. There is an increase in laryngeal and tracheobronchial reactivity. Alveolar macrophages lose their immunoregulatory function, and release reactive metabolites (e.g. superoxide), elastase and other proteolytic enzymes. The resulting loss of elastic recoil together with increased small airway narrowing are reflected in an increased closing capacity which, coupled with a reduced FRC, increases $P(A-a)O_2$. Epithelial permeability is increased.

4. Cessation of smoking for even 1 week will reverse the effects of nicotine and carbon monoxide, improve ciliary function, reduce laryngeal reactivity and restore platelet function. With abstinence up to 8 weeks there is continued improvement in ciliary function with reduction in sputum production. Small airway function improves and there is a reduction in post-operative pulmonary morbidity (bronchospasm, purulent sputum and pyrexia, segmental pulmonary collapse, pneumonia necessitating antibiotic therapy). Normal immune function is restored.

5. Emphasize the benefits of abstinence from smoking for several weeks pre-operatively. Treat respiratory tract infections, and consider chest physiotherapy and bronchodilators to correct reversible airway narrowing. Anticholinergic drugs (glycopyrrolate, pirenzepine, ipratropium) are useful in premedication as they will influence both airway tone and secretions. Benzodiazepines may be used to produce sedation with minimal cardiovascular and respiratory depression. A smooth induction technique is more important than choice of induction agent. Airway manipulation at light planes of anaesthesia may cause coughing, breathholding, laryngospasm and desaturation. Opioids and neuromuscular blockers that cause minimal histamine release may be advantageous. The commonly used inhalational agents have bronchodilator properties and may be used safely for maintenance of anaesthesia. Total intravenous anaesthesia and central neural blockade may be useful alternatives.

Key references:

Erskine RJ, Hanning CD. Do I advise my patient to stop smoking pre-operatively? *Current Anaesthesia and Critical Care* 1992; **3**:175–180.

Beckers S, Camu F. The anesthetic risk of tobacco smoking. *Acta Anaesthesiol Belgica* 1991; **42**:45–56.

Answers to 7.6

1. Take three aliquots of cerebrospinal fluid (CSF) and compare the first and third. If the lumbar puncture was traumatic the blood content of the third aliquot will be much less than the first. The composition of normal CSF from lumbar puncture is as follows:

Appearance	Clear, colourless + no clot
Pressure with patient recumbent	6–18 cmH$_2$O
Cell count	≤ 5 RBC/mm^3
	≤ 5 lymphocytes/mm^3
	No polymorphs
Glucose	50–65% of blood glucose
Protein	0.15–0.40 g/L
IgG	< 15% of total CSF protein
Oligoclonal bands	None

The presence of >100 RBC/mm^3 and no xanthochromia on centrifugation is diagnostic of subarachnoid haemorrhage (SAH). The presence of xanthochromia, a yellow coloration of the CSF, can be due to:

- haemolysis of blood six hours after a subarachnoid bleed and later from altered haemoglobin;
- systemic jaundice due to unconjugated bilirubin;
- large amounts of pus or tumours which cause local stasis of CSF. They are associated with a high protein content.

2. Computed Tomography (CT) scan. LP is contraindicated if an intracranial mass or intracranial hypertension is suspected. The change in CSF pressure may cause a shift of brain tissue. The cerebellar tonsils may cone through the foramen magnum. This results in ischaemia of the brainstem and death.

3. The Glasgow Coma Score (GCS) (*see* Table 7.6) is an internationally agreed physiological scoring system for the assessment of neuro-logical status. It is stated as a total score from 3 to 15 or as the three parts, e.g. 465.

Table 7.6 Glasgow Coma Score

	Score
Eyes open:	
Spontaneously	4
To speech	3
To pain	2
Nil	1
Best motor response:	
Obeys commands	6
Localizes pain	5
Flexion withdrawal	4
Decerebrate flexion	3
Decerebrate extension	2
Nil	1
Best verbal response:	
Orientated	5
Confused conversation	4
Inappropriate words	3
Incomprehensible sounds	2
Nil	1

Coma is defined as a GCS of <8. On admission this patient had a GCS of 8 or 251 (2+5+1).

4. The reperfusion injury is decreased by the calcium channel blocker nimodipine. This reacts with PVC and light and must be given via a central vein. Central venous pressure measurement may help in fluid management. This is important for maintaining normo-volaemia and cerebral perfusion pressure (CPP) and preventing cerebral vasospasm.

$$CPP = MAP - ICP$$

MAP = mean arterial pressure
ICP = intracranial pressure.

5. The preconditions are that the patient is in apnoeic coma and that the cause is irremediable structural brain damage due to a disorder that can lead to brain death. All three conditions (a, b, and c) are necessary.

Key reference:

Pallis C. *ABC of Brain Stem Death*. BMJ, London 1989; 10–13.

Answers to 7.7

1. The following are general signs of upper airway obstruction.

- RS: tachypnoea, stridor, suprasternal supraclavicular and subcostal indrawing, nasal flaring, the use of accessory muscles, paradoxical breathing;
- CVS: tachycardia and cyanosis;
- CNS: anxiety, distress.

2. Croup (acute laryngotracheobronchitis) and epiglottitis account for 98% of acute upper airway obstructions in children of this age.

3. and 4. Comparison of croup and epiglottitis:

	Croup	*Epiglottitis*
Commonest cause	Parainfluenza virus	*Haemophilus influenzae* B
Incidence	Common	Rare
History		
Onset	Slow (days) Viral prodrome	Sudden (hours)
Age	6 m to 5 yr	1 yr to 6 yr
Sore throat	Minor	Severe
Drinking	Yes	No, swallowing is painful
Examination		
Cough	Severe (barking)	Minor or absent
Speech	Hoarse, as vocal cords swollen	Quiet, as throat is painful
Stridor	Harsh	Soft
Temp.	<39°C	>39°C
Appearance	Unwell	Toxic, due to septicaemia. Tripod stance: sitting, neck extended, chin on hands. Drooling saliva
Intubation rate of those admitted to hospital	5%	>80%
Average duration of intubation	5 days	2 days

5. Only (b). Initial management consists of assessment by history, examination and pulse oximetry. This must be done with the minimum amount of stress. Sudden complete airway obstruction may be precipitated by:

- upsetting the child, e.g. separating the child from the parents, doing X-rays;
- siting a venous cannula or taking blood;
- lying the patient supine;
- inspecting the throat with a spatula.

If the child appears stable and settles quickly with rest, oxygen and nebulized adrenaline just observe. If there is any risk of epiglottitis or evidence of incipient respiratory failure (cyanosis, increasing agitation or somnolence) active intervention is required to secure the airway. An ENT surgeon should be present in case an emergency tracheotomy becomes necessary. Induction with halothane and oxygen is by an experienced anaesthetist whilst the child is on the parent's lap. The obstruction will slow induction. When anaesthesia is adequate an i.v. cannula is sited and atropine given. Direct laryngoscopy may show the cherry red swelling of epiglottitis. A tracheal tube, 0.5–1.0 mm smaller than normal for that child, is inserted. If the glottic opening is not visible a colleague can press gently on the chest. The anaesthetist may then see a bubble appear on the epiglottis and insert the tube through it. If intubation is difficult the oral tube should not be changed for a nasal tube. IPPV or spontaneous ventilation is continued until there is a good leak and the anatomy looks normal. Epiglottitis is treated with cefotaxime or chloramphenicol and blood cultures are sent. Dexamethasone may help post-extubation oedema.

Key reference:

Wilmott RW (ed). *Pediatric Clinics of North America* WB Saunders Company, Philadelphia, April 1994; 41:265–276.

Answers to 7.8

1.

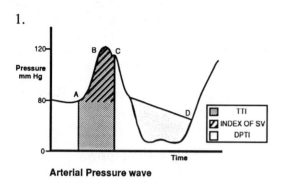

Arterial Pressure wave

2. Measurements obtainable include:

• Real time pulse rate, SBP, DBP and mean arterial blood pressure (MAP). The system overestimates SBP, underestimates DBP but maintains an accurate MAP. As one monitors arteries that are more peripheral, the SBP reading becomes greater and the MAP and DBP fall. In extreme peripheral vasoconstriction (e.g. following hypothermic cardiopulmonary bypass) the radial arterial pressure waveform may give a lower blood pressure than that in the femoral artery.
• A steep AB gradient (dp/dt) indicates a strong left ventricular contraction.
• A low dicrotic notch, C, and steep downslope or rapid diastolic run-off suggests a low systemic vascular resistance or hypovolaemia.
• A change in SBP of >10 mmHg occurring with ventilation may indicate hypovolaemia.
• The area under the systolic ejection phase is an index of the stroke volume.
• Areas DPTI (diastolic pressure time index) and TTI (tension time index) represent the cardiac oxygen supply and demand. The endocardial viability ratio DPTI/TTI is normally >1 and if <0.7 indicates that ischaemia is likely.

3. Following intra-arterial injection of thiopentone the risk is the deposition of thiopentone crystals causing thrombosis of the vessel and ischaemia in the perfused area. Leave the needle or cannula *in situ*. The following may be injected intra-arterially:

• α-blockers, e.g. phentolamine;
• papaverine, a directly-acting vasodilator;
• procaine, a directly-acting vasodilator which buffers the thiopentone and relieves the pain;
• heparin;
• saline.

Stellate ganglion or brachial plexus block cause vasodilatation.

Other complications of arterial lines include:

• infection, both local and systemic;
• arterial thrombosis with consequent ischaemic damage to the perfused area;
• disconnection can cause haemorrhage at a rate of 500 ml/min from the radial artery. Lines and cannulae should be Luer-locked and visible;
• local haematoma and nerve damage;
• emboli, e.g. from a brachial artery cannula to the radial artery.

4. Normal saline with heparin (0.5–1 unit/mL) to prevent clotting in the cannula. Dextrose is avoided as it increases the risk of local infection. Fast flush devices are pressurized to approximately 300 mmHg and deliver about 3 mL/h through a flow restrictor.

Key reference:

Hutton P, Prys-Roberts C (eds). *Monitoring in Anaesthesia and Intensive Care*. WB Saunders Company Ltd, London 1994;121–144.

Answers to 7.9

1. (a) Modified Sengstaken-Blakemore tube.
1. (b) i. Uncontrollable variceal haemorrhage.
   ii. Active variceal bleeding, when definitive treatment cannot be immediately arranged or the patient requires transfer to another unit.

2. Identify aspiration and inflation ports. Check integrity of balloons by inflating with a measured volume of air, and check pressures. Cold, lubricated tubes are easier to pass. Avoid sedation. Position the patient on the left side with head down tilt to minimize risk of aspiration. The tube should be inserted to 60 cm and suction applied to the gastric port. Aspiration of a large volume of blood usually confirms position; the gastric balloon should then be inflated (approx. 300 mL). The tube should be withdrawn until resistance is felt at the gastro-oesophageal junction. The oesophageal balloon is then inflated to a pressure of 40 mmHg, which is usually sufficient to tamponade the varices without compromising arterial supply to the oesophageal mucosa. The tube must be secured to the patient's forehead to prevent displacement. Check the position with a chest X-ray. Allow the gastric channel to drain freely and apply continuous low suction to the oesophageal aspiration port. The balloon should not be kept inflated longer than 24 hours.

3. *Oesphageal rupture* caused by inflation of the gastric balloon in the oesophagus.
Oesophageal ulceration with prolonged balloon inflation at high pressures.
Airway obstruction following deflation/rupture of the gastric balloon, and migration of the oesophageal balloon into the oropharynx.
Aspiration pneumonia, particularly in encephalopathic patients. The risk can be reduced by prior insertion of a cuffed tracheal tube.

4. Liver cirrhosis accounts for 90% of oesophageal varices in the United Kingdom. Other causes include hepatic vein thrombosis (Budd-Chiari syndrome), portal vein thrombosis, pancreatic tumours, myelofibrosis, Hodgkin's disease and hepatic fibrosis from schistosomiasis.

5. *Resuscitation:* Establish large bore vascular access and restore intravascular volume. Blood (O Rh –ve, if necessary) should be given as soon as possible. Transfusion should be guided by CVP monitoring. Fresh frozen plasma and clotting products should be used to correct any clotting abnormality. Diagnosis is confirmed by upper GI endoscopy.
Treatment options include:
Sclerotherapy of varices –Treatment of choice for acute bleeding following resuscitation. Ethanolamine or sodium tetradecyl sulphate can be injected via an endoscope. Repeated sclerosant injections at intervals cause progressive variceal obliteration and minimize rebleeding.
Vasopressin infusion – Lowers portal pressure by splanchnic vasoconstriction. Intra-arterial infusion confers no advantage. Rebleeding is common.
Other drugs – Somatostatin, octreotide, and propranolol have been shown to reduce portal pressure but their place in the emergency treatment of variceal bleeding has not been established. Pentagastrin and metoclopramide have also been reported to control acute variceal bleeding.
Balloon tamponade – Useful when vasopressin and sclerosant therapy prove ineffective.
Embolization – Requires selective catheterization after percutaneous transhepatic portography.
Surgery – Oesophageal transection with anastomosis or a porto-caval shunt are the commonest emergency surgical procedures.

Key references:

McCormick PA, Burroughs AK, McIntyre N. How to insert a Sengstaken-Blakemore tube. *British Journal of Hospital Medicine* 1990; **43**:274–277.

Worthley LIG. *Synopsis of Intensive Care Medicine* 1st ed. Churchill Livingstone, Edinburgh 1994; 533–537.

Answers to 7.10

1. (a) Inferior myocardial infarction.

1. (b) The ECG shows Q waves and ST segment elevation in the inferior leads, II, III and AVF. During an acute myocardial infarction (MI) the ECG evolves through 3 stages – T wave peaking followed by T wave inversion, ST segment elevation and the appearance of new Q waves.

2. Assess Airway, Breathing and Circulation and institute basic and advanced life support if necessary. Reassure patient and give supplemental oxygen via a facemask. Give GTN (sublingual/spray) for coronary vasodilatation. Opioid analgesia is almost always required. Diamorphine in 1 mg boluses can be titrated against the patient's needs. An antiemetic (e.g. cyclizine) may be necessary. Early use of aspirin and thrombolysis reduces mortality. Intravenous nitrates may be required to treat continuing pain. Monitor continuously and investigate on coronary care unit. Heparin given s.c. until the patient mobilizes will reduce the incidence of DVT.

3. Complications include:

* *Extension of infarction:* Recurrent MI at the same site occurs in 10% of patients in the first fortnight. This is commoner in non-Q wave infarctions.
* *Post-infarction ischaemia:* This is associated with increased mortality. Patients with post-infarction angina who are refractory to medical management must undergo early catheterization and revascularization.
* *Arrhythmias:* Sinus bradycardia is common after inferior MI. Supraventricular tachycardias may be compensatory and consequent upon hypovolaemia or pump failure. Ventricular extrasystoles may herald the onset of ventricular tachycardia and must be treated with lignocaine. Atrioventricular conduction block at the level of the AV node (commoner than infranodal) occurs in 20% of inferior MIs. First degree heart block is the most frequent type but complete heart block occurs in 5%.

* *Left ventricular failure:* Initial treatment includes oxygen, diuretics and morphine. In severe cases invasive monitoring of both CVP and PWCP may be necessary. Intravenous nitrates to lower PWCP and inotropes may be required. Intra-aortic balloon counterpulsation is useful when cardiogenic shock supervenes.
* *Pericarditis:* The pericardium is affected in about 50% of MIs but pericarditis is not always clinically significant. The pain is relieved by NSAIDs. A delayed autoimmune phenomenon, Dressler's syndrome, may present up to 12 weeks later. This pericarditis is accompanied by fever, leucocytosis and, sometimes, pericardial or pleural effusions.
* *Other:* Rupture of ventricular wall, papillary muscles or interventricular septum, left ventricular aneurysm. Mural thrombi are rare in inferior infarctions.

4. If surgery is undertaken within six months of myocardial infarction, the peri-operative re-infarction rate is 5–86%; mortality 23–86%. This is 1.5–10 times higher than when the MI and surgery are separated by more than six months. After six months the peri-operative infarction rate is 2 – 6%. Rao *et al.* (*Anesthesiology* 1983: **59**:499–505) showed that invasive monitoring and rapid correction of cardiovascular parameters both intra-operatively and for 72 hours post-operatively reduced the peri-operative re-infarction rate to 5.8% when surgery took place within 3 months of MI. The type of MI (Q-wave or non-Q-wave), thrombolysis, coronary angioplasty and residual left ventricular function will also influence outcome.

Key references:

Miller RD (ed). *Anesthesia* 4th ed. Churchill Livingstone, New York 1994; 939–940.
Mangano DT. Perioperative cardiac morbidity. *Anesthesiology* 1990; **72**:153–184.

Answers to 7.11

1. Platelet count, prothrombin time (PT), activated partial thromboplastin time (APTT) and thrombin time (TT). If the PT, APTT or TT are abnormal, further tests should be done. A reptilase test will identify heparin coagulopathy and fibrinogen levels and fibrinogen degradation product (FDP) titres will identify disseminated intravascular coagulation. Massive blood transfusion is defined as transfusion of the patient's total blood volume (70 mL/kg in an adult) within 24 hours. The commonest cause of bleeding following a massive blood transfusion is dilutional thrombocytopenia. There is a poor correlation between the degree of bleeding and the platelet count. Spontaneous bleeding is rare if the platelet count is above 20 000/μL but post-operatively or following trauma a bleeding diathesis is likely if the count is less than 75 000/μL. The decision to give platelets must follow assessment of the individual risks and benefits for each patient; e.g. the consequences of bleeding following cardiac surgery or neurosurgery may be more devastating than knee surgery. At levels of 100 000/μL, platelets may still be indicated if there is clinical bleeding and evidence that the quality of the platelets is poor, e.g. if the patient has been on aspirin therapy in the last two weeks.

2. Red cell concentrate (RCC) has a haematocrit (packed cell volume, PCV) of 0.65 and is produced by removing plasma from whole blood (PCV 0.4). Therefore it does not contain as much plasma proteins or coagulation factors. If a massive blood loss is replaced with only RCC there will be a relative deficit of plasma proteins, which are necessary to maintain colloid osmotic pressure, and dilution of coagulation factors, leading to more haemorrhage.

3. Blood that has been collected normally in standard anticoagulant has plasma removed to give a PCV of 0.9 and SAG-M is then added until the PCV is 0.6. SAG-M (optimal additive solution) is an acronym for **s**odium chloride (140 mmol/L, **a**denine (1.5 mmol/L), **g**lucose (50 mmol/L). M stand for added **m**annitol. Stored blood degenerates and the minimum standard for viable blood is a red cell survival of 70% at 24 h post-transfusion. The adenine and glucose help maintain the level of ATP which is necessary for the sodium/potassium pump and the phosphorylation of spectrin protein that maintains the integrity of the cell wall. The sodium/potassium pump is important, as a rise in intracellular sodium is followed by water which causes swelling and fragility of the cell. Mannitol offsets this. Compared to whole blood SAG-M has:

- decreased viscosity due to the absence of plasma proteins so transfusion is quicker but it does not maintain colloid osmotic pressure and intravascular volume so well;
- an increase in shelf life from 28 to 35 days;
- no coagulation factors; so dilutional coagulopathy is more common.

Whole blood maintains most factors for 21 days but factors V and VIII decrease to 50% by day 1 and day 14 respectively. Its platelets do not function after 48 h. Fresh frozen plasma (FFP) contains all the coagulation factors. Cryoprecipitate is prepared from FFP and has higher concentrations of factors I, VIII, XIII, von Willebrand and fibronectin.

4. 7–10 000/μL. Each unit contains 50 mL of plasma including some clotting factors and this should be taken into account when treating coagulopathy. It will also contain some red blood cells and these can cause Rhesus sensitization.

Key reference:

Contreras M (ed). *ABC of Transfusion* 2nd ed. BMJ Publishers, London 1992; 38–40.

Answers to 7.12

1. Adult myasthenia gravis (MG), which is a myopathy affecting 1 in 20 000 adults. It is characterized by muscle weakness that deteriorates with repetitive muscle contraction. It usually presents with diplopia. 85% of patients develop involvement of the laryngeal, pharyngeal, facial, respiratory or limb muscles. The maximum effect occurs within three years of onset. It is an autoimmune disease associated with SLE, rheumatoid arthritis and thyroiditis. Antibodies to acetylcholine receptors (AChR) occur in 90% of patients. These are mainly IgG and do not occur in any other disease. Diagnosis is confirmed by giving the patient edrophonium ('Tensilon'), a short-acting anticholinesterase (AChE) which causes a dramatic improvement in muscle power within 30 s.

2. MG is treated by:

- Anticholinesterases: for symptomatic relief of mild MG; pyridostigmine is longer-acting than neostigmine so gives more stable control; antimuscarinics are often necessary initially but can often be tapered off.
- Immunosuppression: azathioprine helps in 45% of patients but takes 3 months to work; steroids can cause improvement in days in up to 80% of patients but have numerous side effects.
- Plasmapheresis helps in 45% of patients by reducing the concentration of AChR antibodies, but requires access to large veins.

3. Myasthenic (MC) and cholinergic (CC) crises. MC, a worsening of the myasthenic condition, can be provoked by emotional upset, infection, overexertion, or drugs (magnesium containing enemas or aminoglycosides). CC (excessive AChE effects) may present with collapse, confusion, vomiting, sweating and salivation. Differentiation may be difficult. A test dose of edrophonium (with immediately available respiratory support) should improve a MC and exacerbate a CC. 70% of adult patients with MG have thymic hyperplasia and 10% have thymomas. 50% are improved by thymectomy and a further 46% develop complete remission. Trans-sternal surgery gives better results than transcervical as more thymus can be excised but it is more invasive and often requires post-operative ventilation.

4. Pre-operative risk factors include:

- respiratory muscle involvement which leads to chest infections and respiratory failure;
- bulbar involvement (pharynx and larynx) which predisposes to aspiration pneumonitis and airway obstruction. It may require a gastrostomy feeding tube.

5. Characteristic drug responses in MG are:

- a normal response to thiopentone: because of the inherent muscle weakness (especially if the pre-operative dose of AChE is omitted), intubation may be possible without a muscle relaxant;
- resistance to suxamethonium: use 2–3 times the normal dose for a rapid sequence induction; there is an increased risk of dual block;
- increased sensitivity to nondepolarizing muscle relaxants: use 10–20% of the normal dose and monitor the result clinically and by peripheral nerve stimulator;
- reversal agents: risk of cholinergic crisis.

6. The need for post-operative ventilation in MG patients is difficult to predict but factors include: the operation, duration of the disease >6 years, vital capacity of <2.9 L, pyridostigmine doses >750 mg/day, and chronic respiratory disease other than that due to MG.

Key reference:

Baraka A. Anaesthesia and myasthenia gravis. *Canadian Journal of Anaesthesia* 1992; 39:476–486.

OSCE cycle 8 – answers

Answers to 8.1

1. Pseudocholinesterase variant **or** allergy to suxamethonium.

2. No. If a patient says that they are allergic to a drug this must be taken seriously until the history can be confirmed. A family history suggests a plasma cholinesterase variant. The reason for the previous admission to ITU may have been either pathology or unrelated to the use of suxamethonium, e.g. for the stabilization of pre-eclampsia.

3 and 4. Refer to Table 8.1

Table 8.1 Major abnormal PChE genotypes

	DN	*FN*	*Frequency*	*Clinical prolongation*
$E_1^u E_1^u$	80	60	97%	none
$E_1^u E_1^a$	60	50	3%	none/minimal
$E_1^a E_1^a$	20	20	1:3000	+++
$E_1^f E_1^f$	65	35	very rare	+
$E_1^s E_1^s$	80	60	very rare	+++

5. Alternatives to suxamethonium for anaesthesia for Caesarean section include:

- regional or infiltration technique. However, this may need to be converted to a general anaesthetic;
- high dose vecuronium;
- priming, although the large inter-patient variation means that the priming dose may fully paralyse some patients while having little effect on others;
- awake intubation.

Notes on plasma cholinesterase (PChE)

PChE is a tetrameric glycoprotein that is synthesized in the liver and found in all tissues except erythrocytes. It has no proven function but may be involved in detoxifying esterases present in the diet. It hydrolyses suxamethonium, normally terminating its action within 3–5 minutes. Prolonged action beyond this is diagnosed by peripheral nerve stimulator (PNS) which may show dual block. Causes include:

- pregnancy, maximum on the third day post-partum and lasting up to eight weeks;
- liver disease, renal disease, bronchial and gastrointestinal carcinoma and burns;
- inhibition of PChE, e.g. by bambuterol, ecothiopate eyedrops and trimetaphan;
- abnormal PChE due to genetic variation. The PChE gene is on chromosome 3 at location q26 and all relevant variants are due to mutations at this one gene.

Initial management is maintenance of anaesthesia to prevent awareness and IPPV until muscle power returns as assessed by PNS. Recovery can be hastened by the administration of fresh frozen plasma or purified serum cholinesterase but the former has inappropriate risks for a benign disease and the latter is not readily available in the UK. Chemical inhibition analysis (Table 8.1) may confirm the result but can miss rarer variants. If clinical evidence supports a diagnosis of abnormal PChE, chromosomal studies may be necessary to identify a rare genetic variant. The family should be appropriately investigated and counselled. The use of suxamethonium in future anaesthetics is not absolutely contraindicated provided that the risks of using suxamethonium as a long-acting muscle relaxant are taken into account.

Key reference:

Pantuck EJ. Plasma cholinesterase: Gene and variations. *Anesthesia and Analgesia* 1993; 77:380–386.

Answers to 8.2

1. He is polycythaemic, probably secondary to long-standing hypoxaemia. His white cell count is raised so it is important to exclude or treat any chest infection.

2. He has a type B pattern of chronic respiratory failure. He is acidaemic. There is a primary respiratory acidosis that is partially compensated by a metabolic alkalosis. He is hypoxaemic with a PaO_2 of less than 8 kPa.

3. He may stop breathing as he has a hypoxaemic respiratory drive. Normally, central chemoreceptors respond to $PaCO_2$ stimulating the respiratory centre in order to control body pH within narrow limits. This ensures enzymes (which are proteins) work in optimal conditions. If central chemoreceptors become insensitive to increases in $PaCO_2$ then the primary drive to ventilation becomes hypoxaemia. A PaO_2 below 8 kPa stimulates mainly the carotid body but also the aortic chemoreceptors, causing hyperventilation via the respiratory centre. This raises the PaO_2 as per the Ideal Alveolar Gas Equation:

$$PAO_2 = PIO_2 - \frac{PACO_2}{R} + F$$

PAO_2 = partial pressure of oxygen in an ideal alveolus

PIO_2 = partial inspired pressure of oxygen

$PACO_2$ = partial pressure of carbon dioxide in an ideal alveolus

R = respiratory quotient

F = small correction factor

This patient is retaining carbon dioxide. This is long-standing as there is a compensatory metabolic alkalosis shown by a raised standard bicarbonate and base excess. Renal compensation occurs slowly over days and respiratory compensation over minutes. The CSF will have normalized and the central chemoreceptors will have reset to a high $PaCO_2$. Increasing this patient's inspired O_2 concentration will reduce

his hypoxaemic drive and the hypoventilation will cause further hypercapnia and acidosis and may result in cardiac arrest. Volatile agents cause a dose dependent decrease in the ventilatory response to carbon dioxide but as little as 0.1 MAC will ablate the hypoxaemic ventilatory response. It is important to ensure adequate post-operative washout of volatiles. The administration of oxygen post-operatively should be by a fixed performance device such as a Venturi type mask.

4. Blood urea, glucose and electrolytes, ECG and a chest X-ray would be appropriate. Chronic obstructive airways disease usually co-exists with ischaemic heart disease as smoking is the primary aetiology in both. Right ventricular failure may occur as chronic hypoxaemia leads to pulmonary hypertension.

Notes on chronic obstructive airways disease
COAD describes a group of lung diseases that often co-exist:

Chronic bronchitis is defined symptomatically by a productive cough most days for three months of the year for two consecutive years. Classically this is the blue bloater who is obese, hypercapnic and hypoxic with compensatory bicarbonate retention and polycythaemia (Type B respiratory failure). They are prone to RVF, have a decreased ventilatory sensitivity to carbon dioxide and may have a hypoxic respiratory drive.

Emphysema is defined histopathologically as dilatation of those parts of the lung distal to the terminal bronchioles. Classically this is the pink puffer who is thin and may have normal arterial gases or a low $PaCO_2$ (Type A respiratory failure). They have a normal ventilatory response to carbon dioxide but a low transfer factor.

Asthma is defined functionally by reversible episodic airway obstruction.

Key reference:
Vickers MD, Jones RM (eds). *Medicine for Anaesthetists* 3rd ed. Blackwell Scientific Publications, 1989; 151–153.

Answers to 8.3

1. The jugular venous pulse (JVP) is best examined with the subject reclining comfortably at 45° with his head supported on one pillow. Clothing must be removed from the neck and chest and over-flexion of the neck avoided to prevent kinking of the vein. When the neck is viewed tangentially, the top of the JVP, which is the transition point between distended and collapsed vein, can normally be seen just above the clavicle. It must be distinguished from the carotid pulsation. Since the jugular vein communicates directly with the right atrium, the jugular venous pressure, which is the mean vertical height of the column of venous blood above the manubriosternal junction, reflects right atrial pressure (RAP). It is assumed that the manubriosternal angle lies 5 cm above the right atrium, irrespective of the position of the subject. The upper limit of normal RAP is approximately 9 cmH_2O (JVP= 4 cm).

2. The JVP, which varies with respiration and posture, disappears when light digital pressure is applied to the neck and can be accentuated by gentle pressure over the right hypochondrium (hepato-jugular reflex). The arterial pulse shows none of the above features. The arterial pulse is a sharp, localized, single pulse whereas the JVP comprises two waves per cardiac cycle.

3.

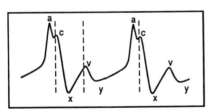

4. 'a' wave = rise in atrial pressure during atrial systole; 'x' descent = initially due to atrial relaxation which is followed by further down-sloping due to the tricuspid valve and floor of the atrium being pulled downwards during right ventricular systole; 'v' wave = venous return to the right atrium with the tricuspid valve closed, reaching a peak at the end of ventricular systole; 'y' descent = passive atrial emptying with an open tricuspid valve and relaxed right ventricle; 'c' wave = transmitted pulsation from carotid artery which may be superimposed on the 'x' descent; 'H' wave = seen between trough of 'y' descent and 'a' wave during slow atrial filling, reflects stiffness of right atrium.

5. Prominent 'a' waves may be seen when there is an increased resistance to atrial emptying such as in tricuspid stenosis/atresia, decreased compliance/hypertrophy of the right ventricle and pulmonary hypertension. Cannon waves are seen in complete a-v dissociation when the atrium contracts against a closed tricuspid valve. No 'a' waves are seen in atrial fibrillation. Prominent 'v' waves are seen with tricuspid regurgitation and atrial septal defects.

Notes

1. The jugular vein is a deep structure and is not usually visible when venous pressure is normal but the pulsations are transmitted to the skin of the neck. When a subject with a normal right atrial pressure lies supine the top of the JVP cannot be seen although the vein is distended; with the subject sitting upright, the top of the JVP is usually obscured by the sternum. In disease, the angle at which the patient reclines may have to be varied to visualize the top of the JVP.

A simplified *aide memoire* is 'a' = atrial contraction; 'x' descent = atrial relaxation; 'v' = atrial filling; 'y' descent = atrial emptying.

Important causes of a raised JVP include congestive heart failure, pericardial disease, hypervolaemia, superior vena caval obstruction (nonpulsatile) and pulmonary embolism.

Key reference:

Braunwald E (ed). *Heart Disease* 4th ed. W B Saunders Company, Philadelphia 1992; 18–20.

Answers to 8.4

1. Pall (BB100F) breathing system filter which is both a heat and moisture exchanger (HME) and a microbial filter.

2. It consists of a pleated hydrophobic membrane which is made of resin-bonded ceramic fibres. This provides a large surface area for heat and moisture exchange and a low airflow resistance. It has very small pores that prevent the passage of liquids. The filter has an internal volume of 90 mL and weighs 44 g. HME performance is maintained even at high gas flows, it resists passage of secretions and bacterial/viral filtration efficiency is greater than 99.999%.

3. Simple hygroscopic devices (e.g. Engström Edith) and composite devices (e.g. Intersurgical Filtaguard, Dar Hygrobac) made up of a hygroscopic layer and a felt filter layer. The Dar Hygroster is a newer composite filter that combines a spiral hygroscopic element with a pleated hydrophobic membrane.

4. Maintenance of airway humidity and temperature in patients in whom the normal humidification mechanisms are by-passed as a result of tracheal intubation, prevention of contamination of breathing systems and ventilators in theatres, ITUs and during resuscitation and transport ventilation.

5. Cold water humidifiers, hot water humidifiers, nebulizers, closed system anaesthesia with low fresh gas flows, instillation of saline into the trachea and humidification of driving/entrained gas in jet ventilators have been described.

6. Heat loss, moisture loss from the airway resulting in mucosal damage and impairment of the mucociliary escalator, decreased surfactant activity, increased atelectasis, reduction in functional residual capacity and static compliance with consequent impairment of oxygenation.

Notes

re 3. The hygroscopic HMEs are made of wool, foam or paper-like material and may be impregnated with moisture-retaining chemicals such as calcium or lithium chloride. They have large pores and offer little resistance to gas flow but have poor filtration properties. The felt layer of composite filters can be subjected to an electrical field (electret felt) which increases filtration efficiency and hydrophobicity.

re 5. *Cold water humidifiers*: gas is passed over the surface of the water or bubbled through it. The level of humidification is limited by the surface area of the gas/water interface and microbial colonization is a risk. Cheap, simple to use.
Hot water humidifiers: generate water vapour and heat the humidified gas/water electrically to achieve a preset temperature. Versatile but risk of thermal and electrical hazards.
Nebulizers: produce a mist of supersaturated droplets of water, usually at room temperature. Delivery of large volumes of water may result in increased airway resistance and water overload. Expensive.

re 6. Under normal conditions 250 mL of water as saturated vapour and 350 kcal of heat (latent heat of vaporization) are lost from the lungs each day. Up to 33% of basal heat production in infants may be required to heat and humidify inspired gases, and ventilation with dry compressed medical gases may result in a marked drop in core temperature.

Key references:

Hedley RM, Allt-Graham J. Heat and moisture exchangers and breathing filters. *British Journal of Anaesthesia* 1994; **73**:227–236.

Shelly MP, Lloyd GM, Park GR. A review of the mechanisms and methods of humidification of inspired gases. *Intensive Care Medicine* 1988; **14**:1–9.

Answers to 8.5

1. Transurethral resection (TUR) syndrome.

2. Presenting signs and symptoms include:

- CVS: initially there is a phase of intra-vascular hypervolaemia with an increase in systolic and pulse pressures but this can be masked by intra-operative haemorrhage. Following redistribution of irrigation fluid to the extracellular fluid (ECF) there tends to be intravascular hypovolaemia with a reduced CVP and cardiac output. ECG changes include bradycardias, ventricular tachycardia and ST depression. Angina may occur.
- RS: pulmonary oedema, tachypnoea, dyspnoea and cyanosis.
- CNS: visual disturbances, irritability, irrational behaviour, nausea and seizures.
- Skin: abnormal sensations, e.g. prickling.
- GU: anuria which may be masked by bladder irrigation post-operatively.
- Disseminated intravascular coagulopathy.

3. The volume absorbed depends on the number and size of open venous sinuses, the duration of resection and the pressure of the irrigating fluid. Guidelines (which may reduce the incidence but do not guarantee prevention of the TUR syndrome) include:

- the pre-operative serum sodium should be normal;
- limit irrigating pressure to 60–70 cmH$_2$O;
- limit resection time to one hour;
- only give saline-containing intravenous fluids;
- regional anaesthesia reduces blood loss and allows earlier recognition of symptoms by talking to the patient;
- post-operative irrigation should be with saline not glycine.

4. Plasma sodium. 1% ethanol. The end-breath concentration continuously reflects the volume of irrigation fluid absorbed.

Notes on TUR syndrome

Minor CNS and CVS effects occur due to absorption of irrigation fluid in up to 25% of TUR operations and rarely they are fatal. The irrigation fluid is forced intravascularly through open prostatic veins and also extravascularly through small perforations in the bladder or prostatic capsule. With the latter, effects are more delayed and prolonged. The commonest irrigating fluid is 1.5% glycine. 2.1% glycine is iso-osmolar but is optically inferior.

The pathophysiology of the TUR syndrome is complicated and includes fluid and electrolyte shifts, haemodilution and the metabolic effects of glycine. Osmolarity changes tend to be small and postmortem cerebral oedema is uncommon so it is unlikely that hypo-osmolarity is a significant factor. Severe hyponatraemia is associated with severe symptoms and a poor prognosis but this may be a marker rather than a cause of the syndrome.

Glycine is an inhibitory neurotransmitter acting on chloride channels. With its metabolites it can cause irritability, nausea and visual disturbances and may be the sole cause of the CNS effects in the TUR syndrome.

The dilution of plasma proteins disturbs the Starling equilibrium, causing accumulation of water in the liver and lungs.

General treatment is supportive including oxygen and IPPV as necessary. Colloid and vasoconstrictors are appropriate for the intravascular hypovolaemia and low cardiac output and this may be complicated if a spinal is wearing off.

Specific treatment includes diuretics. Hypertonic saline is controversial as it may cause pulmonary oedema. Anuria is common and renal failure may occur.

Key reference:

Hahn RG. The transurethral resection syndrome. *Acta Anaesthesiologca Scandinavica* 1991; **35**:557–567.

Answers to 8.6

1. The obvious severity of his burns should not distract from the initial priority of assessment of the airway, breathing and circulation. Inhalation injury, aspiration due to impaired consciousness, hypovolaemia and trauma must be recognized and treated. Hypotension at this stage is unlikely to be due to burns. Vasodilatation due to carbon monoxide or cyanide or hypovolaemia due to trauma should be suspected. Once resuscitation has started, clothing is removed to allow full assessment and prevent further burns. Powdered chemicals should be brushed away. Acids should not be neutralized by adding alkalis as the reaction releases heat, causing more damage. They should be washed away with water. The patient should then be covered to minimize hypothermia. This is exacerbated by an evaporative loss from the burnt area of up to 200 ml/m^2/h (normal 15 ml/m^2/h). The pathophysiology is complex. Endogenous mediators cause a huge systemic inflammatory response greater than that in trauma or sepsis. The increase in vascular permeability and oedema is not limited to burnt tissues. Water and protein are also lost from the open wounds so intravascular volume falls and hypovolaemic shock ensues.

2. The area of burnt skin is gauged by the 'rule of nines', i.e. the body is divided into sections each being a multiple of 9% of total body surface area (BSA). The back represents 18%. This rule does not apply below 14 years of age as the head is proportionately larger. Instead, Lund and Browder paediatric charts should be used. At all ages the palmar surface of the patient's hand including the fingers represents 1%. This can be used for assessing irregularly shaped burns.

3. Intravenous fluids are given if burns exceed 15% in adults or 10% in children. There are many i.v. regimens: none is exact. Perfusion should be monitored and fluids altered accordingly.

One guideline is [wt (kg) x % burns x 2 ml] over 8 h and the same volume repeated over the next 16 h. This is in addition to maintenance fluids and starts at the time of the burn. Superficial burns (erythema) are not included in this calculation. It is accepted that i.v. volume replacement is mandatory to maintain perfusion but the benefit of colloid over crystalloid in the first 24 h is not proven and less important.

4. Management and prognosis are dependent on the % BSA, the depth (see Table 8.6) and the anatomical region affected by the burn.

Table 8.6 Classification of burns by depth

	Superficial	*Partial thickness*	*Full thickness*
Injury depth	Superficial	Outer dermis	Dermis +/– deeper tissue
Skin colour	Red, wet, weeping	Pink or mottled	Waxy white, leathery, dark or charred
Oedema	Minimal	Yes	No
Blisters	No	Yes	No
Painful	Yes	Yes	No

5. In 60% burns the basal energy expenditure (BEE) may double. This hypercatabolic state requires active nutritional support. Core temperature rises 1–2°C due to resetting of the hypothalamus. Cooling causes the BEE to increase to maintain this pyrexia so ambient temperature should be kept at 30°C. Humoral and cellular immunity are impaired. Wound sepsis and pneumonia are the major causes of late death. Antibiotics given i.v. do not penetrate the coagulated zone or the vasoconstricted zone around it. They cause the emergence of resistant strains and should be reserved for proven infection. Prophylactic topical antibiotics are used: dead tissue is removed surgically.

Key reference:

Kaufman L (ed). *Anaesthesia Review 10*. Churchill Livingstone, Edinburgh 1993;149–162.

Answers to 8.7

1. Down's syndrome (trisomy 21, T21) and finger clubbing. The characteristic facies is well known: flat face, slanting eyes, brachycephaly (round rather than ovoid head), small ears and, in common with 20% of the normal population, epicanthic folds. There may be a single transverse palmar crease and short, broad hands and fingers. Chromosomal abnormalities occur in 0.6% of live births and Down's is the commonest (0.15%). Only trisomies 21, 18 and 13 survive to birth. Trisomies 18 and 13 only survive a few weeks but most children with Down's syndrome survive into adulthood.

2. Finger clubbing is present when the normal angle between the nail and the dorsum of the finger is >180°. The nail bed is fluctuant due to increased vascularity. The nails' curvatures are increased both lengthways and side-to-side. Congenital clubbing is rare and has no associated pathology. The cause of clubbing is not known but its associations include:

- squamous cell bronchial carcinoma;
- chronic suppurative lung disease, e.g. lung abscess, cystic fibrosis, bronchiectasis and empyema;
- pulmonary fibrosis, e.g. cryptogenic fibrosing alveolitis;
- tuberculosis;
- pleural and mediastinal tumours, e.g. mesothelioma;
- congenital cyanotic heart disease (CCHD) and subacute bacterial endocarditis (SBE);
- inflammatory bowel disease;
- cirrhosis and chronic liver disease.

Clubbing does not occur with chronic bronchitis or emphysema. It only occurs in cor pulmonale because of the associated lung pathology. In this child the likely causes are SBE or CCHD. Clubbing usually takes months to develop so it is not seen in infants with CCHD or in acute bacterial endocarditis.

3. Intubation problems with Down's include:

- large tongue with a small mouth, mandible and maxilla;
- atlanto-axial subluxation with instability, which occurs in up to 15%;
- subglottic stenosis, so use an endotracheal tube 1 mm smaller than expected for age.

4. Congenital heart disease (CHD) occurs in about 1% of live births. 40% of children with Down's syndrome have CHD including:

- endocardial cushion defects in 40%;
- ventricular septal defects in 25%;
- patent ductus arteriosus in 10%;
- tetralogy of Fallot in 10%.

There is an increased risk of developing pulmonary hypertension with Down's syndrome. This may develop secondary to obstructive sleep apnoea in the absence of a primary heart defect. More than 80% of the cardiac defects are treated surgically. Even small amounts of air may cause a paradoxical embolus through a septal defect which by-passes the pulmonary circulation and lodges in cerebral vessels. People with Down's syndrome also have an increased risk of thyroid and neoplastic disease, strabismus, cataracts and seizures. There are no proven abnormal reactions to anaesthetic agents.

5. Post-operative problems include:

- increased post-operative stridor and laryngospasm;
- increased susceptibility to respiratory tract infections due to immunodeficiency and pulmonary oedema;
- generalized hypotonia and obstructive sleep apnoea.

Key reference:

Kobel M, Creighton RE, Steward DJ. Anaesthetic considerations in Down's syndrome. *Canadian Anaesthetists' Society Journal* 1982; **29**:593–599.

Answers to 8.8

Ideally all patients undergoing day stay surgery must be interviewed and examined post-operatively by both the surgeon and the anaesthetist. They, together with the nurse, must ensure that the patient fulfils criteria for discharge from the day stay unit. The details of these criteria may vary slightly from unit to unit.

- The patient should be awake and be orientated in time, place and person.
- The patient should be able to change his/her own clothes and ambulate, without feeling dizzy or lightheaded. Most anaesthetic and sedative drugs affect baroreceptor sensitivity but recovery of the reflex is rapid.
- The operative site must be inspected. There should be no abnormal swelling, bleeding or compromised circulation at the operative site.
- He/she should be able to tolerate oral fluids without nausea or vomiting.
- Blood pressure, pulse, respiratory rate and temperature should remain stable for at least 30 minutes before discharge.
- The patient's pain should be controllable with simple oral analgesics. A prescription for appropriate analgesic medication to be taken at home must be issued and clear instructions given. Dietary instructions must also be given.
- The patient should not have had more than minimal nausea or vomiting over the preceding 30 min. A prescription for anti-emetic medication may be necessary.
- If central neural blockade was performed as part of the anaesthetic technique, it must be ascertained that the patient is able to micturate and there is return of motor power, sensation and proprioception prior to discharge.
- No new signs or symptoms should have developed since the operation.
- Although a battery of tests has been described to assess recovery of cognitive sensory and psychomotor function after general anaesthesia, there are no standardized guidelines at present. These tests are usually too labour intensive and time-consuming to be of real benefit in a busy day stay unit.
- The patient must be escorted home by a responsible adult. Patients are usually warned not to drive, operate machinery or undertake complex mental tasks for at least 24 hours.
- The patient should be given a telephone number to contact the hospital on, in case complications were to develop at home. Some units use postal questionnaires for post-operative follow up.
- Arrangements for follow up outpatient clinics must be made before discharge.

Notes

Cognitive function tests:
Processing: mental arithmetic, reaction time testing (choice reaction time, simulated car driving tests).
Integration: critical flicker fusion test.
Memory tests: word span.
Learning: word lists.

Sensory function tests:
  Maddox Wing test
  Vigilance test
  Stimulus detection

Psychomotor function tests:
  Trieger dot test
  Post box test
  Bender Gestalt Track Tracer Test

Key references:

Klepper ID, Sanders LD, Rosen M (eds). *Ambulatory Anaesthesia and Sedation*. Blackwell Scientific Publications, Oxford 1991; 63–168.

Miller RD (ed). *Anesthesia* 4th ed. Churchill Livingstone, New York 1994; 2237–2240.

Answers to 8.9

1. (a) Direct current defibrillator.

1. (b) The defibrillator is a capacitor which consists essentially of two plates separated by an insulator. It stores electric charge which when required, can be released in a controlled fashion. When the defibrillator is discharged, a short pulse of a large current of high voltage is transmitted through a pair of large electrodes (paddles). The amount of energy stored will depend both on the charge and the potential.

2. Regular maintenance checks of defibrillator output and a daily functional test are important. Gel pads must be placed on the patient's chest both to reduce chest wall impedance and to minimize risk of tissue damage from burns. The two gel pads must not touch each other.

Paddles of the appropriate size must be selected (13 cm diameter paddles for adults) and correct paddle position must be ensured. Anterolateral placement is usual with one paddle placed over the apex in the mid-axillary line and the other parasternally below the right clavicle. Alternative paddle position (e.g. anteroposterior) may be considered if defibrillation is unsuccessful.

The correct energy level must be selected and the charge button activated. The energy levels currently recommended by the ERC for the first three shocks during advanced life support are 200 J, 200 J and 360 J respectively. Charging must not take place with the paddles dangling in mid air–the paddles must either be in their cradles or on the patient's chest.

The paddles must be placed on the gel pads and firm pressure applied. Once the defibrillator is charged it is important to ensure that nobody is in contact with the patient or the trolley before discharging the shock. (The energy delivered is enough to cause cardiac arrest!)

Once the shock is delivered the paddles must be kept on the patient's chest or returned to the cradle for recharging. Defibrillation at end-expiration will minimize thoracic impedance. A short delay may occur before the ECG signal returns following defibrillation, due to the high impedance retained by the electrodes during this time.

3. Ensure the 'lead select' switch is appropriately switched depending on whether leads or paddles are being used to monitor the ECG. Adhesive silver/silver chloride electrodes give a better ECG signal than paddles but ensure that the leads are firmly connected both at the patient and machine ends. If paddles are used, they must make proper contact with the electrode–chest wall coupling medium and the gain must be turned up sufficiently. Remember that a diagnosis of asystole carries a poorer prognosis than ventricular fibrillation (VF) and if there is any doubt at all, resuscitation must proceed as for VF.

4. The Automatic Implantable Cardioverter Defibrillator (AICD) is implanted under general anaesthesia in those patients in whom ventricular arrhythmias are unresponsive to medical and surgical treatment. The sophisticated AICDs can function as pacemakers, cardioverters and defibrillators. AICDs can detect changes in heart rate and ECG morphology and deliver a cardioverting or defibrillating current of 23–38 J to terminate ventricular tachyarrhythmias. A period of 5–20 s is taken for sensing and a further 5–15 s is needed to charge the capacitors before giving the shock. If the first shock is unsuccessful in treating VF, the AICD will recharge and deliver between three to six further shocks, depending on the model. Special care is necessary in the post-operative period as the AICD is not activated until several days after surgery.

Key references:

Advanced Life Support Working Party of the European Resuscitation Council. Guidelines for advanced life support. *Resuscitation* 1992; **24**:108–109.

Zaidan JR. Pacemakers. *Refresher Courses in Anesthesiology* Vol 21. The American Society of Anesthesiologists, Inc. 1993; 1–12.

Answers to 8.10

1. Acute aspirin poisoning may result in a compensated or uncompensated respiratory alkalosis or a metabolic acidosis or a combination of these. Following absorption it is hydrolysed to salicylate which has multiple effects. It causes a respiratory alkalosis by direct stimulation of the respiratory centre. Renal compensation then occurs with urinary loss of sodium, bicarbonate, potassium and water. The plasma bicarbonate falls and the $PaCO_2$ and pH return toward normal. The salicylate then causes a metabolic acidosis by:

- uncoupling oxidative phosphorylation in skeletal muscle, increasing the oxygen consumption and CO_2 and heat production;
- derangement of carbohydrate metabolism resulting in accumulation of organic acids;
- renal impairment due to poor perfusion causing accumulation of inorganic acids;
- accumulation of its acidic metabolites.

This results in a picture of uncompensated respiratory acidosis with a high $PaCO_2$ and a low pH and plasma bicarbonate. This is exacerbated by higher toxic doses which directly depress the respiratory and vasomotor centres. Cardio-respiratory collapse results.

2. Serum levels may be deceptively low as salicylate is taken up by tissues. Clinical findings are more important and include:

- initially tinnitus, nausea, vomiting;
- hyperventilation (tetany is unusual and hypoventilation is a late ominous sign);
- restlessness that may progress to coma;
- dehydration (poor perfusion, tachycardia);
- vasodilatation, fever and sweating (unless too dehydrated);
- arrhythmias due to acidosis, hypokalaemia;
- cerebral oedema with fits, a late sign;
- coagulopathy due to platelet effects, rare in acute aspirin intoxication.

3. Dehydration occurs due to hyperventilation and renal losses in response to the respiratory alkalosis, sweating and vomiting. Hypernatraemia occurs as water loss exceeds sodium loss. Hypo- and hyperglycaemia can occur. Fluid is replaced by dextrose with potassium as the total body potassium is low.

4. Ipecacuanha causes vomiting by gastric irritation and stimulation of the chemoreceptor trigger zone. Vomiting may not occur, especially if the patient has taken an antiemetic or been given charcoal which absorbs the ipecacuanha. The dose may be repeated or gastric lavage instituted. Contraindications to the use of ipecacuanha include:

- ingestion of corrosive poisons, e.g. alkalis;
- patients who, by the time they vomit, may be comatose and not protect their airway;
- ingestion of hydrocarbons (turpentine, furniture polish) as these can cause a haemorrhagic aspiration pneumonitis if inhaled;
- ingestion of a central stimulant as it may provoke a fit.

5. Gastric lavage is done with the largest possible tube, i.e. about 36 FG in an adult and 24 FG in a child. It is unlikely to be of use >4 hours after ingestion unless an antiemetic is ingested, e.g. opioids, aspirin (up to 24 h) or a tricyclic antidepressant (up to 8 h). A safe airway is a prerequisite, i.e. the presence of a cough reflex or an tracheal tube. Gastric lavage also allows installation of charcoal, desferri-oxamine (for iron poisoning) and Fuller's earth (for paraquat poisoning). Other methods of eliminating aspirin include forced alkaline diuresis and multiple dosing of activated charcoal. Haemodialysis is effective and allows correction of altered biochemistry.

Key reference:

Jaimovich DG, Vidyasagar D (eds). *The Pediatric Clinics of North America,* WB Saunders, Philadelphia 1993; **40**:407–429.

Answers to 8.11

1. Questions should be directed at eliciting the following information: time of onset with respect to timing of procedure, nature of headache, severity, radiation, effect of posture, other aggravating or relieving factors, presence of nausea, vomiting, visual and auditory disturbances.

2. Post-dural puncture headache (PDPH) may be severe, and interfere with parent–child bonding; the patient may display a wide range of emotions. A full explanation of the reason for the PDPH, reassurance that it is often self-limiting, discussion of the management options and regular assessment are important. Breast feeding should be encouraged and psychological support provided as necessary. A horizontal position will be the most comfortable (mobilize whenever possible) and it is prudent to maintain adequate oral/intravenous hydration (although there is no evidence that it relieves headache). Simple analgesics will treat mild to moderate pain effectively. Limited evidence suggests that caffeine (oral or i.v.) and DDAVP may be useful adjuncts. If initial conservative management fails, epidural blood patching, which is safe and effective for the treatment of PDPH, must be offered.

3. Two experienced anaesthetists are required. Strict asepsis must be maintained. The epidural space is identified in an adjacent space and 30 mL of autologous blood are withdrawn from an arm vein by the second operator. 10 mL are sent for blood culture and 20 mL are injected into the epidural space over 2 minutes. Injection should be stopped for 30 s if discomfort or parasthesiae are experienced by the patient and then resumed. The patient must remain supine during the injection and for 30 min after. The patient should be advised not to strain or lift heavy objects for a week afterwards.

Notes

1. PDPH commonly occurs within 48 hours of dural puncture. It is throbbing in nature, of varying severity, aggravated by the upright position and relieved when recumbent, typically fronto-occipital and may radiate to the neck and shoulders. Neck stiffness, nausea, vomiting, visual and auditory disturbances (diplopia, tinnitus etc.) may be present.

PDPH is thought to be caused by a combination of ongoing CSF leakage and reflex cerebrovascular dilatation. Relief of the low pressure headache by manual abdominal compression is a useful diagnostic test. Spontaneous resolution is not uncommon. Rarely it causes cranial nerve palsies, subdural haematomata and may be incapacitating. The onset of PDPH may sometimes be delayed and rarely it may persist for one week or longer.

Headache unrelated to anaesthesia is common following delivery (39%). Important but rare causes that need exclusion are paranasal sinusitis, cortical vein thrombosis (1:3000–1:6000 deliveries) and intracranial tumours, haemorrhage and vascular malformations.

2. Abdominal binders and the prone position have been shown to raise pressure in the epidural space but are uncomfortable and unpopular.

3. A success rate of 89% with epidural blood patching has been reported, whilst a second blood patch was successful in 97.5%. Blood should not be injected epidurally in the presence of systemic infection. Epidural patching with Dextran 40 has also been successful.

Key references:

Shnider SM, Levinson G (eds). *Anesthesia for Obstetrics* 3rd ed. Williams and Wilkins, Baltimore 1993; 437–439.

Stride PC, Cooper GM. Dural taps revisited. *Anaesthesia* 1993; **48**:247–255.

Answers to 8.12

1. Rules of thumb regarding children include:

- birthweight (3.5 kg) doubles by 5 months (7 kg) and trebles (10.5 kg) by a year;
- 1–10 years: weight (kg) = 2(Age + 4);
- estimated blood volume is:
    - 80–90 mL/kg from 0 to 3 months;
    - 75–80 mL/kg from 3 to 12 months;
    - 70–75 mlLkg after 12 months

i.e. an estimated weight of 18 20 kg and a blood volume of 1.3 to 1.5 L. Up to 40% of children having tonsillectomies lose 10% of their estimated blood volume. If the child is still bleeding three hours later he will have lost more than this 10% (130 mL) and will need a blood transfusion. He should be given oxygen and one unit of blood should be cross-matched urgently. He should be resuscitated fully before the induction of anaesthesia.

2. Children tend to swallow the blood so the amount visible is not a good indicator of the total amount lost. Initially they compensate well and changes in blood pressure and heart rate may be small. The average systolic blood pressure in children is about 80 + (2 x age) in mmHg. Poor perfusion is indicated by cold, pale, cyanosed or mottled peripheries with constricted veins and no return of capillary flush within two seconds. Tachypnoea may occur due to increasing catecholamines. The maximum respiratory rate per minute is 40 at 1 month, 25 at 1 year and 20 at 5 years. Agitation or drowsiness may occur but all these signs may be masked by the effects of the previous anaesthetic.

4. There are three main problems at induction: hypovolaemia, a full stomach and difficult intubation. Hypovolaemia causes difficulty with venous access and cardiovascular instability on induction. This is complicated by the presence of residual anaesthetic so no premedication is given and the induction dose should be reduced. Swallowed blood in the stomach may be aspirated or complicate intubation. Intubation may be difficult in the presence of blood clots in the pharynx and a swollen laryngopharynx from the previous surgery and intubation.

5. An experienced anaesthetist should be present due to the risks mentioned and the quick onset of cyanosis in children. Included in the standard equipment are two large bore suckers, two laryngoscopes and a range of tracheal tubes. The two main methods of induction are:

(a) Pre-oxygenation and a rapid sequence intra-venous induction using cricoid pressure and suxamethonium. The advantages include familiarity with the technique and rapid securing of the airway. The disadvantage is the potential for losing the airway when the child is not breathing spontaneously. If the anaesthetist is unable to intubate the child ventilation by a mask may be difficult due to the presence of airway oedema and clot.

(b) A gaseous induction with halothane and oxygen in the left lateral head down position. When anaesthesia is deep enough to allow suction of blood the airway is assessed by laryngoscopy. The child may be intubated on its side or cricoid pressure applied, the patient turned supine and then intubated. The main advantage is maintenance of the airway at all times. Disadvantages include the cardiovascular depression with halothane (more common than when this technique was used with ether), the slow induction if the airway is narrowed, the risk of laryngospasm if intubated too early and the difficulty of intubating the child in the left lateral position which is not a technique familiar to many anaesthetists.

After securing the airway a wide bore gastric tube should be placed and aspirated. Awake extubation should be performed in the left lateral head down position.

Key reference:

Nimmo WS, Rowbotham DJ, Smith G (eds). *Anaesthesia*. 2nd ed. Blackwell Scientific Publications, Oxford 1994: 937–938.

OSCE cycle 9 – answers

Answers to 9.1

1. The causes of early post-operative hypox-aemia [PaO_2 <8 kPa (60 mmHg) or SaO_2 <90%] include:

- inadequate replacement of blood loss;
- myocardial depression;
- wound pain/supine position/restrictive bandaging, reducing alveolar ventilation;
- impaired gas exchange due to reduced FRC, increased shunt and increased V/Q mismatch;
- abolition of hypoxic pulmonary vaso-constriction by anaesthetic agents;
- diffusion hypoxia;
- post-hyperventilation hypoxia;
- impaired ventilatory response;
- residual muscle paralysis;
- airway obstruction/bronchospasm;
- pre-existing lung disease.

2. It is difficult in the early phase to diagnose hypoxia clinically. Cyanosis is difficult to see or quantify. The rate and depth of breathing are not totally helpful although slow shallow breathing may point to depressed central control. Measuring arterial oxygenation is the only reliable method of detection and assessment of the hypoxic state. Continuous monitoring of SaO_2 with pulse oximetry is both useful and practical.

3. Ensure the airway is patent. Airways obstruction may occur due to mechanical factors at oropharyngeal level, or be due to laryngospasm or bronchospasm. Observe the respiratory pattern and auscultate the chest. Clear oropharynx of secretions and optimize airway with chin lift/jaw thrust/head tilt man-oeuvres. Use an oropharyngeal or naso-pharyngeal airway if required. Assess level of residual neuromuscular blockade. If significant, this may necessitate continuation of mechanical ventilation until the muscle relaxant wears off, or further doses of reversal agent. Hypo-ventilation from opioid-induced central respiratory depression may be treated with naloxone. Repeat doses may have to be titrated against response. Ensure that blood loss has been adequately replaced and the patient is haemodynamically stable. Relieve mechanical factors that may cause hypoventilation. Oxygen therapy by facemask should continue throughout the recovery period. (In patients with obesity, heart or lung disease and operations on the thorax or abdomen it is prudent to continue oxygen therapy for 3 days after surgery.) Nurse the patient in the recovery position to minimize the risk of aspiration. Post-operative chest physiotherapy will help improve lung volumes.

4. Causes of late post-operative hypoxaemia:

- mechanical ventilatory abnormalities;
- VC and FRC are reduced post-operatively;
- abdominal wounds, pain and supine posture contribute;
- small airway closure and impaired cough mechanism lead to retention of secretions and atelectasis;
- impaired gas exchange;
- impaired respiratory control usually due to opioids given for pain relief;
- impairment of rib cage movement and hypotonia of the upper airway musculature during REM sleep.

Hypoxaemia during the later post-operative period is related temporally to increased production of catecholamines, tachycardia, arrhythmias, myocardial ischaemia and hypertension.

Key references:

Jones JG, Sapsford DJ, Wheatley RG. Postoperative hypoxaemia: mechanisms and time course. *Anaesthesia* 1990; **45**:566–573.

Atkinson RS, Adams AP (eds). *Recent Advances in Anaesthesia and Analgesia* Vol 17. Churchill Livingstone, Edinburgh 1992; 103–117.

Answers to 9.2

1. Abdominal pain, a pulsatile abdominal mass and hypovolaemic shock equal a ruptured abdominal aortic aneurysm.

2. No. He may have a fixed pacemaker, be on ß-blockers or have diabetic autonomic neuropathy.

3. Only (d) is appropriate.

Notes on ruptured abdominal aortic aneurysms

90% rupture into the retroperitoneal space and if the haemorrhage is limited by tamponade the patient may survive long enough to allow surgical repair. Untreated mortality is 90% at 6 weeks. The high treated mortality (50%) is related to the systolic blood pressure at diagnosis and the time taken to control the haemorrhage by aortic cross-clamping. Hypotension, especially if refractory to fluid challenge, reflects the severity of the rupture and the patient's cardiovascular reserve. Co-existing diseases are the rule and any delay in surgically controlling the haemorrhage causes further ischaemic organ damage. Initial management aims to maintain adequate perfusion of vital organs until the bleeding is controlled. Specific guidelines for fluid replacement are controversial and each patient will have different requirements. A mean arterial pressure of 65 mmHg is a reasonable aim but not proven. Aggressive fluid resuscitation should be tempered by the risk of disrupting the retroperitoneal tamponade, causing dilutional coagulopathy and delaying surgery. Surgical and anaesthetic preparation are best achieved simultaneously in theatre. Anaesthetic preparation must include:

- 100% oxygen;
- siting a large bore intravenous cannula and sending blood for cross-matching of 10 units.

Four units of group O blood should be sent for immediately;
- i.v. fluids to maintain organ viability;
- non-invasive blood pressure and ECG.

A pulse oximeter should be attached but may not work if there is severe vasoconstriction. The insertion of arterial and central venous lines should not delay surgery. Prior to clamping of the aorta anything which may disrupt the tamponade should be avoided: placement of a nasogastric tube and urinary catheterization should be deferred till the patient is anaesthetized; movement of the patient should be gentle; induction of anaesthesia should be smooth to ensure no coughing. Induction should start when the patient's skin has been fully prepared and draped and the surgical staff are scrubbed and ready. On induction there may be a precipitous drop in blood pressure as the tamponade effect of the abdominal muscles is reduced by paralysis. The specific technique for maintenance is not important but care must be taken of the cardiovascular parameters and the risk of awareness. The replacement of blood loss by itself is a challenge and the presence of a second anaesthetist is invaluable. If peripheral lines are difficult, central venous access may be gained using a large bore (8.5 FG) pulmonary artery catheter introducer. Once surgical control is achieved the institution of invasive monitoring is necessary for intra-operative and post-operative blood sampling and cardiovascular monitoring. Peri-operative hypothermia, the surgical stress of the operation, the large blood loss and the presence of co-existing diseases in these patients requires them to be managed post-operatively in the intensive care unit.

Key reference:

Brimacombe J, Berry A. A review of anaesthesia for ruptured abdominal aortic aneurysm with special emphasis on preclamping fluid resuscitation. *Anaesthesia and Intensive Care* 1993; **21**:311–323.

Answers to 9.3

1. Indications for insertion of arterial lines are:

- operations in which the moment to moment monitoring and manipulation of the cardio-vascular system is necessary, e.g. vascular and cardiothoracic surgery, neurosurgery and hypotensive anaesthesia;
- patients who are cardiovascularly unstable and patients with severe cardiovascular disease, e.g. ischaemic heart disease;
- patients who will need frequent arterial blood gases or other blood sampling.

2. The commonest cause of overdamping is air bubbles in the monitoring line which is why lines should be transparent to assess this. Other causes are clots, kinking of the cannula or lines, and the cannula abutting the vessel wall.

3. Examination of the waveform alone is inadequate to diagnose overdamping. There is a wide variation of waveform between patients. Check the line for bubbles, clots and kinking. Check and manipulate the cannula. Flush the system, ending the flush during diastole. This has three functions:

- it may remove bubbles;
- if it doesn't flush, the line must be blocked or kinked or the bag isn't pressurized;
- it will confirm if the system is overdamped.

If damping is optimal the resulting waveform produced should overshoot below diastolic once, rise above diastolic by 6% of flush value and then settle into the patient's waveform (Fig. 9.3).

Notes on invasive pressure monitoring

The complex arterial waveform can be represented by Fourier analysis as a group of sine waves or harmonics. To ensure accurate reproduction, summing of the first ten harmonics is required. The normal pulse is less than

Fig. 9.3 Effects of damping on square waves

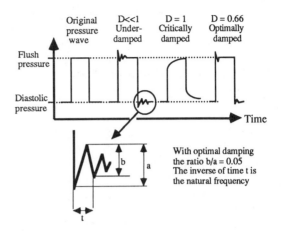

120/minute (2 Hz) so the system must respond accurately to frequencies from 2 Hz to 20 Hz. The saline filled line will oscillate in response to a pressure change: it is a second order system and is characterized by:

- a natural frequency, f_o, at which it will oscillate freely and resonate. To minimize this amplification of the signal, the input frequency should be <66% of f_o;

- a damping coefficient (D) which is an index of the tendency of the system to minimize oscillations;

As D increases, the number of oscillations and the time to a static result decreases. At critical damping (D=1) no overshoot occurs but response time is still prolonged. With a continuously changing input, optimal damping (D=0.66) maintains a 100% response for the maximum frequency and has an initial 6% overshoot.

Key reference:

Gardner RM. Direct arterial pressure monitoring. *Current Anaesthesia and Critical Care* 1990; **1**:239–246.

Answers to 9.4

1. Pulmonary artery flow-directed catheter (PAFC or Swan-Ganz catheter) with a mixed venous saturation oximeter. The right side because 55% of blood flow goes to the right lung and the catheter is flow directed.

2. Basic channels are:

- pulmonary artery lumen, which opens at the tip and measures pulmonary artery pressure (PAP) and pulmonary artery occlusion pressure (PAOP);
- central venous pressure (CVP) lumen, which opens 30 cm proximal to tip;
- balloon lumen for inflating balloon at tip;
- thermistor wires to thermistor which lies just proximal to the balloon.

Modifications of the basic PAFC

- Injection port separate but adjacent to the central venous pressure (CVP) port for closed system injection for cardiac output measurement.
- Pacemaker lumen to allow pacing via the PAFC.
- Two fibreoptic channels for continuous monitoring of mixed venous oxygen saturation by reflectance oximetry.
- Lumen for right ventricular thermal filament to allow continuous cardiac output thermodilution measurements by a stochastic system identification technique.
- The right ventricular ejection fraction PAFC uses a rapid response thermistor and a specialized monitoring system.

3. CVP, PAP, PAOP, tip temperature and mixed venous oxygen saturation ($S\bar{v}O_2$) are measured directly. The following are derived:
- Cardiac output (Qt) by thermodilution
- Stroke volume $= \dfrac{Qt}{\text{Heart rate}}$

- Systemic vascular resistance (SVR)
$$= \frac{(\text{Mean arterial pressure} - \text{CVP})}{Qt} \times 80$$
- Pulmonary vascular resistance (PVR)
$$= \frac{(\text{Mean PAP} - \text{PAOP})}{Qt} \times 80$$

- Oxygen consumption (VO_2)
$= (CaO_2 - C\bar{v}O_2) \times Qt$
CaO_2 = arterial oxygen content
$\qquad = Hb \times 13.8 \times SaO_2$
(SaO_2 = arterial oxygen saturation)
$C\bar{v}O_2$ = mixed venous oxygen content
$\qquad = Hb \times 13.8 \times S\bar{v}O_2$

- Oxygen flux or delivery (DO_2)
$= CaO_2 \times Qt$

4. $S\bar{v}O_2$ is measured by continuous reflectance oximetry via fibreoptic channels.
$$S\bar{v}O_2 = SaO_2 - \frac{VO_2}{Hb \times 13.8 \times Qt}$$

VO_2, Hb and SaO_2 are assumed constant. Analysis of $S\bar{v}O_2$ indicates the adequacy of tissue oxygenation of the body as a whole and does not guarantee regional oxygenation. It reflects the balance between oxygen supply and demand in an analogous way to $PaCO_2$ reflecting the balance between CO_2 production and elimination. Normal $S\bar{v}O_2$ is 75% but can be raised by:

- blood shunting past tissues, e.g. sepsis;
- left to right intracardiac shunts;
- decreased VO_2 in hypothermia, carbon monoxide or cyanide poisoning.

Key reference:

Barash PG (ed). *ASA Refresher Courses in Anesthesiology*. JB Lippincott, Philadelphia 1993; **21:** Ch 15.

Answers to 9.5

1. (a) Permanent pacemaker *in situ* with fractured ventricular pacing lead.

1. (b) Check the patient's pacemaker registration card to ascertain the pacemaker type, mode, rate and the clinical condition that necessitated pacemaker implantation. Ask the patient when the device was last checked. (Note that pacing thresholds may change between clinic visits; the newer lithium batteries usually have a 5–10 year life-span.) Ensure that the initial symptoms have not recurred. A full history and physical examination with particular reference to the CVS is mandatory. In addition to its contribution to the cardiorespiratory evaluation the chest X-ray will help locate the pulse generator and atrial/ventricular leads, and identify the pacemaker model. An ECG will establish whether the patient is dependent on the pacemaker all the time to maintain the cardiac rhythm, and will detect pacemaker malfunction. Drugs acting on the conducting system must be considered, and serum potassium concentration must be checked.

2. Damage to the internal mechanism or reprogramming may occur leading to pacemaker failure. Ventricular fibrillation may be induced by current channelled along the pacemaker electrode. Burning of myocardium at the tip of the electrode may render subsequent pacing ineffective.

3. If the use of diathermy is unavoidable, use bipolar diathermy, with the smallest possible current in short bursts. The diathermy should not be used within 15 cm of the pacemaker and the current should be directed away from the pulse generator. The indifferent ground plate should be placed such that a line drawn between the active and indifferent electrodes of the diathermy is perpendicular to a line drawn between the pacemaker electrode in the ventricle and the pacemaker generator. Magnets placed over demand pacemakers convert them to fixed rate pacemakers and minimize interference from diathermy but this can be dangerous as modern programmable pacemakers may be reprogrammed. Electively reprogramming the pacemaker to fixed rate non-demand mode (e.g. VOO) prior to surgery must be considered. Pacemaker settings must be checked after surgery.

4. Pacemakers may be affected by acute changes in potassium concentration, muscle artefacts and lithotripsy beams. Movement-sensing rate responsive pacemakers may be affected by changes in position, vigorous surgical manipulation, convulsions or post-operative shivering although fasciculations induced by suxamethonium are unlikely to cause a tachycardia. Pacemakers that measure thoracic impedance may be influenced by rate and depth of mechanical ventilation. Drugs interfering with cardiac conduction, intra-operative changes in blood pH and temperature may also influence rate responsive pacemakers.

5. If after pacemaker failure the intrinsic rate and rhythm are sufficient to maintain adequate cardiac output and peripheral perfusion, monitoring and close observation is all that is required. If bradycardia or heart block results in inadequate cardiac output, a bolus dose of isoprenaline followed by an infusion may restore ventricular rhythm. Transcutaneous pacing at 70 bpm may be employed intra-operatively, the output being increased until capture is confirmed on the ECG. If unsuccessful, emergency transvenous pacing may be necessary. In the absence of any escape rhythm and cardiac output, the appropriate cardiac arrest protocol must be followed.

Key references:

Barash PG (ed). *ASA Refresher Courses in Anesthesiology* . JB Lippincott, Philadelphia 1993; **21**:1–12.

Bloomfield P, Bowler GMR. Anaesthetic management of the patient with a permanent pacemaker. *Anaesthesia* 1989; **44**:42–46.

Answers to 9.6

The following characteristics of the arterial pulse must be noted: rate, rhythm, amplitude, character and waveform. Useful information can be obtained by palpation of an arterial pulse in many clinical conditions. These include:

- *Coarctation of the aorta:* brachial pulses are bounding, rise rapidly and have a large volume. Exaggerated pulsations may be felt in the supraclavicular fossa, and over the chest wall and scapulae due to well developed collateral channels. The systolic and pulse pressures in the lower extremities are reduced with a slow rate of rise and a late peak, and there is radio-femoral delay.
- *Fixed obstruction to left ventricular outflow:* a slow rising small-volume pulse, best felt in the carotids, is characteristic of aortic stenosis. Turbulence may also cause a carotid thrill. Supravalvular aortic stenosis causes a stronger and more rapidly rising pulse in the brachial arteries of the right side and the blood pressure is higher on the right side.
- *Aortic regurgitation:* the characteristic water hammer pulse (Corrigan's sign) consists of an abrupt upstroke followed by a rapid collapse in systole but no dicrotic notch. It may be exaggerated by elevating the patient's arm. Bisferiens pulse, characterized by two systolic peaks separated by a distinct mid-systolic dip, may be felt in mixed aortic valve disease.
- *Cardiac tamponade and constrictive pericarditis:* may result in pulsus paradoxus in which the pulse volume shows an exaggerated decrease during inspiration and increase during expiration. Pulsus paradoxus may also be seen in asthma due to the superimposition of swings in intrathoracic pressure upon arterial pressure. Normally, the difference between the two pressures does not exceed 10 mmHg during quiet respiration.

- *Left ventricular failure:* pulsus alternans is a sign of severe myocardial depression. There is alternation between strong and weak pulses in a regular rhythm. Palpation should be carried out with the breath held in mid-expiration to avoid respiratory superimposition on pulse amplitude.
- *Increased left ventricular stroke volume*: this results in an increase in pulse volume. Bounding arterial pulses may be felt in patients with a patent ductus arteriosus or other arterio-venous fistula (increased run off) or in hyperkinetic states such as thyrotoxicosis, pregnancy and fever.
- *Hypovolaemia:* a dicrotic pulse may be felt in hypotensive patients with reduced peripheral resistance. May also be present in cardiac tamponade, severe heart failure and hypovolaemic shock. The second peak of this pulse is in diastole, immediately after the second heart sound.
- *Premature ventricular contractions:* these occurring every other beat result in pulsus bigeminus in which the rhythm is usually irregular and there is alternation in the strength of the pulse. The compensatory pause following a premature beat is succeeded by a pulse which is stronger than normal.
- *Peripheral vascular disease:* asymmetry of popliteal pulses indicates ileo-femoral obstruction. Absence or weakness of radial, posterior tibial or dorsalis pedis pulses on one side suggests arterial insufficiency.
- *Normal ageing process/hypertension:* with the increase in arterial stiffness and vascular resistance there is an increase in pulse velocity, and the pulse contour has a rapid upstroke with increased amplitude.

Key references:

Braunwald E (ed). *Heart Disease* 4th ed. WB Saunders Company, Philadelphia 1992; 21–25.

Munro J, Edwards C (eds). *Macleod's Clinical Examination* 8th ed. Churchill Livingstone, Edinburgh 1990; 88–91.

Answers to 9.7

1. 100% oxygen while you quickly assess his airway, breathing and circulation (ABC).

2. The scenario may be due to more than one cause but the following should be considered:

- pneumothorax or haemothorax;
- lobar consolidation, collapse or contusion;
- fat embolism syndrome;
- hypovolaemic shock;
- head injury;
- sepsis;
- cardiac tamponade or contusion.

3. A delayed petechial rash over the chest, axilla, neck or conjunctiva.

4. With respiratory and neurological signs, this suggests fat embolism syndrome (FES). Alveolar deadspace increases as does shunt later. *Arterial blood gases*: an increased alveolar–arterial oxygen difference reflecting hypoxaemia and hypocarbia. Hyperventilation is caused by hypoxaemia and stimulation of lung J-receptors by emboli so hypocarbia may persist after the hypoxaemia has been corrected.
Chest X-ray may initially be normal but classically FES produces a 'snowstorm' effect of diffuse infiltrates and may progress to ARDS.
ECG: may show arrhythmias or signs of right ventricular strain, e.g. prominent S waves or ST changes in leads V_1 to V_4 or RBBB.

5. If supplementary oxygen improves his clinical condition he may not need ventilation. However, he is still at risk and should be monitored in a high dependency unit or ITU. General indications for ventilatory support include:

- PaO_2 <60 mmHg (8 kPa) despite O_2 therapy;
- $PaCO_2$ >60 mmHg;
- respiratory rate of >30/minute.

Specific conditions in the trauma scenario that warrant a low threshold for instituting mechanical ventilation include:

- multiple injuries;
- intestinal perforation;
- aspiration pneumonitis;
- major thoracic injury, e.g. flail chest or multiple broken ribs.

Notes on fat embolism syndrome (FES)

This syndrome occurs mainly in adults (99%) following trauma but can occur with some haemoglobinopathies, diabetes mellitus and collagen diseases. Following trauma, bone marrow and tissue thromboplastin may be embolized from the fracture site causing activation of complement and the extrinsic pathway and embolic damage to all organs. The onset is sudden. A quarter present in the first 12 h but 15% do not present until 48 h and the diagnosis may be confused by concomitant operations, shock, and head injury. CNS signs vary from restlessness to fits and coma. Tachypnoea, tachycardia and a pyrexia up to 40°C are common. No test is pathognomonic. Organ biopsy is traumatic. Blood, sputum and urine testing for fat are not accurate. Fat staining of aspirate from broncho-alveolar lavage obtained by fibrescope is reported as accurate. Scoring systems for clinical diagnosis have been devised. Operative fixation of major fractures before 24 h reduces the progression to ARDS five-fold. The management of FES is supportive and steroids. If FES progresses to ARDS the mortality is only 10%. Ethanol and other lipolysing agents show no benefit.

Key references:
Chastre J, Fagon J, *et al.* Bronchoalveolar lavage for rapid diagnosis of the fat embolism syndrome in trauma patients. *Annals of Internal Medicine* 1990; **113**:583–588.

Rockwood CA, Green DP, Bucholz RW (eds). *Fractures in Adults* 3rd ed. JB Lippincott, Philadelphia 1991; 341–351.

Answers to 9.8

1. Pulmonary artery flow-directed catheter (PAFC or Swan-Ganz catheter).

2. There are no absolute indications for the insertion of a PAFC. Indications include:

- management of a low cardiac output with signs of right ventricular failure, e.g. high central venous pressure (CVP);
- distinguishing cardiogenic shock from adult respiratory distress syndrome (ARDS);
- monitoring and optimizing the cardio-vascular and oxygenation responses to inotropic and vasoactive drugs;
- monitoring and manipulating the cardio-vascular status during major cardiovascular surgery, e.g. aortic aneurysm repair;
- for operations when the patient is at risk due to severe cardiovascular disability, e.g. immediately post myocardial infarction or if in cardiac failure.

3.

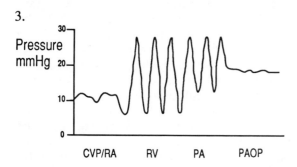

4. Complications not related to actual insertion:

- local infection and septicaemia, so replace or remove catheter after 48 h;
- pulmonary artery rupture may be caused by flushing the line while wedging or using more than 1.5 mL to inflate the balloon;
- arrhythmias are more common with ice-cold injectate which confers little clinical advantage over room temperature injectate;
- pulmonary infarction may occur if the catheter is left wedged in the pulmonary artery so the pulmonary artery pressure wave should be monitored continuously;
- mural thrombus, thrombophlebitis, venous thrombosis and embolism.

Notes on the PAFC

There are no outcome studies proving an improvement in mortality, morbidity or length of hospital stay due to insertion of a PAFC. There are therefore no absolute indications for the insertion of a PAFC peri-operatively or in the Intensive Care Unit. However, there are well documented risks and contraindications. Each patient should be assessed individually with respect to the benefits and risks for that patient. Peri-operative factors to consider are the patient's cardiorespiratory status, the length and possible cardiovascular stress of the operation and the ability of the anaesthetist to interpret the results and provide treatment. Complications during insertion include pneumothorax, heart block, arrhythmias, arterial puncture, air embolus, bleeding, and endocardial valve damage. Contraindications to the insertion of a PAFC include:

- lack of appropriate operator skill, knowledge or equipment;
- presence of a transvenous pacemaker;
- presence of an artificial tricuspid or pulmonary valve;
- coagulopathy;
- heart block (but can insert a PAFC with integral pacemaker wires).

Key reference:

Wheatly S, Pollard B. Inserting a pulmonary artery catheter. *Current Anaesthesia and Critical Care* 1992; 3:108–116.

Answers to 9.9

1. Clear the airway with suction and by jaw thrust and chin lift. Ventilate by mask with 100% oxygen.

2. Even in preterm babies 100% oxygen is safe for resuscitation for short periods. If no improvement after one minute, then intubate.

3. Initially less than 40 cmH$_2$O but more if ventilation is inadequate. Healthy neonates may generate negative pressures of 100 cmH$_2$O during the initial inflation of their lungs. Initial neonatal resuscitation may require similar pressures but then the chest compliance increases markedly and ventilation becomes possible with a uncuffed tube at low pressures. The low functional residual capacity (FRC) and doubled oxygen consumption causes a quick fall in PaO$_2$ if apnoeic. Closing capacity exceeds FRC until the age of 6 years so closure of the smaller airways occurs during normal breathing. If ventilating, a positive end-expiratory pressure should be applied.

4. Internal diameter   2.5–3.0 mm
   Length to lips   8.0–9.0 cm

5. The neonate has:

- a relatively large tongue and small mouth. The neonate is thus an obligatory nasal breather and an oral airway may not help;
- small airway tissues that are compressible. The airway is readily collapsed by manual pressure so only the bony parts should be held and overextension, flexion and rotation of the neck should be avoided;
- a prominent occiput, relatively large head and a short neck. This may require a raise behind the shoulders during mask ventilation and intubation;

- a floppy epiglottis that is directed posteriorly at 45° and a more anterior and cephalad larynx situated at the C2/C3 level (C5/C6 in the adult). A curved laryngoscope placed anterior to the epiglottis may not reveal the cords. A straight-bladed laryngoscope displacing all of the relatively large tongue to the left side of the mouth can be positioned distal to the epiglottis and the blade withdrawn, staying posterior to the epiglottis until the glottis is visualized. The tube may need a stylet to displace its tip anteriorly as the larynx is more anterior and cephalad;
- vocal cords that slope upwards and backwards. This may hinder the passage of the tube and it may impact against the anterior inner part of the cricoid;
- a cricoid cartilage as the narrowest part of the airway that is circular in cross-section. An uncuffed tube has a similar cross-section and provides an adequate seal to prevent aspiration and allow positive pressure ventilation. A leak should be present to prevent ischaemia of the cricoid mucosa, or subglottic scarring and stenosis may result. The narrowest part of the adult airway is the glottis which is diamond shaped and a tracheal cuff is necessary to produce a seal to prevent aspiration. The adult has a lower total chest compliance and so also requires a cuff to prevent a leak when applying IPPV;
- a smaller glottic–carinal distance. The tube is placed only 2.5–3 cm through the cords and the position secured. Accidental extubation or bronchial intubation may occur if the head is rotated to one side;
- main bronchi that deviate from the carina symmetrically. Bronchial intubation therefore occurs equally to the right and left.

Key reference:
Advanced Life Support Group. *Advanced Paediatric Life Support.* BMJ Publishing Group, London 1993; 52–57.

Answer 9.10

1. Winged Tuohy epidural needle, plastic epidural catheter, epidural filter and connector with Luer-Lok fittings, plastic loss of resistance syringe.

2. (a) Valveless internal vertebral venous plexus, arteries supplying the spinal cord, lumbar ventral and dorsal spinal nerve roots, epidural fat and fibrous connective tissue strands.

2. (b) The tactile method, which depends on the loss of resistance to air or saline (contained in a freely running syringe) upon entry into the epidural space, is currently the most popular. The hanging drop technique is preferred by some to locate the thoracic epidural space. It relies on a drop of water that is suspended in the hub of the needle being sucked into the needle due to the artefactual negative pressure caused by tenting of the dura by the needle.

3. (a) The ideal epidural test dose should reliably and unequivocally detect inadvertent intrathecal, intravascular or subdural injection within five minutes without subjecting the mother or foetus to additional dangers. (No such ideal exists.)
   (b) A test dose of 3–5 ml of bupivacaine (strength not specified) containing adrenaline is recommended by the manufacturer's Data Sheet. Bupivacaine with adrenaline contains 5.5 µg/mL of adrenaline (adrenaline tartrate PhEur 10.0 µg/mL).

4. (a) Absence of flow of blood or cerebrospinal fluid with the open end of the catheter held below the level of the epidural puncture.
   (b) Negative aspiration.
   (c) Injection of just 1 mL of air can be detected by precordial Doppler monitoring, if intravascular. Although it is difficult to arrange on a labour ward and interpretation is subject-

ive, it may be useful in situations where even small doses of adrenaline are contraindicated.

5. (a) Local anaesthetic toxicity either from an absolute overdose or an inadvertent intravascular injection.
5. (b) Total spinal anaesthesia
5. (c) Profound hypotension and cardiovascular collapse.

Notes
2. (a) The internal vertebral venous plexus communicates with the systemic circulation via the internal iliac veins, the intercostal and azygos veins and cerebral sinuses. Often the lower part of the anterior spinal artery is only fed by the single anterior radicular artery of Adamkiewicz.
2. (b) Other methods include Odom's glass adapter (modified by Brooks) and Dawkins' gravity indicator, both of which rely on sub-atmospheric epidural pressures. Spring-loaded devices which rely on loss of resistance to injection (e.g. Oxford indicator) have been used. The characteristic hiss of air is said to be indicative of entry into the epidural space and the sound can be amplified by covering the syringe with a rubber diaphragm and attaching it to a stethoscope. Free flow of a running infusion attached to the epidural needle upon entry into the epidural space has also been described.

3. A good discussion of the vexed issue of epidural test doses is found in the first reference below.

Key references:

Shnider SM, Levinson G (eds). *Anesthesia for Obstetrics* 3rd ed. Williams and Wilkins, Baltimore 1993; 137–141.

Shah JL. Identification of the epidural space. *British Journal of Hospital Medicine* 1991; **46**:60–62.

Answers to 9.11

1. Causes of post-operative hypertension include:

- airway obstruction, hypoxia, hypercarbia;
- pain from urinary retention, the surgical site or, if pre-operative trauma, other sites;
- pre-operative hypertension;
- raised intracranial pressure: systemic hypertension occurs to maintain cerebral perfusion (Cushing response). There is usually an associated reflex bradycardia.

Causes of post-operative agitation include:

- hypoxaemia or hypotension of any cause;
- emergence from anaesthesia;
- pain from any cause;
- metabolic causes: hypoglycaemia, hyperglycaemia, uraemia, hyponatraemia;
- residual curarization;
- pulmonary or fat embolism;
- intracranial pathology, e.g. after neurosurgery;
- delirium tremens.

2. There are many causes for this scenario so one must first exclude those causing immediate danger to the patient by assessing the patient's airway, breathing and circulation (ABC) and giving oxygen. Having ensured that the patient is safe one may then systematically diagnose and treat the problem. The initial part of the ABC is verbal communication with the patient: 'Are you all right?' A coherent sensible answer means oxygen is being carried to the brain by circulating blood and may also tell you the diagnosis, e.g. 'My leg hurts'. If the ABC assessment is normal but the patient does not answer coherently check the pulse oximeter to exclude hypoxia. Important points to note in the history are:

- previous history of hypertension, alcohol and drug abuse, and mental state;
- premedication and whether antihypertensive drugs were withheld that day;
- nature of the surgery, e.g. neurosurgery;
- history of intra-operative cerebral insult, e.g. surgery, hypotension or hypoxia;
- intra-operative analgesia.

Residual anaesthetic may mask physical signs. Examination should include:

- CNS: to exclude seizures, the twitching muscular movements associated with partial curarization, stroke;
- RS: to exclude pneumo- or haemothorax;
- abdomen: to exclude bladder distension. If a catheter is present, check that it is draining well and, if not, flush it.

3. Generally, post-operative hypertension should be assessed and treated appropriately as risks include:

- left ventricular strain predisposing to myocardial ischaemia, arrhythmias, LV failure and infarction;
- surgical bleeding: cardiac tamponade following cardiac surgery, raised intracranial pressure after neurosurgery and hypovolaemic shock if a large wound is involved;
- cerebrovascular bleeding.

4. One situation when treatment of a high blood pressure may be deleterious is following clipping of a cerebral artery aneurysm. Postoperatively there may be a Cushing response to maintain perfusion of ischaemic parts of the brain and to overcome cerebral artery spasm. Obtunding this response may cause a cerebral ischaemic deficit.

Key reference:

Miller RD (ed). *Anesthesia* 4th ed. Churchill Livingstone, Edinburgh 1994; 2320–2321.

Answers to 9.12

1. The basic requirements are:

- control of O_2 concentration of inspired gas;
- prevention of excess accumulation of CO_2;
- no resistance to spontaneous breathing;
- efficient/economical use of O_2;
- acceptability to patients.

2. In 1970, MJ Leigh classified the methods of oxygen delivery into fixed performance and variable performance systems.

Fixed performance systems: These give a fixed FIO_2 independent of patient factors such as ventilatory pattern. They can be subdivided into High flow (e.g. venturi systems) and Low flow (e.g. anaesthetic breathing systems). Peak inspiratory flow is provided either by the high O_2 flow or the incorporation of a reservoir bag.

Variable performance systems: These employ air–oxygen mixtures with O_2 flow rates less than peak inspiratory demand; performance is influenced by patient factors. These can be subdivided into No capacity (e.g. nasal cannulae at low flows), Small capacity (e.g. MC, Hudson masks) and Large capacity (Pneumask, Oxyaire, oxygen tent, incubator) systems.

3. A= Hudson variable performance oxygen mask. B= Nasal cannulae. C= HAFOE (High Air Flow Oxygen Enrichment) fixed performance oxygen mask.

Hudson mask: This provides a higher FIO_2 than nasal cannulae at low flows because the mask serves as a 100–200 mL reservoir of O_2. A snug fit must be ensured to minimize loss of O_2 flow. This is a valveless system and the side holes serve as expiratory ports and help entrain room air during inspiration. An FIO_2 of up to 0.6 can be predictably achieved with a normal ventilatory pattern. There is no significant further increase in FIO_2 with flow rates >8 L/min. There is some compensation for hypoventilation with a greater FIO_2 being delivered at lower levels of ventilation.

If a reservoir bag is attached to the mask and a nonrebreathing valve is used an FIO_2 approaching 1.0 may be achieved.

Nasal cannulae: These simple devices have two prongs, one being placed in each nostril. They are well tolerated by patients at flow rates between 0.25–6 L/min. An FIO_2 between 0.24 and 0.44 can be reliably achieved, with a normal ventilatory pattern. Oxygen must be humidified at the higher flow rates as long term use of dry gas may result in mucosal dehydration, irritation and nose bleeds. Prolonged pressure from the prongs may traumatize nasal mucosa.

Venturi type (HAFOE) mask: Gas entrainment based on the Bernoulli effect provides the peak inspiratory demand. A tight fit is not necessary, performance is independent of ventilatory pattern and an FIO_2 up to 0.65 can be reliably obtained. The high flow is less economical but rebreathing is minimized. As the required FIO_2 increases, air entrainment decreases, resulting in a net decrease in total gas flow. This could lead to the patient's peak flow requirements outstripping the mask's flow capability.

4. *Respiratory depression:* may occur with uncontrolled O_2 therapy in those with ventilatory failure from COAD, who are dependent on their hypoxic ventilatory drive.

Absorption atelectasis: a high FIO_2 leads to nitrogen washout and loss of alveolar splinting, particularly in those with decreased V/Q ratios.

Pulmonary oxygen toxicity: prolonged exposure to a high FIO_2 may result in alveolar damage by oxygen free radicals.

Retrolental fibroplasia and *bronchopulmonary dysplasia* in neonates.

Key references:

Benumof JL (ed). *Clinical Procedures in Anesthesia and Intensive Care* 1st ed. JB Lippincott Company, Pennsylvania 1992; 63–71.

Oh TE (ed). *Intensive Care Manual* 3rd ed. Butterworths Ltd, Sydney 1990; 128–134.

OSCE cycle 10 – answers

Answers to 10.1

1. Peripheral nerve stimulation: a train of four (TOF) ratio <0.7, fade with 50 Hz tetanus for 5 s and fade with double burst stimulation (DBS$_{3,3}$). However, the absence of fade when sought by sight or touch with these techniques does not guarantee adequate recovery from neuromuscular blockade. This requires assessment by mechanomyograph or electromyography.

2. No.

3. Head lift for 5 s. This requires voluntary effort and is not performed well if in pain, e.g. following an abdominal operation.

4. Neuromuscular blockade (NMB) may be prolonged because of:

- hypothermia: a reduction of core temperature from 36.5°C to 34.5°C doubles the duration of action of atracurium and vecuronium;
- myasthenia gravis;
- renal failure or hepatic failure;
- respiratory acidosis or metabolic alkalosis;
- drugs, e.g. volatile agents, gentamicin;
- electrolyte imbalance, e.g. low potassium, sodium or calcium levels or high magnesium levels;
- biological variation.

Notes on NMB and recovery

The duration and intensity of NMB are very variable between patients and with many factors, as indicated above. Safe recovery from NMB requires that patients can maintain their airway, swallow secretions, cough and ventilate so as to maintain normal blood gases. This is assured by a TOF ratio ≥0.7, and the ability to sustain a 50 Hz tetanus for 5 s or to raise their head for 5 s. The muscles of the upper airway are more sensitive to NMB than the diaphragm and ventilation can be adequate even though the patient cannot maintain an airway or swallow their secretions. External appearances of swallowing do not guarantee the ability to complete this manoeuvre. 50 Hz tetanus is painful and only reliably detects fade manually if TOF ratio is <0.3. The detection of fade of TOF by vision or touch is only reliable if TOF ratio <0.4. This may be due to the middle two responses confusing the comparison of the first and fourth responses. This led to the development of DBS.

DBS$_{3,3}$ is two bursts of three stimuli each at 50 Hz and separated by 750 ms. The two tetanic bursts are each perceived as one response. A faster tetanus is painful and above 100 Hz, in the presence of volatile agents, fade can occur without neuromuscular blockade. DBS is more painful than TOF stimuli which are usually painless. Manual DBS$_{3,3}$ is more reliable than manual TOF stimuli at detecting fade and reliably indicates a TOF ratio <0.5 but does not guarantee a TOF ≥0.7. Absence of fade as assessed manually or visually by 50 Hz tetanus, DBS or TOF does not guarantee adequate reversal of NMB. Manual DBS$_{3,2}$ has two stimuli in the second burst and so has integral fade and will detect a TOF ratio <0.8 reliably. Unfortunately it will also show fade at levels above 0.7 and may lead to the inappropriate use of reversal agents.

The ability to reverse NMB adequately is inversely proportional to the value of T1, the first response of the TOF, at reversal. Vecuronium and atracurium are rapidly reversed by 50 µg/kg neostigmine when T1 >10% of the pre-relaxant control or when there are spontaneous movements.

Key references:

Bevan D *et al*. Reversal of neuromuscular blockade. *Anesthesiology* 1992; **77**:785–805.

Shorten GD. Postoperative residual curarisation: incidence, aetiology and associated morbidity. *Anaesthesia and Intensive Care* 1993; **21**:782–789.

Answers to 10.2

1. International Society for the Study of Hypertension in Pregnancy classification:

- Gestational hypertension and/or proteinuria developing after 20 weeks gestation in a previously normotensive nonproteinuric woman.
- Chronic hypertension, incidentally associated with pregnancy, diagnosed before, during or persisting after pregnancy.
- Unclassified hypertension, found at the first antenatal visit after 20 weeks gestation, in a woman whose past hypertensive history is unknown.
- Eclampsia.

2. Pre-eclampsia is defined as a pregnancy complicated by hypertension with either proteinuria or oedema or both. Hypertension is defined as a diastolic blood pressure (phase IV) ≥90 mmHg on two occasions at least 4 h apart or a single recording ≥110 mmHg. Severe hypertension is defined as a diastolic pressure ≥110 mmHg on two occasions at least 4 h apart or a single recording ≥120 mmHg. Proteinuria is defined as ≥ ++ on reagent dipstick testing of two clean caught midstream samples taken six hours apart or greater than 0.3 g in a 24-hour collection. Oedema is manifested by accelerated weight gain in the third trimester.

3. Admission to hospital is essential if the mother is symptomatic or has proteinuria. Bedrest is not of proven value. It is important to remember that abrupt reductions in perfusion pressure may adversely affect both mother and child and that volume expansion may be required before vasodilators are used. A gradual reduction of blood pressure is favoured. Long term treatment is usually with methyl-dopa, 1–3 g daily, in divided doses. It has a good safety record in pregnancy but may cause sedation and postural hypotension. Sublingual nifedipine (10 mg, repeated at 30 min) is useful in short term treatment but may cause headaches and palpitations. Hydralazine is currently popular.

It may cause a tachycardia, either resting or reflex, and may necessitate the addition of a ß-blocker. Labetalol in divided doses blunts the rise in blood pressure without significant effects on the foetus and is therefore safe in short term use. Diazoxide, nitroprusside and GTN are not widely used.

4. Well-conducted epidural anaesthesia is safe and probably the method of choice. It does not have deleterious effects on the cardiac output if the patient is adequately hydrated and it suppresses the vasoactive response to pain. In addition, it reduces circulating endogenous catecholamines with resultant decrease in LV stroke work. With adequate intravascular volume expansion epidurals may reduce uterine artery vasospasm and increase intervillous blood flow, thus benefiting the foetus.

The main risks with general anaesthesia ar difficulties with airway management and the exaggerated pressor response to intubation which may cause rises in ICP, cerebral haemorrhage and cardiac failure. Drugs used to blunt the pressor response to tracheal intubation include lignocaine, nifedipine, alfentanil, α- and β-blockers and magnesium sulphate. A combination of these agents may be used. A standard obstetric general anaesthetic with rapid sequence induction must be carried out. Careful monitoring of intravascular volume status and provision of adequate post-operative analgesia are important. Delivery cures the condition. Post-operative laryngeal oedema may occur.

Key references:

Atkinson RS, Adams AP (eds). *Recent Advances in Anaesthesia and Analgesia* Vol 17. Churchill Livingstone, Edinburgh 1992; 137–155.

Barash PG (ed) *ASA Refresher Courses in Anesthesiology* . JB Lippincott, Philadelphia 1992; **20**:143–154.

Answers to 10.3

1. Arterial blood gases can only be fully assessed with the clinical condition of the patient. Specific treatment depends on the reversibility and nature of the disease and whether it is improving or deteriorating. Specific information required in this patient would be his age, clinical condition and his inspired oxygen concentration (FIO_2).

2. This patient is alkalaemic with a primary respiratory alkalosis. At a PaO_2 of 60 mmHg (8 kPa) the chemoreceptors are stimulated and hyperventilation occurs which reduces the $PaCO_2$. This offsets the hypoxia as described by the alveolar gas equation. The hypoxia will also directly depress the respiratory centre. There is no renal compensation so the diagnosis is acute respiratory failure. Causes of hypoxaemia with hypocapnia include chest infection, pulmonary oedema and pulmonary embolus, pneumothorax and venous admixture (shunt).

3. The low $PaCO_2$ implies hyperventilation and an increased work of breathing. Normally, the work of breathing is only 2% of the energy consumption of the body. If lung compliance decreases, as in pneumonia, this proportion may increase to 20%. Also, infection increases the CO_2 production (increasing the respiratory workload) and O_2 consumption (which reduces respiratory muscle oxygenation). When the respiratory work load exceeds his capacity for respiratory work the $PaCO_2$ will rise. The pulse oximeter gives the arterial oxygen saturation which depends on the PaO_2 and the position of the oxyhaemoglobin dissociation curve. It does not reflect $PaCO_2$ levels. A relatively small increase in FIO_2 can compensate for the hypoxia caused by hypoventilation so this management may allow the patient to become grossly hypercapnic and acidaemic. He may then become more settled but this is CO_2 narcosis and he is about to become apnoeic, hypoxic and arrest. He should be monitored clinically for his ability to perform the work of breathing as reflected by his respiratory rate, use of accessory muscles of respiration and general condition. If an FIO_2 >60% is required to maintain oxygenation (equivalent to a 20% shunt on the iso-shunt diagram – *see* Fig. 10.3) there should be a low threshold for intubation and IPPV.

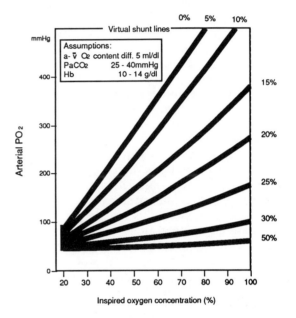

Fig. 10.3. The iso-shunt diagram. Redrawn from **Benatar** SR, Hewlett AM and Nunn JF. The use of iso-shunt lines for control of oxygen therapy. *BJA* 1973; **45**:711.

4. The shunt can be conveniently calculated by plotting the initial FIO_2 and PaO_2 values. Assuming the shunt remains constant, the FIO_2 that will give a normal PaO_2 can be predicted. This graph explains why an FIO_2 of 30% is used during general anaesthesia: following induction, shunt increases from the physiological (< 5%) up 15 or 20% and it requires an FIO_2 of 30% to counteract this. Changes in respiratory function can be monitored. This helps predict successful weaning from mechanical ventilation (which is unlikely if shunt >20%).

Key reference:

Nunn JF. *Nunn's Applied Respiratory Physiology* 4th ed. Butterworth-Heinemann Ltd, Oxford 1993; 183–184.

Answers to 10.4

1. Clear the airway and give 100% oxygen.

2. Methylene blue is used to identify the parathyroid glands at surgery and will cause cyanosis but no dyspnoea or agitation. Haemorrhage into the wound is a medical emergency causing blockage of the airway and needs to be recognized and dealt with immediately. The wound sutures or clips are removed and the clot evacuated. Damage to the recurrent or superior laryngeal nerves can occur during surgery and post-operatively the presence of damaged tissue and locally released potassium can impair their function. Unilateral recurrent laryngeal nerve palsy causes stridor but bilateral damage leads to complete airway obstruction. Partial obstruction can occur due to laryngeal mucosal oedema secondary to venous congestion but this usually presents the following day. Very rarely, tracheal collapse occurs due to removal of supporting tissue during the thyroidectomy. Removal of thyroid tissue may result in hypocalcaemia and tetany. Excess thyroxine causes osteoporosis and the sudden reduction in thyroxine may cause a massive uptake of calcium into the skeletal system. If parathyroidectomy is carried out or the parathyroid glands are damaged during thyroidectomy then the reduction in para-thormone may also cause tetany but this usually occurs two or three days later. Tetany of the vocal cords can cause obstruction. Thyroid storm is discussed below and can cause cyanosis due to the high oxygen utilization. Thyrotoxicosis may present as cardiac failure although this should have been controlled before surgery.

3. Hypocalcaemic tetany.

4. *Trousseau's sign:* a blood pressure cuff inflated above systolic blood pressure for two minutes will exacerbate latent tetany and produce carpopedal spasm.

Chvostek's sign: tapping the facial nerve at the facial notch in the mandible precipitates twitching of the ipsilateral facial muscles.
The QT interval may be prolonged.

5. Intravenous calcium gluconate.

Notes on thyrotoxic crisis (thyroid storm)

This is caused by an excessive release of thyroid hormones into the circulation resulting in a sudden increase in metabolic rate. It may be precipitated by any acute medical or surgical event or trauma. It has a mortality of 20%. It may present as pyrexia, tachypnoea, tachycardia, arrhythmias, nausea, vomiting, delirium or coma. Oxygen consumption rises and pulmonary oedema can occur so the patient may be cyanosed despite oxygen therapy. The differential diagnosis includes sepsis, phaeochromocytoma and malignant hyperthermia. The diagnosis is clinical as thyroid function tests are too slow and will not distinguish between thyroid storm and thyrotoxicosis. The initial management is treatment of the initial cause and oxygen, intravenous fluids and drugs. ß-blockers will reduce the catecholamine mediated symptoms but should be used carefully if there is cardiac failure or asthma. Thiouracils will decrease the synthesis of thyroxine in the thyroid gland and can be given orally or by nasogastric tube. Iodine will inhibit the release of thyroid hormones and steroids will stop the peripheral transformation of thyroxine to triiodothyronine. Tepid sponging and antipyretics may be necessary if the pyrexia does not settle. Dantrolene has been used.

Key reference:

Mason RA. *Anaesthesia Databook* 2nd ed. Churchill Livingstone, London 1994; 566–569.

Answers to 10.5

1. (a) Hyperparathyroidism
1. (b) Malignancy with metastases to bone which may be seen with carcinomas of the breast, prostate, kidney, ovary, thyroid, colon and bronchus (hypercalcaemia is caused by bone metastases or ectopic PTH secretion).

2. Raised plasma PTH with a normal or low phosphate level is strongly suggestive of hyper-parathyroidism.
A hypochloraemic alkalosis with a low albumin and hypokalaemia would be suggestive of metastases. The phosphate and alkaline phosphatase levels are usually raised.

3. Other causes of hypercalcaemia include: myelomatosis, sarcoidosis, hyperthyroidism, excess of vitamins A and D, thiazide diuretics, milk-alkali syndrome, prolonged immobilization, calcium exchange resins in haemodialysis.
(If the plasma albumin is high at the same time, the hypercalcaemia may simply reflect dehydration or a sample taken after application of a venous tourniquet.)

4. Emergency treatment is warranted when the plasma calcium is very high (>3.5 mmol/L) or the patient is symptomatic with polydipsia, polyuria, vomiting and clouding of consciousness. Options include:

- Intravenous rehydration with 0.9% saline infusion. Large volumes of up to 3–4 L per day are required in most cases and is best undertaken with CVP monitoring. Plasma electrolytes must be checked at regular intervals, and concurrent hypokalaemia and hypomagnesaemia must be corrected.
- Frusemide by slow intravenous injection/infusion. Thiazide diuretics that the patient may be taking must be stopped.
- Intravenous diphosphonates are the treatment of choice for hypercalcaemia of malignancy. The dose of disodium pamidronate should be titrated against the plasma calcium level. It is administered by slow i.v. infusion. It inhibits bone resorption and osteoclastic activity.
- Prednisolone is useful in the treatment of hypercalcaemia caused by sarcoidosis, myeloma and vitamin D excess. It is of little value in the treatment of hypercalcaemia from other causes.
- EDTA 15–50 mg/kg i.v. is the most rapid way available to acutely lower serum ionized calcium. It is reserved for use in life threatening situations because of the risk of acute renal failure.
- Mithramycin and calcitonin may be used but have short lived actions. Intravenous phosphate has been used to lower plasma calcium but is dangerous.

After the plasma calcium is lowered and the patient is no longer acutely ill, a cause for the hypercalcaemia must be investigated. Parathyroidectomy must be advised, after correction of the reversible disturbances, in patients with hypercalcaemia of parathyroid origin.

5. Effects of hypercalcaemia on the ECG include:

- shortening of ST segment;
- shortening of QTc interval;
- amplitude of U wave–normal or increased.

Hypercalcaemia shortens ventricular systole and decreases the duration of the effective refractory period. It decreases the duration of phase 2 of the action potential. The decrease in the QaTc interval shows a strong correlation with increase in plasma calcium level and it has been suggested that the ECG may be a useful method of screening for hypercalcaemia.

Key references:

Kumar P, Clark M (eds). *Clinical Medicine* 3rd ed. Bailliere Tindall, London 1994; 430–432.

Thys DM, Kaplan JA (eds). *The ECG in Anesthesia and Critical Care*. Churchill Livingstone, New York 1987; 175–176.

Answers to 10.6

1. Second degree heart block – Mobitz type I (Wenckebach phenomenon).

2. Atrioventricular (AV) conduction block is said to exist when the atrial impulse is conducted with delay or is not conducted at all to the ventricle at a time when the AV junction is not physiologically refractory. AV conduction block can be classified in two ways:
Based on the standard surface ECG they can be classified into first, second and third degree AV blocks. Second and third degree heart blocks can be further classified into Type A (QRS duration ≤0.11 s) and Type B (QRS duration ≥0.12 s). In Type A the block lies above the bifurcation of the bundle of His. The block is usually in the AV node itself. In Type B, the block lies below the bifurcation and carries a poorer prognosis.

First degree AV block: PR interval >0.2 s. The rhythm is regular and all the beats are conducted to the ventricles. The conduction defect need not be confined to the AV node and may involve the internodal pathway and the bundle of His. His bundle ECGs may show an increased AH interval, HV interval or both.

Second degree AV block: With second degree heart block a proportion of the atrial impulses are not conducted to the ventricles. This is sub-classified into Mobitz Type I and Mobitz Type II. Mobitz Type I block = gradually lengthening PR interval until a P wave occurs that is not followed by a QRS complex. Mobitz Type II block = PR interval is constant but QRS complexes are intermittently dropped.

Third degree AV block: There is total disruption of impulse conduction between the atria and the ventricles. The atria fire independently and usually an escape focus in the distal conducting system fires at its intrinsic rate resulting in AV dissociation.

3. AV nodal dysfunction: anatomical (congenital, degenerative, infiltrative); functional (ischaemia, acidosis). Drugs (neostigmine, propranolol, halothane, fentanyl, digoxin). Increased vagal (occulocardiac reflex) or decreased sympathetic (hypothermia) tone.

4. *Sick sinus syndrome (Tachy-brady syndrome):* This is the commonest indication for permanent pacemaker implantation. A variety of SA and AV nodal defects may occur alone or in combination. These include sinus arrest, sino-atrial block, severe bradycardia or alternating tachycardia and bradycardia.

Complete AV block: Unless congenital and asymptomatic, complete heart block invariably requires permanent pacing.

Second degree heart block, Mobitz Types I and II: Type I was previously considered to be benign but is now a recognized indication for permanent pacing. Type II block often progresses to complete heart block and is therefore an indication for permanent pacing.

Acute myocardial infarction (MI): Newly acquired bundle branch block in the presence of transient complete AV block *may* require permanent pacing. Patients who develop conduction blocks after an anterior MI usually have extensive myocardial damage and a poor prognosis.

Other: Symptomatic atrial fibrillation with a slow ventricular response and symptomatic hypersensitive carotid sinus syndrome may require permanent pacing.

Key references:

Braunwald E (ed). *Heart Disease* 4th ed. WB Saunders Company, Philadelphia 1992; 710–718.

Thys DM, Kaplan JA (eds). *The ECG in Anesthesia and Critical Care*. Churchill Livingstone, New York 1987; 58–62.

Answers to 10.7

1. A line drawn from the anterior superior iliac spine to the pubic tubercle marks the inguinal ligament. The femoral artery can be palpated at its mid-point. If the femoral vein is entered first, the needle is directed laterally to enter the artery. The femoral sheath is an extension of the extra-peritoneal fascia (iliac fascia behind and transversalis fascia in front). This fuses around the femoral vessels in the femoral triangle. The femoral sheath also contains the femoral canal which is medial to the femoral vein allowing it to expand during exercise. The canal contains Cloquet's lymph node and the femoral branch of the genitofemoral *n.* (L1).

2. The three nerves of a '3-in-1' block are the femoral, the obturator and the lateral cutaneous femoral (lateral cutaneous nerve of the thigh). These are branches of the lumbar plexus that forms in the psoas muscle. The femoral *n.* is its largest branch. It comes from the posterior divisions of the anterior primary rami of L2,3,4. It descends through the pelvis in a fascial compartment (psoas and iliacus fascias behind and transversalis fascia in front). It passes deep to the inguinal ligament and enters the femoral triangle lateral to, but separate from, the femoral sheath which contains the femoral artery. The cutaneous branches of the femoral *n.,* i.e. the anterior and medial femoral cutaneous *n.* and the saphenous *n.,* supply the regions that the great (long) saphenous vein follows. The obturator *n.* supplies an area on the medial aspect of the thigh or knee. The needle is inserted 1 cm lateral to the femoral artery in a cephalad direction at 45° to the skin. The distance between the artery and nerve is often more than 1–2 cm so it is important to confirm the nerve's location by paraesthesiae or peripheral nerve stimulation. The needle is then presumed to be in the nerve's fascial compartment. The needle is fixed and local anaesthetic is injected with intermittent aspirations. At the same time the operator presses below the injection point to prevent distal spread of solution and to facilitate proximal spread toward the lumbar plexus. The femoral *n.* divides at or just above the inguinal ligament. A large volume (20–30 mL) is used to ensure these and the obturator *n.* and lateral cutaneous femoral *n.* are all blocked.

3. In addition to the 3-in-1 block, complete block above the knee requires a posterior cutaneous nerve of the thigh (S2,3) block. This nerve escorts the sciatic *n.* (L4,5 S1,2,3) to the thigh so in practice they are blocked together. At the knee the sciatic *n.* forms the tibial *n.* and the common peroneal *n.* These supply those areas below the knee that are not supplied by the saphenous branch of the femoral *n.* Combining a 3-in-1 and a sciatic *n.* block anaesthetizes the whole lower limb.

4. The ilio-inguinal *n.* is the collateral branch of the ilio-hypogastric *n.* which is the anterior primary ramus of L1. They supply the skin of the upper part of the buttock, the area above the inguinal ligament, the anterior one third of the scrotum and the root of the penis (or mons pubis). With the subcostal *n.* (T12) they can be blocked 1–2 cm medial to the anterior superior iliac spine. Injections from 2 cm superior to 2 cm inferior to this point have been described. It is important to inject the local anaesthetic throughout the different inter-muscular planes as the nerves first travel between the internal oblique and transversus muscles and then pierce the former to lie under the external oblique. This may be aided by a short bevel (45°) needle that clicks through the layers. A fan injection is also made over the pubic tubercle to block the genitofemoral and intercostal *n.* branches that supply the medial inguinal area.

Key reference:

Wildsmith JAW, Armitage EN (eds) *Principles and Practice of Regional Anaesthesia* 2nd ed. Churchill Livingstone, Edinburgh 1993;161–163, 189–195.

Answers to 10.8

1. Mitral stenosis (MS) with pulmonary hypertension. 99% of MS is due to rheumatic heart disease and most patients give a history of rheumatic fever. Normal valve size is 5 cm², symptoms occur at 2 cm² and stenosis is severe at <1 cm². MS causes a progression of pathological changes as the pressure increases from the left atrium (LA) back to the right ventricle (RV). In MS the underused left ventricle (LV) is small and may be compressed if there is RV dilatation. The left ventricular stroke volume (LVSV) is further limited by its preload that is dependent on LA function, heart rate (HR) and the degree of stenosis. LA function depends on sinus rhythm and LA filling pressure. To overcome the stenosis the LA dilates and hypertrophies.

2. Aortic valve disease. This occurs with mitral disease in 40% of rheumatic valve lesions. Solitary MS occurs in 50%.

3. Atrial fibrillation (AF). This is due to stretching and ischaemia of the dilated LA. In a normal heart, LA contraction is responsible for up to 30% of ventricular filling but in MS it is responsible for up to 40% as blood needs to be forced through the stenotic valve. LA pressure will increase if RV output exceeds that which the LA can handle. This can occur with fever or pregnancy or if LA function deteriorates as in AF. Pulmonary venous and capillary pressure follow LA pressure and if this exceeds colloid osmotic pressure (about 25 mmHg) pulmonary oedema results which manifests as exertional dyspnoea, orthopnoea, paroxysmal nocturnal dyspnoea, haemoptysis and recurrent bronchitis. If the LA pressure remains raised it may cause a reactive pulmonary hypertension resulting in a low cardiac output and right ventricular hypertrophy, dilatation and failure. The lung compliance then falls and spirometry may show a restrictive pattern.

4. The following suggest severe MS:

- Low cardiac output: small pulse pressure, malar flush or peripheral cyanosis.
- Immobility of the valve cusps: the opening snap (OS) disappears and the loud first heart sound softens.
- An early OS <0.09 s after the aortic second sound indicates a left atrial pressure >20 mmHg.
- Long diastolic murmur or thrill.
- Pulmonary hypertension: palpable and loud pulmonary second sound. Prominent 'a' wave of JVP (if not in AF).
- Right ventricular hypertrophy, dilatation or failure: parasternal heave, raised JVP, peripheral oedema.
- Tricuspid incompetence: giant 'v' waves on JVP and pulsatile liver.
- Graham-Steel murmur of pulmonary incompetence (rare).

5. None. Pulmonary hypertension is present so pulmonary artery wedge pressure doesn't reflect LA pressure. Insertion may cause AF. Fluid management is crucial as overloading can cause pulmonary oedema or precipitate AF by LA dilatation. Tachycardia reduces the LV filling time by shortening diastole, causing CO to fall. LVSV is limited so bradycardia causes a decrease in CO. Acidosis, hypoxia, hypercarbia and nitrous oxide should be avoided as pulmonary vascular resistance may increase, so reducing LA filling. The poor pulmonary compliance and pulmonary hypertension are better managed by IPPV rather than spontaneous ventilation except for very short procedures. Spinal block is contraindicated as venous return and LA filling may fall and the limited CO may not be able to compensate for any hypotension.

Key reference:

Mason R. *Anaesthesia Databook* 2nd ed. Churchill Livingstone, London 1994; 294–296.

Answers to 10.9

1. (a) Blood filter (Pall Ultipor).

1. (b) This is a screen filter with a filtration surface of 25 square inches. The filter is made of woven polyester with a pore size of 40 µm, which is folded to increase surface area and is contained within a 2-inch square polypropylene housing.

2. There are two basic types of microaggregate filters: screen and depth. Combination filters are also available.

- *Screen filters:* These function as sieves with a fixed pore size, usually 40 µm. Micro-aggregate debris that is larger than the pore size is intercepted and retained on the upstream side of the filtration surface. The mesh is fixed, the fibres cannot be displaced and channelling does not occur. These are probably more convenient for routine clinical application.
- *Depth filters:* A depth filter provides both a screening function and an adsorptive function whereby particles adhere to the filtration surface. The filters are made of dacron, nylon, polyester, cotton or similar material. Channelling may occur, resulting in some blood by-passing the filter mechanism. Whilst they do not have a true pore size they are able to remove particles down to 10 µm size. They have been found to clog more rapidly than screen filters with consequent reduction in flow rates.
- *Combination filters:* These combine the advantages of screen and depth filters. They filter particles down to 20 µm (e.g. Fenwal filter).

3. Microfilters in extra-corporeal circuits have been shown to reduce arterial embolization and post-operative neurological dysfunction.

Minimizing nonhaemolytic febrile reactions in patients requiring repeated transfusions. The reduction in febrile reactions correlates with the reduction in leucocyte count achieved by a combination of centrifugation and micro-filtration.

Transfusions to neonates with pulmonary dysfunction (post-transfusion pulmonary emboli have been implicated in neonatal pulmonary hypertension).

Large volume blood transfusions >5 units. (The controversy of whether microaggregate debris contributes to the development of ARDS is still unresolved but on current evidence microfiltration is probably advisable.)

4. Disadvantages include:

- Cost: when considering cost, it must be remembered that filters may have to be changed a number of times during a massive transfusion.
- Large priming volumes and slow flow rates.
- Haemolysis occurs with some depth filters, particularly with ageing blood at high flow rates.
- Removal of viable platelets and complement activation have also been reported.

Notes

Microaggregates range in size between 20 and 120 µm. They form in stored blood and consist of nonviable platelets and white cells held together by strands of fibrin. They increase in size and number with prolonged storage. Microaggregate accumulation is not significant in blood that is less than one week old. Both micro- and macroaggregates have been found in SAG-M blood. The standard blood giving set contains a screen filter of pore size 170–230 µm. It removes visible clots and offers minimal resistance but microaggregates can pass through easily.

Key references:

Rossi EC, Simon TL, Moss GS (eds). *Principles of Transfusion Medicine.* Williams & Wilkins, Maryland 1991; 643–645.

Kox WJ, Gamble J (eds). *Fluid Resuscitation.* Bailliere Tindall, London 1988; 649–666.

Answers to 10.10

1. Anaphylactoid reaction. The clinical features (urticaria, bronchospasm and cardiovascular collapse) resemble those of immediate immune mediated hypersensitivity but this cannot be termed anaphylaxis without proof from laboratory tests. Anaphylactic reactions are mediated by IgG or IgE antibodies and are Type B (not dose related, worse with repeated exposure, clinical features unlike normal pharmacological response) adverse reactions.

2. Stop injection of thiopentone. Summon help. Airway and Breathing – administer 100% O_2, consider tracheal intubation and IPPV.
Circulation – adrenaline 50–100 µg i.v. is the first line drug with further boluses/continuous infusion as necessary. Intravascular volume expansion must be achieved with rapid colloid infusion. External cardiac compression may be needed to maintain cardiac output.
Adrenaline-resistant bronchospasm may be treated with i.v. salbutamol, terbutaline or aminophylline. Hydrocortisone/methyl prednisolone may be of benefit in the treatment of bronchospasm/cardiovascular collapse, but there is little evidence to support their use. Antihistamines may be helpful in some cases. Blood for arterial blood gas analysis and a clotting screen must be taken. Severe acidosis may be treated with $NaHCO_3$.

3. *Mast cell tryptase*: Released from immunologically activated mast cells but not basophils, white or red blood cells. In reactions to anaesthetic agents this test appears to be highly specific and sensitive for anaphylaxis. Blood is sampled 1 h after the start of the reaction when resuscitation is usually over.
Plasma histamine: Levels >100 ng/mL (when done within 10 min) suggest allergy but do not establish cause. Methylhistamine assay is useful because it is more stable, remains elevated longer and can be measured in urine.
Others: Complement-activation tests have been found to be of little value in evaluating adverse reactions to anaesthetic drugs. The usefulness of sequential measurements of IgE in anaphylaxis has not been validated.
Skin testing: Cheap, rapid, reliable, simple and essential. Intradermal (diluted drug is injected intradermally) or prick testing (dermis is pricked through **un**diluted drug placed on skin) is usually carried out 4–6 weeks later.
Radioimmunoassays (RIA): Measure circulating IgE and are useful in identifying drugs causing reactions during anaesthesia. RIA inhibition tests may be used to verify the results. The diagnostic yield is improved when skin testing is combined with RIA tests.
Passive transfer testing (PT), Basophil degranulation (BD), Histamine release from leucocytes (HRL): Not widely available and are regarded as research tools. PT and HRL have the advantage of measuring cell bound IgE. **Note:** There is no valid **predictive** test for anaphylaxis at present and routine screening of patients for specific drug antibodies prior to anaesthesia is not recommended.

4. The patient should be given a letter to be shown to subsequent anaesthetists, indicating the drug concerned, the nature of the reaction and the tests used to confirm the diagnosis. A 'medic alert' bracelet should be worn. Full resuscitation facilities must be available when subsequent anaesthesia is undertaken. Drugs which show positive skin tests must not be used. Local and volatile anaesthetic techniques are safest. Pretreatment with H_1, H_2 blockers and steroids is recommended. If required, i.v. agents with a low incidence of anaphylactoid reactions (e.g. etomidate, alfentanil, vecuronium) should be chosen.

Key references:

Fisher M, Baldo BA. Anaphylaxis during anaesthesia: current aspects of diagnosis and prevention. *European Journal of Anaesthesiology* 1994; **11**:263–284.

Association of Anaesthetists of Great Britain and Ireland. *Working Party report on Anaphylactic reactions associated with Anaesthesia,* September 1990, London.

Answers to 10.11

1. The normal daily nitrogenous load for a 70 kg adult is about 700 mosmol. The kidneys can produce a maximally concentrated urine of 1200–1400 mosm/L. Therefore the minimum obligatory urine output that is compatible with adequate excretion under normal conditions is 500 mL/day. In sepsis or trauma the nitrogenous load and the obligatory urinary volume may be higher. As a rule of thumb, a urinary output of 0.5 mL/kg is the minimum allowed before active treatment is started.

2. Serum osmolarity may be calculated as:
$$2[Na^+] + 2[K^+] + [urea] + [glucose].$$

This approximates to plasma osmolality if the presence of gross hyperproteinaemia, hyperlipid-aemia or osmotically active substances such as mannitol or ethanol are excluded. Sodium and its anions account for 90% of plasma osmolarity which is normally 280–295 mosm/L. Under normal conditions the water content and osmolality of the body is regulated by the osmoreceptors of the anterior hypothalamus. Above an osmolality of 280 mosm/kg the hypo-thalamus secretes antidiuretic hormone (ADH) in increasing amounts. ADH causes the collecting tubules in the kidneys to become more permeable to water, increasing its absorption and limiting diuresis. Administering water inhibits ADH release and causes a diuresis. Conversely, a good diuresis suggests an adequate fluid input. However, this is only true when the control mechanisms are able to function correctly. The presence of renal disease, diuretic drugs, hyperglycaemia and diabetes insipidus can overcome this control. In this patient the serum osmolarities on admission and 48 hours later were 295 and 364 mosm/L respectively. This large change is due to either excessive water loss or to administration of sodium, or both. Examination of the urine shows a huge volume with a low osmolality and pathological retention of sodium in the face of hypernatraemia. The diagnosis is diabetes insipidus secondary to the subarachnoid haemorrhage. The large volume of urine does not confirm an adequate intake.

3. The neurological damage which occurs with a subarachnoid haemorrhage (SAH) includes the intracranial pressure effects, the ischaemic vasospasm due to extravascular blood and damage which occurs as blood reperfuses ischaemic tissue. The reperfusion injury is more severe if the blood sugar during reperfusion is high. Therefore, during the initial management of SAH and head trauma, hyperglycaemia is avoided by not using dextrose containing solutions and by having all other i.v. fluids contain sodium. It is important to maintain cerebral perfusion pressure (mean arterial pressure minus intracranial pressure). The volume of i.v. crystalloids is usually restricted to avoid exacerbating cerebral oedema. Hypovolaemia is avoided by using sodium containing colloids. Mannitol may exacerbate dehydration and hypernatraemia. However, these reasons alone would not account for such a sudden severe hypernatraemia and the diagnosis remains as diabetes insipidus.

4. An antidiuretic hormone analogue such as desmopressin can be given i.v., orally or by nasal spray. The urine output will return to normal within 2–4 h, confirming the diagnosis. Hypertension may occur.

5. The hypovolaemia caused may result in acute tubular necrosis. If the patient deteriorates and organ donation becomes a possibility the hypernatraemia will have to be corrected before brainstem testing can proceed.

Key reference:

Kumar P, Clark M (eds). *Clinical Medicine* 3rd ed. Baillière Tindall, London 1994; 820–821.

Answers to 10.12

1. (a) Retrobulbar block needle and ocular compression weight.

1. (b) The retrobulbar block needle is used to deposit local anaesthetic (LA) agents within the extraocular muscle cone to provide ocular anaesthesia. An ocular compression device (Buys bag/ Honan's balloon) is used to soften the globe and spread the LA solution. It also promotes akinesia of the periorbital muscles, particularly after peribulbar block.

2. *Retrobulbar block:* In the classical technique a 35 mm needle is passed beyond the globe to enter the muscle cone. Although the 'up and in' position of the globe was originally described, the primary gaze or 'down and out' positions are now recommended to minimize trauma to the optic nerve and vessels.
Peribulbar block: LA is injected through short 25 mm needles extra-conally with minimal trauma to orbital structures.
Subconjunctival block: Useful for anterior segment surgery. Following instillation of LA eye drops a small volume of anaesthetic is injected under the superior bulbar conjunctiva.
Sub-Tenon's anaesthesia: Topical anaesthesia is followed by an incision in the conjunctiva through the Tenon's fascia down to sclera. A blunt cannula is passed through this incision into the posterior sub-Tenon's space to instil LA. This provides good operating conditions and minimizes the risks of retrobulbar block.

3. Amethocaine or oxybuprocaine eye drops provide topical anaesthesia. Subsequent injections through anaesthetized conjunctivae are painless. A mixture of lignocaine 2% and bupivacaine 0.5–0.75% is popular as it provides the good penetration and fast onset of lignocaine and a longer duration of action. Hyaluronidase improves dispersion through connective tissue, promotes spread of anaesthetic, enhances block and reduces need for additional injections. Carbonation of lignocaine does not improve quality of block. The addition of adrenaline does not improve or extend eye anaesthesia produced by bupivacaine. Adjustment of pH with NaHCO$_3$ has been shown to reduce onset time of peribulbar blocks with both lignocaine and bupivacaine.

4. *Retrobulbar block:* It has to be combined with a painful facial nerve block to prevent the shutting of the eyelids interfering with surgery and provide *orbicularis oculi* akinesia which prevents increases of IOP. Intraconal injection increases risk of injury to globe, optic nerve and blood vessels.
Peribulbar block: Dual injections and larger volumes (6–20 mL) of LA are used. Orbital pressure is higher and compression for 10–20 min is required. Slow diffusion of solution into the muscle cone delays onset of block. Poor akinesia may necessitate further injections.

5. *Retrobulbar haemorrhage,* either arterial or venous – the rise in pressure may result in central retinal artery occlusion and loss of vision. *Globe perforation* – risk is increased in myopic eyes with an axial length greater than 26 mm. *Injury to optic nerve* may lead to blindness. *Inadvertent injection* of local anaesthetic into the optic nerve sheath and spread to the optic chiasma may result in bilateral amaurosis. Retrograde ophthalmic arterial injection could lead to passage of LA into the thalamus and midbrain. *Subdural and subarachnoid spread* of LA has been reported to cause brainstem anaesthesia, and respiratory arrest.
Other: subconjunctival oedema and haemorrhage, ptosis, entropion, diplopia and temporary extra-ocular muscle dysfunction have been reported.

Key references:

Wong DHW. Regional anesthesia for intraocular surgery. *Canadian Journal of Anaesthesia* 1993: **40:**635–657.

Berry CB, Murphy PM. Regional anaesthesia for cataract surgery. *British Journal of Hospital Medicine* 1993: **49:**689–701.

Index of topics